International Law and Global Governance

This book explores the methods through which international law and its associated innovative global governance mechanisms can strengthen, foster and scale up the impacts of treaty regimes and international law on the ability to implement global governance mechanisms.

Examining these questions through the lens of the Sustainable Development Goals (SDGs), the book looks at environmental, social and economic treaty regimes. It analyses legal methodologies as well as comparative methods of assessing the relationship between the SDGs and treaty regimes and international law. Contradictions exist between international treaty regimes and principles of international law resulting in conflicting implementation of the treaty regimes and of global governance mechanisms. Without determining these areas of contest and highlighting their detrimental impacts, the SDGs and other efforts at global governance cannot maximize their legal and societal benefits. The book concludes by suggesting a path forward for the SDGs and for international treaty regimes that is forged in a solid understanding and application of the advantages of global governance mechanisms, including reflections from the COVID-19 pandemic experience.

Addressing the strengths, gaps and weaknesses related to treaty regimes and global governance mechanisms, the book provides readers with a comprehensive understanding of this increasingly important topic. It will be of interest to students, researchers and practitioners with an interest in sustainability and law.

Alexandra R. Harrington is a Visiting Professor at Albany School of Law, Executive Director of the Center for Global Governance and Emerging Law, Research Director of the Centre for International Sustainable Development Law and Director of Studies for the International Law Association of Colombia.

I0894767

International Law and Global Governance

Treaty Regimes and Sustainable Development Goals Implementation

Alexandra R. Harrington

Routledge
Taylor & Francis Group
LONDON AND NEW YORK

First published 2021
by Routledge
2 Park Square, Milton Park, Abingdon, Oxon OX14 4RN

and by Routledge
52 Vanderbilt Avenue, New York, NY 10017

Routledge is an imprint of the Taylor & Francis Group, an informa business

British Library Cataloguing-in-Publication Data
A catalogue record for this book is available from the British Library

Library of Congress Cataloging-in-Publication Data
A catalog record has been requested for this book

ISBN: 978-0-367-23535-2 (hbk)
ISBN: 978-0-367-75391-7 (pbk)
ISBN: 978-0-429-29332-0 (ebk)

Typeset in Times New Roman
by KnowledgeWorks Global Ltd.

Dedication

To the memory of my beloved Mother, Barbara, and pup, Churchill.

Contents

Acknowledgments

This book is the result of support and encouragement from a number of people and sources, without whom it could not have been written.

From the outset, the support of the Fulbright Program and Fulbright Canada for the topic of the book and of the Balsillie School of International Affairs in hosting me first as Fulbright Canada Research Chair in Global Governance and then as Fulbright Foundation Special Fellow must be acknowledged, although words hardly seem enough to thank these institutions and the incredible people who are a part of them. At Fulbright Canada, special thanks are owed to Mr. Brad Hector. The warmth and kindness shown to me by everyone at the Balsillie School was overwhelming and special thanks are owed to Ms. Tiffany Bradley, Ms. Joanne Weston, Prof. John Ravenhill, and Prof. Anne Fitzgerald. Additionally, during my Fulbright terms the University of Waterloo, and particularly the School of Environment, Enterprise and Development, kindly invited me to become a member of the thriving community of scholars there.

The journey of writing this book has taken me to many countries and I have been lucky to find colleagues and friends along the way, particularly Prof. Frederic Megret, Prof. Marie-Claire Cordonier Segger, Prof. Markus Gehring, Mr. Freedom-Kai Phillips, Prof. Amar Khoday, Prof. Maya Prabhu, Prof. Sumudu Atapattu, Prof. Christina Voigt, Prof. Valentina Duran Medina, Prof. Timiebi Aganaba-Jeanty, Prof. Danshera Cords, Prof. Connie Mayer, Dean Alicia Ouellette, Prof. David Pratt, Prof. Christian Sundquist, Prof. Barbara Mikołajczyk, Prof. Agnieszka Bielska-Brodziak, Vice Rector Barbara Janusz-Pawletta, Prof. Emmanuella Doussis, Prof. Ilaria Espa, Ms. Emily Morison, Ms. Tara Atleo, Dr. Elisabeth Ruthman, Mr. Rex Ruthman, Dr. Gabrielle Dumas-McBath and Dr. William O'Dwyer. Special recognition must go to my students, past and present, for their curiosity and encouragement, especially Anthony Cove, Claudia Cadenillas, Corey James Benziger, Viktoria Yudchits, Megan Goss, Jenni Barra, Lavinia Bhaskaruni Gabrielle Bruno and Nichole Scholl.

My family has, as always, been a constant source of encouragement, without which the process of writing this book would have been far more difficult. Special thanks in the US to George Harrington, Michael Devlin and

Robert Reicher and Norman Mokhiber and Mia Ebert, to the Harrington, McNerney and Manley families in the UK, and to the Stryja family – Magdalena, Mikołaj and Kajetan – in Poland for always supporting me. To Onchan Inkhamfong I owe more than I can ever say.

In the process of writing this book several people were lost, including my beloved mother, Barbara Mokhiber Harrington, who was my first editor and inspiration, as well as Churchill the faithful and laugh-inducing Bernese Mountain Dog. It is my hope that they find this work a small tribute.

Acronyms/Abbreviations

2030 Agenda	Transforming our world: the 2030 Agenda for Sustainable Development
Abidjan Convention	Convention for Co-Operation in the Protection and Development of the Marine and Coastal Environment of the West and Central African Region
African Charter	African Charter of Human and Peoples' Rights
African Commission	African Commission on Human and Peoples' Rights
American Convention	American Convention of Human Rights
Bamako Convention	Bamako Convention on the Ban of the Import into Africa and the Control of Transboundary Movement and Management of Hazardous Wastes within Africa
Barcelona Convention	Convention for the Protection of the Marine Environment and the Coastal Region of the Mediterranean and Its Protocols
Basel Convention	Basel Convention on the Control of Transboundary Movements of Hazardous Wastes and Their Disposal
Cartagena Convention	Convention for the Protection and Development of the Marine Environment of the Wider Caribbean Region
Cartagena Protocol	Cartagena Protocol on Biosafety to the Convention on Biological Diversity
CAT	Convention against Torture and Other Cruel, Inhuman or Degrading Treatment or Punishment
CBD	Convention on Biological Diversity
CEDAW	Convention on the Elimination of All Forms of Discrimination against Women
CERD	International Convention on the Elimination of All Forms of Racial Discrimination

CITES	Convention on the International Trade in Endangered Species of Flora and Fauna
CMS	Convention on the Conservation of Migratory Species of Wild Animals
CoP	Conference of the Parties
COVID-19	SARS-CoV-2
CRC	Convention on the Rights of the Child
DSB	World Trade Organization Dispute Settlement Body
DSU	World Trade Organization Dispute Settlement Unit
EC	European Commission
EU	European Union
EEZ	Exclusive Economic Zone
EIA	Environmental Impact Assessment
Escazu Convention	Regional Agreement on Access to Information, Public Participation and Justice in Environmental Matters in Latin America and the Caribbean
Espoo Convention	UNECE Convention on Environmental Impacts in the Transboundary Context
FAO	Food and Agriculture Organization
GATS	General Agreement on Trade in Services
GATT	General Agreement on Tariffs and Trade
Helsinki Convention	Convention on the Protection of the Marine Environment of the Baltic Sea Area
HLPF	High Level Political Forum on the Sustainable Development Goals
IATTC Convention	Convention for the Establishment of an Inter-American Tropical Tuna Commission
IBRD	International Bank for Reconstruction and Development
ICAO	International Civil Aviation Organization
ICCPR	International Covenant on Civil and Political Rights
ICESCR	International Covenant on Economic, Social and Cultural Rights
ICJ	International Court of Justice
IDA	International Development Agency
IFC	International Finance Corporation
IHRs	International Health Regulations
IMF	International Monetary Fund
Inter-American Commission	Inter-American Commission on Human Rights
Inter-American Court	Inter-American Court of Human Rights
IRENA	International Renewable Energy Agency
ITLOS	International Tribunal for the Law of the Sea

IUCN	International Union for the Conservation of Nature
Jeddah Convention	Regional Convention for the Conservation of the Red Sea and Gulf of Aden Environment
Kyoto Protocol	Kyoto Protocol to the United Nations Framework Convention on Climate Change
Marrakech Agreement	Marrakech Agreement Establishing the World Trade Organization
Migrant Workers Convention	International Convention on the Protection of the Rights of All Migrant Workers and Their Families
MDGs	Millennium Development Goals
MIGA	Multilateral International Guarantee Agency
Montreal Protocol	Montreal Protocol on Substances that Deplete the Ozone Layer
Moon Treaty	Agreement Governing the Activities of States on the Moon and Other Celestial Bodies
MoP	Meeting of the Parties
Nagoya Protocol	Nagoya Protocol on Access to Genetic Resources and the Fair and Equitable Sharing of Benefits Arising from Their Utilization to the Convention on Biological Diversity
Nairobi Convention	Convention for the Protection, Management and Development of the Marine and Coastal Environment of the Eastern African States
NDC	Nationally Determined Contribution
OAS	Organization of American States
OECD	Organisation for Economic Co-operation and Development
OSPAR	Convention for the Protection of the Marine Environment of the North-East Atlantic
Paris Agreement	Paris Agreement on Climate Change
PoPs	Persistent Organic Pollutants
Ramsar Convention	Convention on Wetlands of International Importance Especially as Waterfowl Habitats
Rotterdam Convention	Rotterdam Convention on Prior Informed Consent Procedure for Certain Hazardous Chemicals and Pesticides in International Trade
SADC	Southern African Development Community
SBSTA	Subsidiary Body for Scientific and Technical Advice to the UNFCCC
SBSTTA	Subsidiary Body for Scientific, Technical and Technological Advice to the CBD

SDGs	Sustainable Development Goals
SEA Protocol	Strategic Environmental Assessment Protocol to the Espoo Convention
SIDS	Small Island Development States
SRFC	Sub-Regional Fisheries Commission
Stockholm Convention	Stockholm Convention on Persistent Organic Pollutant
TRIMS	World Trade Organization Agreement on Trade-Related Investment Measures
TRIPS	World Trade Organization Agreement on Trade-Related Aspects of Intellectual Property Rights
UDHR	Universal Declaration of Human Rights
UN	United Nations
UNCAC	United Nations Convention against Corruption
UNCLOS	United Nations Convention on the Law of the Sea
UNECE	United Nations Economic Commission for Europe
UNEP	United Nations Environment Programme
UNFCCC	United Nations Framework Convention on Climate Change
UNGA	United Nations General Assembly
UNOOSA	United Nations Office for Outer Space Affairs
UNSC	United Nations Security Council
UNSG	United Nations Secretary General
Vienna Convention	Convention for the Protection of the Ozone Layer
VNR	Voluntary National Review
Waigani Convention	Convention to ban the importation into island countries of hazardous and radioactive wastes and to control the transboundary movement and management of hazardous wastes within the South Pacific Region
WIM	Warsaw International Mechanism for Loss and Damage associated with Climate Change Impacts under the UNFCCC
WHO	World Health Organization
WTO	World Trade Organization

1 Introduction

Global governance has become a popular concept across fields and disciplines, yet the sources of and contouring mechanisms for it often resemble a chimera more than a set of regimes. While this uncertainly or fuzziness might be useful in some contexts, it does not allow a robust understanding of global governance regimes, their abilities to evolve and grow over time, and the ways in which they can be used to shape the future of international law and its implementation.

Critical questions in this context remain unaddressed and, without an examination of their potential answers, the ability to advance international law regimes, especially soft law regimes, through global governance mechanisms is inevitably hindered. How can treaty regimes and international law facilitate the implementation of global governance mechanisms? How can treaty regimes and international law hinder the successful implementation of global governance mechanisms? The answers to these questions are unknown although the international community has devoted many resources – political, legal and economic – to global governance mechanisms.

This book studies methods through which international treaty law and its associated innovative global governance mechanisms – such as those found in treaty regimes and their domestic authorities/stakeholders – can strengthen, foster and scale up the impacts of treaty regimes and international law on the ability to implement global governance mechanisms. By way of a modern, concrete example, the book examines these questions through the lens of the 2015 Sustainable Development Goals (SDGs). The SDGs have been selected as an area of focus because they contain soft and hard law elements, relate to a number of international treaty regime topics and associated governance mechanisms, and offer a blank slate upon which to conduct analysis for current and future implementation. Additionally, the SDGs are time-limited in the sense that they are intended to achieve results by 2030, necessitating the rapid entrenchment of their terms as part of global government mechanisms as well as national governance mechanisms and policies.

At the same time, there exist inherent contradictions between international treaty regimes and principles of international law that function in tandem for global governance mechanisms to be properly implemented. For example, environmental treaties and human rights treaties often speak of furthering essential rights and freedoms, however they can be interpreted as giving primacy to different constituencies, resulting in conflicting implementation of the treaty regimes themselves and of global governance mechanisms. Without determining these areas of contest and highlighting the inherent interconnections rather than contradictions, the SDGs will not be able to maximize their legal and societal benefits. This, in turn, could be detrimental to other efforts at global governance in the future, at a time when all governance options must be available to a world crippled by the pandemic and seeking to determine a path to normality. Thus, this book addresses the gaps and negative areas involving treaty regimes and global governance mechanisms in order to offer readers a holistic understanding of the topic.

The research project of which this book is a result began in 2018, well before the world became familiar with the COVID-19 virus or the existence of a crippling modern-day pandemic. The pandemic and the local, national, regional and global impacts stemming from it are unprecedented and will certainly change the ways in which the SDGs are achieved and the ways in which global governance mechanisms function in the short-term and the long-term. Rather than calling the premise of this book into question, however, the pandemic and its lasting effects highlight the importance of understanding the ways in which international law helps and hinders global governance mechanisms and especially how these lessons can be translated to the SDG context, where there is grave concern over the ability to meet the 2030 targets from many circles.

1.1 Background on the Sustainable Development Goals

1.1.1 *Origins*

The SDGs were created in 2015 as the successor to the Millennium Development Goals (MDGs), the groundbreaking statement regarding the issues following the world into the new millennium in 2000 and the ways in which the international community hoped to address them.[1] As such, it is essential to understand the MDGs before examining the SDGs. From the outset, it should be highlighted that the MDGs, like the SDGs, were time-bound and expired in 2015. This was emphasized as a governance advantage by the United Nations in that it was intended to create a sense of urgency among States and other international actors in terms of implementing

1 See Amir Attaran, "An Immeasurable Crisis? A Criticism of the Millennium Development Goals and Why They Cannot be Measured," [2005] 2(10) PLoS Medicine 318; Simon Dalby, Susan Horton & Rianne Mahon, "Global governance challenged in achieving the Sustainable Development Goals: Introduction," in Simon Dalby, Susan Horton & Rianne Mahon, eds, *Global governance challenged in achieving the Sustainable Development Goals* (Routledge, 2019).

commitments made.[2] Whether this was indeed effective as a strategy is still a matter that is up for debate, although it has been replicated as a model moving forward.

The MDGs articulated eight areas of focus to be undertaken by the international community and State actors during the first 15 years of the millennium. MDG 1 sought to "eradiate extreme poverty and hunger"[3] using targets centering on raising the number of people living above the poverty line,[4] "achiev[ing] full and productive employment and decent work for all, including women and young people,"[5] and reducing the number of those suffering from hunger at the global level by half the 1990 rates.[6] MDG 2 focused on accomplishing access to primary education across the world,[7] using the ability of both genders to access and finish primary education as the target for achievement.[8] In MDG 3, the international community pledged support to the "promot[ion] of gender equality and empower[ing] women,"[9] specifically adopting a target that centered on ensuring access for women and girls to primary and secondary education.[10] The reduction of child mortality was the focus of MDG 4,[11] with the target of achieving a 2/3 reduction in mortality rates for children under age 5.[12]

Health concerns were divided between two goals under the MDGs.[13] In MDG 5, the focus was on maternal health issues and targets were set to significantly reduce global maternal mortality rates as well as ensuring "universal access to reproductive health" measures.[14] A broader set of

2 UN System Task Force on the post-2015 UN Development Agenda, *Review of the Contributions of the MDG Agenda to Foster Development: Lessons for the Post-2015 Development Agenda* (2012) 2.
3 United Nations, *Millennium Development Goals 1*, available at https://www.un.org/millenniumgoals/poverty.shtml.
4 Ibid. at Target 1.A.
5 Ibid. at Target 1.B.
6 Ibid. at Target 1.C.
7 United Nations, *Millennium Development Goals 2*, available at https://www.un.org/millenniumgoals/education.shtml.
8 Ibid. at Target 2.A.
9 United Nations, *Millennium Development Goals 3*, available at https://www.un.org/millenniumgoals/gender.shtml; Sara Rose Taylor & Rianne Mahon, "Gender equality from the MDGs to the SDGs: The struggle continues," in Simon Dalby, Susan Horton & Rianne Mahon, eds, *Global governance challenged in achieving the Sustainable Development Goals* (Routledge, 2019).
10 *Millennium Development Goals 3*, *supra* note 9 at Target 3.A.
11 United Nations, *Millennium Development Goals 4*, available at https://www.un.org/millenniumgoals/childhealth.shtml.
12 Ibid. at Target 4.A.
13 See Alan Whiteside, "From MDGs to SDGs: Health slips in global priorities," in Simon Dalby, Susan Horton & Rianne Mahon, eds, *Global governance challenged in achieving the Sustainable Development Goals* (Routledge, 2019).
14 See MDG United Nations, *Millennium Development Goals 5*, available at https://www.un.org/millenniumgoals/maternal.shtml.

concerns was addressed in MDG 6, which focused on efforts to address communicable diseases including HIV/AIDS, tuberculosis and malaria.[15] Issues relating to "environmental sustainability" were contained in MDG 7, with targets stressing the need to "integrate the principles of sustainable development into country policies and programmes and reverse the loss of environmental resources,"[16] reduce the rate of biodiversity loss,[17] reduce the rate of the population "without sustainable access to safe drinking water and basic sanitation,"[18] and, by 2020, "achieve a significant improvement in the lives of at least 100 million slum dwellers."[19]

Finally, to draw together the strands of the MDGs and provide for their implementation across the international and national communities, MDG 8 provided for the development of global partnerships.[20] Included in this are targets seeking to "develop further an open, rule-based, predictable, non-discriminatory trading and financial system,"[21] incorporate the needs of developing States, Small Island Developing States and land-locked States in implementing the MDGs and assist in creating methods to address these needs,[22] cooperate with the pharmaceutical industry to "provide access to affordable essential drugs in developing countries,"[23] and engage with private actors to provide for technology transfer where appropriate.[24]

In addition, indicators for the measurement of target achievements under the MDG system were established although they were generally lacking in specific aims and quantities of changes caused by the various MDGs.[25] The failure to tie accomplishment of the MDGs to specific timeframes within the 15-year lifespan of the MDGs has been noted as an issue in generating durable implementation and meaning for their terms.[26]

As is evident, the MDGs were largely aspirational, containing a recognition of major issues which were perceived as inhibiting the full development of global society although lacking both hard or soft law enforcement mechanisms and methods of indicating progress toward the articulated

15 See United Nations, *Millennium Development Goals 6*, available at https://www.un.org/millenniumgoals/aids.shtml.
16 United Nations, *Millennium Development Goals 7*, Target 7.A, available at https://www.un.org/millenniumgoals/environ.shtml.
17 Ibid. at Target 7.B.
18 Ibid. at Target 7.C.
19 Ibid. at Target 7.D.
20 United Nations, *Millennium Development Goals 8*, available at https://www.un.org/millenniumgoals/global.shtml.
21 Ibid. at Target 8.A.
22 Ibid. at Targets 8.B, 8.C.
23 Ibid. at Target 8.E.
24 Ibid. at Target 8.F.
25 See United Nations, *Millennium Development Goal 8: Taking Stock of the Global* Partnership for Development (2015).
26 See ibid. at xiii.

targets. The MDGs as a legal framework were soft law, carrying with them a moral force as instruments of the international community and allowing for extreme flexibility in implementation and assessment. However, this arguably represented a critical flaw in the MDGs as well, since the lack of a discernible structure or assessment system, coupled with such high levels of flexibility and interpretive space, created a vacuum for oversight and the inability to tie the MDGs to hard legal, regulatory or organizational systems. Indeed, the MDG review panel convened under the aegis of the UN Secretary General identified issues in drafting and adopting fulsome indicators as measuring mechanisms for the achievement of the various goals as an existential flaw that limited the translation and efficacy of the MDGs at the international and national levels.[27]

At the same time, the review panel itself reiterated the basic governance reality that "monitoring is not implementing," and noted that efforts at oversight for the MDGs were lacking in methods of ensuring and incentivizing implementation of the goals at the international and national levels.[28] An additional structural flaw in the MDG system was that, while there was an intent for the various MDGs to work together where possible, they were constructed in a manner that emphasized siloing particular sectors and issues rather than examining them in a cross-cutting light that would allow for intersectional methods of addressing the topics and generating meaningful change.[29]

By 2015, the MDGs were scheduled to expire and work on the next iteration of them was well underway. The final tally of the MDGs demonstrated significant advances in many of the areas of focus, although much work remained to be done to accomplish the goals as well as to address the institutional and governance issues that had plagued them from the outset.[30] At the same time, the international community increasingly understood that the issues highlighted in the MDGs could not be achieved in a siloed system.[31] Further, there was a recognition that conflicts and the lack of stability undermine the ability the full range of the MDGs and serves as a basis for ongoing inequalities across the environmental, social and economic sectors.[32]

As 2015 loomed on the horizon, official reviews of the MDGs – as well as many commentators and academic reviews – emphasized the need to build stronger tools for the next iteration of the global development agenda.[33] In particular, the United Nations task force assigned to reviewing the MDGs issued a number of suggestions for the future, several of which addressed

27 See ibid. at 3–4.

28 See ibid. at 7–8.

29 See UN System Task Force on the post-2015 UN Development Agenda, *supra* note 2 at 5–7.

30 See United Nations, *Millennium Development Goals Report: 2015* (2015).

31 See ibid. at 8 (emphasizing the cross-cutting issues posed by climate change as hindering accomplishment of the MDGs and their targets).

32 Ibid.; UN System Task Force on the post-2015 UN Development Agenda, *supra* note 2 at 9.

33 UN System Task Force on the post-2015 UN Development Agenda, *supra* note 2.

inherent governance issues.[34] These included the suggestion that the post-2015 agenda "should be tailored to serve as an overarching tool for advocacy on global development priorities, a guide for policies at the national and global level, a framework for global monitoring and progress incentive, and a set of principles and targets that ensure policy coherence and underlie the transformative change suggested by the MDG agenda,"[35] that the next set of goals, targets and indicators should set a higher level of aspirations than used in the MDGs,[36] and that there should be an attempt to balance national needs and priorities with at the very least minimum international standards and expectations for implementation.[37]

1.1.2 *Creation*

In September 2015, the international community officially took the next step on the path opened through the MDGs by adopting the *2030 Agenda for Sustainable Development* during the UN General Assembly meeting.[38] As discussed above, this reflected the culmination of several years of attempts to bridge from the successes and challenges of the MDGs and to address the issues facing the global community 15 years into the new millennium. In designating the theme as sustainable development, the international community overtly signaled the intent to focus on all three of pillars of sustainable development in the implementation of the SDGs.[39] By embracing the pillars and principles of sustainable development through the SDGs the international community also recognized the inherent links between the pillars. In furtherance of this, the *2030 Agenda* begins with the statement of the international community's resolve "between now and 2030, to end poverty and hunger everywhere; to combat inequalities within and among countries; to build peaceful, just and inclusive societies; to protect human rights and promote gender equality and the empowerment of women and girls; and to ensure the lasting protection of the planet and its natural resources. We resolve also to create conditions for sustainable, inclusive and sustained economic growth, shared prosperity and decent work for all, taking into account different levels of national development and capacities."[40]

The *2030 Agenda* established 17 SDGs, accompanied by 169 targets for implementation and, ultimately, supplemented by hundreds of indicators

34 Ibid. at 11.
35 Ibid. at 12.
36 Ibid. at 12–13.
37 Ibid. at 13.
38 UN General Assembly, *Transforming Our World: The 2030 Agenda for Sustainable Development*, A/RES/70/1 (21 October 2015).
39 Ibid. at preamble.
40 Ibid. at para 3.

as an additional layer of oversight and guidance.[41] To guide the implementation of the SDGs, the *2030 Agenda* provided five areas of priority: people, planet, prosperity, peace and partnership.[42] An essential aspect of this is that the achievement of the SDGs is to be accomplished in a way that does not leave anyone behind.[43] While the *2030 Agenda* embraces and is built upon a number of international law principles, agreements and customs, it nevertheless notes the need to move beyond the segmented nature of many of these instruments to create a different method of handling the overwhelming challenges facing the international community and individual States.[44] In this context, it is essential to note the provision that "Sustainable development recognizes that eradicating poverty in all its forms and dimensions, combating inequality within and among countries, preserving the planet, creating sustained, inclusive and sustainable economic growth and fostering social inclusion are linked to each other and are interdependent."[45]

1.1.3 *Goals, targets and indicators*

The MDGs' focus on eradicating poverty has been directly transferred to SDG 1, with the goal to "end poverty in all its forms everywhere."[46] Against this highly aspirational goal, the *2030 Agenda* established seven specific targets and subsequently a series of indicators were adopted.[47] While some of these, for example "by 2030, eradicate extreme poverty for all people everywhere, currently measured as people living on less than $1.25 a day,"[48] are far more difficult to achieve, others are specific and have methods for entrenchment in governance structures. Included in these are "by 2030, reduce at least by half the proportion of men, women and children of all ages living in poverty in all its dimensions according to national definitions,"[49] "by 2030, build the resilience of the poor and those in vulnerable situations and reduce their exposure and vulnerability to climate-related extreme events and other economic, social and environmental shocks and disasters,"[50] and to "create sound policy frameworks at the national, regional and international levels,

41 See generally ibid.
42 Ibid. at preamble.
43 Ibid. at para 4.
44 Ibid. at para 13.
45 Ibid.
46 Ibid. at Goal 1.
47 Ibid.
48 Ibid. at Target 1.1.
49 Ibid. at Target 1.2.
50 Ibid. at Target 1.5.

based on pro-poor and gender-sensitive development strategies, to support accelerated investment in poverty eradication actions."[51]

SDG 2, "end hunger, achieve food security and improved nutrition and promote sustainable agriculture," shifts the focus of the MDGs to a more comprehensive understanding of the food and agriculture sector for current and future generations.[52] Many of the targets established in SDG 2 are scientifically focused but require legal and regulatory review to ensure that land rights without discrimination based on gender or other status exist and are actualized.[53] Additionally, national and international governance elements are involved in Target 2.5's provision "by 2020, maintain the genetic diversity of seeds, cultivated plants and farmed and domesticated animals and their related wild species, including through soundly managed and diversified seed and plant banks at the national, regional and international levels, and promote access to and fair and equitable sharing of benefits arising from the utilization of genetic resources and associated traditional knowledge, as internationally agreed."[54] While the ability of States and the international community to meet the 2020 deadline established in Target 2.5 is unlikely, especially given the pandemic's impacts and restrictions, the intent will still remain in the coming years and may be amplified by the food insecurity issues raised as a result of COVID-19. Further, Target 2.b forms a direct connection with the application and respect of the WTO's agricultural trade requirements, tying it to the governance system of the WTO as well.[55]

The SDGs combined the MDGs health-related focus areas into SDG 3 to "ensure healthy lives and promote well-being for all at all ages."[56] From the outset, it should be noted that many of the target areas under SDG 3 relate to the right to health as a whole and to specific aspects of the right to health as established by human rights law and the WHO, thus potentially allowing them to be tied to several of the human rights governance systems discussed in Chapter 3.[57] Additionally, a number of the topics addressed in the SDG 3 targets, for example those relating to tobacco use, are under the specific governance rubric of the WHO,[58] and others, such as certain pharmaceutical access issues, are at least in part under the governance rubric of the WTO.[59]

Through SDG 4, "ensure inclusive and equitable quality education and promote lifelong learning opportunities for all," the scope of education access targets is significantly broadened from the primary education focus

51 Ibid. at Target 1.b.
52 Ibid. at Goal 2.
53 Ibid. at Target 2.3.
54 Ibid. at Target 2.5.
55 Ibid. at Target 2.b.
56 Ibid. at Goal 3.
57 See generally ibid. at Goal 3 and targets.
58 Ibid. at Target 3.b.
59 Ibid. at Target 3.c.

of the MDGs.[60] This includes equality of access to university as well as to vocational schools, and in many ways links to the specific human rights guaranteed to children and women through the various human rights treaty regimes and governance systems discussed in Chapter 3.

SDG 5, "achieve gender equality and empower all women and girls," builds on the terms of the MDGs to provide a more complete understanding of the forms of discrimination that continue to affect the participation of women across all sectors of society and activity on an equal level.[61] The majority of the SDG 5 targets reflect correlations with provisions of CEDAW and other human rights treaty regimes and governance systems discussed in Chapter 3, allowing them to be part of an already-established system.

A number of SDGs can be seen as outgrowths of the general MDG focus on "environmental sustainability." The first of these is SDG 6, "ensure availability and sustainable management of water and sanitation for all,"[62] which brings together human rights and environmental concerns and treaty regimes such as those discussed in Chapters 2 and 3. This includes targets focusing on the need to coordinate the protection and use of transboundary water resources as well as the right to water.[63]

SDG 7, "ensure access to affordable, reliable, sustainable and modern energy for all," bridges between the three pillars of sustainable development by recognizing energy as having a human rights component, especially in terms of access, an environmental component, particularly in the renewable energy sector, and an economic component, notably in the promotion of clean and renewable energy markets at national and international levels.[64] In this context, Target 7.a links to the energy sector treaty regimes discussed in Chapter 4 by providing that "by 2030, enhance international cooperation to facilitate access to clean energy research and technology, including renewable energy, energy efficiency and advanced and cleaner fossil-fuel technology, and promote investment in energy infrastructure and clean energy technology."[65] Additionally, from a governance system perspective Target 7.b works in conjunction with the technology transfer provisions found in environmental and economic treaty regimes to provide "by 2030, expand infrastructure and upgrade technology for supplying modern and sustainable energy services for all in developing countries, in particular least developed countries, small island developing States, and land-locked developing countries, in accordance with their respective programmes of support."[66]

60 Ibid. at Goal 4.
61 Ibid. at Goal 5.
62 Ibid.at Goal 6.
63 Ibid. at Target 6.5.
64 See ibid. at Goal 7 and targets.
65 See ibid. at Target 7.a.
66 See ibid. at Target 7.b.

SDG 8, "promote sustained, inclusive and sustainable economic growth, full and productive employment and decent work for all," addresses issues that are critical to many of the economic treaty regimes and governance systems discussed in Chapter 4 as well as the employment and working conditions aspects of several human rights treaty regimes and governance systems discussed in Chapter 2.[67] Additionally, it should be noted that there is a connection between the concept of employment and working rights contained in SDG 8 and the concept of just transitions advanced in the *Paris Agreement* in particular as it relates to transitioning away from the traditional energy sources sector. In SDG 9, "build resilient infrastructure, promote inclusive and sustainable industrialization and foster innovation," there is an attempt to encourage the creation of growth in these areas that relies on all three pillars of sustainable development.[68]

SDG 10, "reduce inequality within and among countries," is itself a statement as to the national and international prioritization of addressing and remedying discrimination and unequal statuses in order to allow for a more productive and just society.[69] Of particular note in the context of treaty regimes and governance systems in Target 10.6, seeking to "ensure enhanced representation and voice for developing countries in decision-making in global international economic and financial institutions in order to deliver more effective, credible, accountable and legitimate institutions,"[70] and Target 10.a, "implement the principle of special and differential treatment for developing countries, in particular least developed countries, in accordance with World Trade Organization agreements."[71]

Through SDG 11, "make cities and human settlements inclusive, safe, resilient and sustainable," States and the international community recognize the importance of including political sub-units within the realm of the global development agenda.[72] This demonstrates another area in which the balance between State sovereignty and international concerns is delicately achieved while furthering the focus on those living in cities that was first recognized in the MDGs' emphasis on addressing slums and associated conditions in metropolitan areas. Additionally, while perhaps incongruously, commitments of States and the international community to protect natural and cultural heritage are also contained in Target 11.4.[73] This has connections to the human rights treaty regimes and governance systems discussed in Chapter 3 and the several of the environmental treaty regimes and governance systems discussed in Chapter 2.

67 See ibid. at Goal 8, Targets 8.3, 8.4, 8.7–8.10.
68 Ibid. at Goal 9.
69 Ibid. at Goal 10.
70 Ibid. at Target 10.6.
71 Ibid. at Target 10.a.
72 Ibid. at Goal 11.
73 Ibid. at Target 11.4.

In SDG 12, "ensure sustainable consumption and production patterns," there is an obvious emphasis on economic practices, as well as more subtle attention placed on environmental and human rights practices.[74] For instance, in providing "by 2030, achieve the sustainable management and efficient use of natural resources," Target 12.2 links to environmental treaty regimes and governance systems,[75] as does Target 12.4, "by 2020, achieve the environmentally sound management of chemicals and all wastes throughout their life cycle, in accordance with agreed international frameworks, and significantly reduce their release to air, water and soil in order to minimize their adverse impacts on human health and the environment"[76] and Target 12.5, "by 2030, substantially reduce waste generation through prevention, reduction, recycling and reuse."[77] Likewise, human rights treaty regimes and governance systems can be linked to Target 12.7, "promote public procurement practices that are sustainable, in accordance with national policies and priorities"[78] and Target 12.8, "by 2030, ensure that people everywhere have the relevant information and awareness for sustainable development and lifestyles in harmony with nature."[79]

It is perhaps evident that SDG 13, "take urgent action to combat climate change and its impacts," has strong and durable links to environmental treaty regimes and governance systems, especially the *UN Framework Convention om Climate Change* (UNFCCC).[80] However, what must be noted in the context of SDG 13 is the evolution from the concept of "environmental sustainability" as one element of the MDGs to a sophisticated understanding of climate change and related issues as a set of topics which relate to environment as well as economics and human rights. Indeed, while there are separate SDGs for water and terrestrial concerns as well, these are meant to be reinforcing rather than mutually exclusive.

Thus, SDG 14, "conserve and sustainably use the oceans, the seas and marine resources for sustainable development," contains targets relating to national, transboundary, regional and international bodies of water as well as the ecosystems in which they exist.[81] Included in these targets are issues of pollution, fishing and fisheries practices, the interplay between regulation of these sectors and WTO law and UNCLOS law, and recognition of the particular needs of Small Island Developing States in the marine protection context.[82] These issues extend to environmental, economic and human

74 Ibid. at Goal 12.
75 Ibid. at Target 12.2.
76 Ibid. at Target 12.4.
77 Ibid. at Target 12.5.
78 Ibid. at Target 12.7.
79 Ibid. at Target 12.8.
80 Ibid. at Goal 13.
81 Ibid. at Goal 14.
82 Ibid. at Goal 14 and associated targets.

rights treaty regimes and governance systems as discussed in Chapters 2–4. Further, SDG 15, "protect, restore and promote sustainable use of terrestrial ecosystems, sustainably manage forests, combat desertification, and halt and reverse land degradation and halt biodiversity loss," contains targets touching on all aspects of terrestrial resources, including transboundary lands and shared resources.[83]

Arguably the most wide-ranging and cross-cutting SDG is SDG 16, "promote peaceful and inclusive societies for sustainable development, provide access to justice for all and build effective, accountable and inclusive institutions at all levels."[84] Perhaps more than any other, SDG 16 can be seen as a reaction to the criticisms of and suggestions for the MDGs centering on the need to create stronger mechanisms for accountability and to promote the settlement of conflict as a means to furthering development. Essential for governance entrenchment at all levels are Target 16.3, "promote the rule of law at the national and international levels and ensure equal access to justice for all,"[85] Target 16.5, "substantially reduce corruption and bribery in all their forms,"[86] Target 16.6, "develop effective, accountable and transparent institutions at all levels,"[87] Target 16.7, "ensure responsive, inclusive, participatory and representative decision-making at all levels,"[88] Target 16.8, "broaden and strengthen the participation of developing countries in the institutions of global governance,"[89] Target 16.10, "ensure public access to information and protect fundamental freedoms, in accordance with national legislation and international agreements,"[90] Target 16.a, "strengthen relevant national institutions, including through international cooperation, for building capacity at all levels, in particular in developing countries, to prevent violence and combat terrorism and crime,"[91] and Target 16.b, "promote and enforce non-discriminatory laws and policies for sustainable development."[92] These represent recurrent themes in the treaty regimes and governance systems discussed in Chapters 2–4 and are subject to further examination in Chapter 5.

Finally, SDG 17 expands upon MDG 8 in terms of creating a system for the development of partnerships between public and private sectors, and actors within each.[93] Many of the targets, such as Target 17.4 on debt

83 Ibid. at Goal 15.
84 Ibid. at Goal 16.
85 Ibid. at Target 16.3.
86 Ibid. at Target 16.5.
87 Ibid. at Target 16.6.
88 Ibid. at Target 16.7.
89 Ibid. at Target 16.8.
90 Ibid. at Target 16.10.
91 Ibid. at Target 16.a.
92 Ibid. at Target 16.b.
93 Ibid. at Goal 17.

reduction for developing States,[94] Target 17.6 on technology and information sharing and transfer,[95] and Targets 17.9 and 17.18 on capacity-building[96] are entrenched in the treaty regimes and governance systems discussed in Chapters 2–4. Additionally, it should be noted that some of these provisions, especially those addressing debt and capacity-building, are likely to become more important to achievement of the SDGs *per se* in the aftermath of the COVID-19 pandemic.

1.1.4 *Governance regimes*

Building on the criticisms of the MDGs, the *2030 Agenda* specifically includes implementation as a critical element of the SDG system,[97] while also recognizing the continued place and role of sovereignty and sovereign interests over people and resources.[98] Significantly, in this context a system for periodic review of implementation at all levels was operationalized within the *2030 Agenda* in the form of the High Level Political Forum (HLPF) on the SDGs.[99]

The HLPF meets on an annual basis and in many ways serves a function similar to the Conferences of the Parties convened by many of the treaty regimes discussed throughout this book.[100] During the HLPF, States publicly summarize and address questions regarding their progress toward implementing the SDGs, which functions in tandem with the requirement that States periodically file Voluntary National Reviews (VNRs) of their SDG commitments with the United Nations system.[101] Additionally, the HLPF provides space for discussion and decision-making as needed for major issues facing the international community and impacting on the SDGs as well as allowing the participation of non-State actors through observation of these sessions and the organization of side events.[102]

In the wake of COVID-19, there is deep concern about the ability of States and the international community to maintain the momentum which had been generated during the first five years of the SDGs' existence.[103] Indeed, there is an increasing focus on the period before the pandemic as a discrete area of analysis and SDG implementation on the one hand,

94 Ibid. at Target 17.4.
95 Ibid. at Target 17.6.
96 Ibid. at Targets 17.9, 17.18.
97 Ibid. at para 17.
98 Ibid. at para 18.
99 See ibid. at para 47.
100 United Nations, High Level Political Forum on the Sustainable Development Goals, available at https://sustainabledevelopment.un.org/hlpf.
101 Ibid.
102 Ibid.
103 IISD, *Coronavirus and Its Impacts on the SDGs (20 April 2020)*, available at https://www.iisd.org/events/coronavirus-and-its-impact-sdgs.

featuring quantifiable information and discernible trends, and the period during and after the pandemic as a separate temporal frame that is characterized by the unknown.[104] While it is possible to see this as the result of the largely soft law nature of the SDGs given the flexibility of many SDG commitments, it is the argument of this book that the opposite is true – the structure of the SDGs allows for durability in the face of significant challenges. This can be seen in the many forms of global governance systems across hard and soft law treaty regimes which have and continue to entrench the fundamental terms and premises of the SDGs.

1.2 Book summary

In Chapters 2–4, this book parallels the three pillars of sustainable development – environmental, social and economic – in discussion before turning to analysis of emerging trends, contradictions and future outcomes from treaty regimes and governance systems discussed in Chapter 5. Within each of the pillar-based chapters, treaties are assigned to one of four topic clusters, based on the parameters of the sectors, and each these clusters are subsequently analyzed in terms of (1) purposes and objectives of treaties, (2) governance mechanisms used, (3) dispute settlement mechanisms used, (4) hard law elements in governance systems and, where applicable, (5) soft law elements in governance systems. The intent of each of these categories is to ensure that the critical aspects of organizational structures which promote and entrench the terms of treaty regimes in international and national governance systems are reviewed for areas of overlap and divergence.

In Chapter 2, environmental treaty regimes and associated governance systems are discussed since they represent the pillar with which sustainable development is often most closely associated. Although environmental concerns in the SDGs tend superficially to be clustered in SDGs 13, 14 and 15, in reality environmental issues are truly cross-cutting, playing a vital role in everything from food security concerns under SDG 2 to clean water under SDG 6 to renewable energy under SDG 7 to peace, justice and strong institutions under SDG 16 and beyond. Indeed, as Chapter 2 demonstrates, environmental treaty regimes are exceptionally diverse in context and content, scope and scale, although united by the ways in which international law has shaped them and how these treaty regimes have established governance systems that allow them legitimacy and the ability to meet the current and future needs of their constituencies.

Chapter 2 progresses by reviewing treaty regimes that are categorized into (1) generally focused environmental treaty regimes, (2) pollution-based

104 See United Nations, *Partnerships against Covid-19: Building Back Better Together to Advance the 2030 Agenda* (7 July 2020), available at https://sustainabledevelopment.un.org/hlpf/2020/Partnerships-against-COVID-19.

regimes, (3) species and wildlife regimes, and (4) geographically focused regimes. It then provides an overview of the ways in which governance mechanisms contained in the treaties reviewed have responded to and been impacted by the COVID-19 pandemic as an indicator of the strengths and weaknesses of governance systems in the face of a global emergency. Finally, the Chapter reviews discernible trends across environmental treaty regimes and governance systems that can be used to understand how some SDGs and associated targets are already entrenched in these systems and how these systems may be used as a model for the achievement of the SDGs as long-term legal and policy instruments.

The treaties reviewed in Chapter 2 are the UNFCCC and the *Paris Agreement on Climate Change*/Katowice Outcomes,[105] the *Convention on Biological Diversity* (CBD) and *Nagoya* and *Cartagena Protocols*,[106] the *United Nations Convention on the Law of the Sea* (UNCLOS),[107] the *Antarctic Treaty*,[108] the *UNECE Convention on Environmental Impacts in the Transboundary Context* (*Espoo Convention*),[109] the *Regional Agreement in Access to Information, Public Participation and Justice on Environmental Matters in Latin America and the Caribbean* (*Escazu Convention*),[110] the *Stockholm Convention on Persistent Organic Pollutants*,[111] the *Convention for the Protection of the Ozone Layer* (*Vienna Convention*),[112] the *Montreal Protocol on Substances That Deplete the Ozone Layer*,[113] the *UNECE Convention on Long-Range Transboundary Air Pollution*,[114] the *UNECE Convention on the Protection and Use of Transboundary Watercourses and International Lakes*,[115] the *UNECE European Agreement on Main Inland Waterways of International Importance*,[116] the *Agreement on Cooperation on Marine Oil Pollution Preparedness and Response in the*

105 *United Nations Framework Convention on Climate Change* (1992); *Paris Agreement on Climate Change* (2015); Katowice climate package (2018), available at https://unfccc.int/process-and-meetings/the-paris-agreement/katowice-climate-package.

106 *Convention on Biological Diversity* (1992); *Nagoya Protocol on Access to Genetic Resources and the Fair and Equitable Sharing of Benefits Arising from Their Utilization to the Convention on Biological Diversity* (2010); *Cartagena Protocol on Biosafety to the Convention on Biological Diversity* (2003).

107 *United Nations Convention on the Law of the Sea* (1982).

108 *Antarctic Treaty* (1961).

109 *UNECE Convention on Environmental Impacts in the Transboundary Context* (1997).

110 *Regional Agreement in Access to Information, Public Participation and Justice in Environmental Matters in Latin America and the Caribbean* (2018).

111 *Stockholm Convention on Persistent Organic Pollutants* (2004).

112 *Convention for the Protection of the Ozone Layer* (1988).

113 *Montreal Protocol on Substances That Deplete the Ozone Layer* (1989).

114 *UNECE Convention on Long-Range Transboundary Air Pollution* (1981).

115 *UNECE Convention on the Protection and Use of Transboundary Watercourses and International Lakes* (1996).

116 *UNECE European Agreement on Main Inland Waterways of International Importance* (2015).

Arctic,[117] the *Convention on the Protection of the Rhine*,[118] the *Agreement on the Nile River Basin Cooperative Framework*,[119] the *Convention on the Protection of the Black Sea against Pollution*,[120] the *Convention on Migratory Species of Wild Animals* (CMS),[121] the *Agreement on the Conservation of Gorillas and Their Habitats*,[122] the *Agreement on the Conservation of Albatrosses and Petrels*,[123] the *Agreement on the Conservation of African-Eurasian Migratory Birds*,[124] the *Agreement on the Conservation of Populations of European Bats*,[125] the *Convention on the International Trade in Endangered Species* (CITES),[126] the *International Plant Protection Convention*,[127] the *Convention on Wetlands of International Importance Especially as Waterfowl Habitats* (*Ramsar Convention*),[128] the *Convention on the Conservation of European Wildlife and Natural Habitats*,[129] the *Agreement on the Conservation of Cetaceans of the Black Sea, Mediterranean Sea and Contiguous Atlantic Area*,[130] the *Inter-American Convention for the Protection and Conservation of Sea Turtles*,[131] the *Treaty on the Conservation and Sustainable Management of Forest Ecosystems in Central Africa and to Establish the Central African Forests Commission*,[132] the *Convention for the Conservation of Antarctic Seals*,[133] the *Kuwait Regional Convention for Co-Operation on the Protection of the Marine Environment from Pollution*,[134] the *Convention for the Protection, Management and Development of the Marine and Coastal Environment of the Eastern African States* (*Nairobi Convention*),[135] the *Convention for Co-Operation in the Protection and Development of the Marine and Coastal Environment of the West and Central*

117 *Agreement on Cooperation on Marine Oil Pollution Preparedness and Response in the Arctic* (2013).
118 *Convention on the Protection of the Rhine* (1963).
119 *Agreement on the Nile River Basin Cooperative Framework* (2010).
120 *Convention on the Protection of the Black Sea against Pollution* (1994).
121 *Convention on Migratory Species of Wild Animals* (1979).
122 *Agreement on the Conservation of Gorillas and Their Habitats* (2007).
123 *Agreement on the Conservation of Albatrosses and Petrels* (2004).
124 *Agreement on the Conservation of African-Eurasian Migratory Birds* (1999).
125 *Agreement on the Conservation of Populations of European Bats* (1994).
126 *Convention on the International Trade in Endangered Species* (1975).
127 *International Plant Protection Convention* (1952).
128 *Convention on Wetlands of International Importance Especially as Waterfowl Habitats* (1975).
129 *Convention on the Conservation of European Wildlife and Natural Habitats* (1979).
130 *Agreement on the Conservation of Cetaceans of the Black Sea, Mediterranean Sea and Contiguous Atlantic Area* (1996).
131 *Inter-American Convention for the Protection and Conservation of Sea Turtles* (2001).
132 *Treaty on the Conservation and Sustainable Management of Forest Ecosystems in Central Africa and to Establish the Central African Forests Commission* (2005).
133 *Convention for the Conservation of Antarctic Seals* (1972).
134 *Kuwait Regional Convention for Co-Operation on the Protection of the Marine Environment from Pollution* (1978).
135 *Convention for the Protection, Management and Development of the Marine and Coastal Environment of the Eastern African States* (1996).

African Region (*Abidjan Convention*),[136] the *Convention for the Protection of the Natural Resources and Environment of the South Pacific Region and Related Protocols*,[137] the *Convention on the Conservation of Antarctic Marine Living Resources*,[138] the *Convention for the Protection of the Marine Environment of the North-East Atlantic* (OSPAR *Convention*),[139] the *Convention on the Protection of the Marine Environment of the Baltic Sea Area* (*Helsinki Convention*),[140] the *Convention for the Protection and Development of the Marine Environment of the Wider Caribbean Region* (*Cartagena Convention*),[141] the *Convention for the Protection of the Marine Environment and the Coastal Region of the Mediterranean and Its Protocols* (*Barcelona Convention*),[142] the *Convention for the Protection of the Marine Environment and Coastal Area of the South-East Pacific*,[143] the *Framework Agreement on the Sava River Basin*,[144] the *Agreement on the Cooperation for the Sustainable Development of the Mekong River Basin*,[145] and *Regional Convention for the Conservation of the Red Sea and Gulf of Aden Environment* (*Jeddah Convention*).[146]

Some of these treaty regimes will seem obvious choices to many readers, notably the UNFCCC, CBD, CITES and CMS. These are among the preeminent environmental treaty regimes in international law and serve as the foundation upon which many subsequent treaty regimes have been built. At the same time, these are treaty regimes that continue to grow to meet the challenges of their specializations and their constituencies, including significant growth in the governance realm. Each of these treaties could itself be a book volume case study on governance mechanisms *per se*, and they are mentioned here in reference only to certain aspects which are directly relevant to the SDGs. The choice to include a number of other treaty regimes, including those with a specific species or geographical focus was made to demonstrate the diversity of treaty regimes and attendant governance systems existing in the environmental context. Rather than assuming that the

136 *Convention for Co-Operation in the Protection and Development of the Marine and Coastal Environment of the West and Central African Region* (1984).
137 *Convention for the Protection of the Natural Resources and Environment of the South Pacific Region and Related Protocols* (1986).
138 *Convention on the Conservation of Antarctic Marine Living Resources* (1982).
139 *Convention for the Protection of the Marine Environment of the North-East Atlantic* (1992).
140 *Convention on the Protection of the Marine Environment of the Baltic Sea Area* (1992).
141 *Convention for the Protection and Development of the Marine Environment of the Wider Caribbean Region* (1986).
142 *Convention for the Protection of the Marine Environment and the Coastal Region of the Mediterranean and Its Protocols* (1976).
143 *Convention for the Protection of the Marine Environment and Coastal Area of the South-East Pacific* (1981).
144 *Framework Agreement on the Sava River Basin* (2004).
145 *Agreement on the Cooperation for the Sustainable Development of the Mekong River Basin* (1995).
146 *Regional Convention for the Conservation of the Red Sea and Gulf of Aden Environment* (1982).

discussion should be bounded by the completely global treaty regimes or the better-known treaty regimes, the aim is to highlight the breadth of such regimes and the lessons they can offer in connection with the SDGs.

In Chapter 3, social treaty regimes and associated governance systems are reviewed. Social treaty regimes represent a spectrum of legal and governance concerns, as has been highlighted by the COVID-19 pandemic's impacts on health practice and governance as well as nearly all aspects of the core international human rights system. The connections between social treaty regimes, governance systems and the SDGs are similarly wide-ranging, although the justice and rule of law issues governed by many of the treaty regimes discussed suggest that SDG 16 is more all-encompassing in terms of reflecting and furthering the social treaty regimes.

Chapter 3 progresses by reviewing treaty regimes that are categorized into (1) core human rights treaty regimes, (2) criminal regimes, (3) health and food regimes, and (4) weapons and hazardous substances regimes. It then provides an overview of the ways in which governance mechanisms contained in the treaties reviewed have responded to and been impacted by the COVID-19 pandemic as an indicator of the strengths and weaknesses of governance systems in the face of a global emergency. Finally, the chapter reviews discernible trends across social treaty regimes and governance systems which can be used to understand how some SDGs and associated targets are already entrenched in these systems and how these systems may be used as a model for the achievement of the SDGs as long-term legal and policy instruments.

The treaties reviewed in Chapter 3 are the *International Covenant on Civil and Political Rights* (ICCPR),[147] the *International Covenant on Economic, Social and Cultural Rights* (ICESCR),[148] the *Convention on the Rights of the Child* (CRC),[149] the *International Convention on the Protocol of the Rights of All Migrant Workers and Members of Their Families*,[150] the *International Convention on the Elimination of All Forms of Racial Discrimination* (CERD),[151] the *Convention on the Elimination of All Forms of Discrimination against Women* (CEDAW),[152] the *Convention against Torture and Other Cruel, Inhuman and Degrading Treatment or Punishment*,[153] the *International Convention on the Protection of All Persons from Enforced Disappearance*,[154]

147 *International Covenant on Civil and Political Rights* (1976).

148 *International Covenant on Economic, Social and Cultural Rights* (1976).

149 *Convention on the Rights of the Child* (1989).

150 *International Convention on the Protocol of the Rights of All Migrant Workers and Members of Their Families* (1990).

151 *International Convention on the Elimination of All Forms of Racial Discrimination* (1969).

152 *Convention on the Elimination of All forms of Discrimination against Women* (1981).

153 *Convention against Torture and Other Cruel, Inhuman and Degrading Treatment or Punishment* (1978).

154 *International Convention on the Protection of All Persons from Enforced Disappearance* (2010).

the *United Nations Convention against Corruption* (UNCAC),[155] the *United Nations Convention against Transnational Organized Crime*[156] and its *Protocol to Prevent, Suppress and Punish Trafficking in Persons, Especially Women and Children*,[157] *Protocol against the Smuggling of Migrants by Land, Sea and Air*,[158] and *Protocol against the Illicit Manufacturing of and Trafficking in Firearms, Their Parts and Components and Ammunitions*,[159] the *United Nations Convention against Illicit Traffic in Narcotic Drugs and Psychotropic Substances*,[160] the *Inter-American Convention against Corruption*,[161] the *African Union Convention on Preventing and Combating Corruption*,[162] the *Constitution of the World Health Organization*,[163] the *Constitution of the Food and Agriculture Organization*,[164] the *Treaty on the Prohibition of Nuclear Weapons*,[165] the *Convention on Cluster Munitions*,[166] the *Convention on the Prohibition of the Development, Production, Stockpiling and Use of Chemical Weapons and on Their Destruction*,[167] the *Arms Trade Treaty*,[168] the *African Nuclear Weapon-Free-Zone Treaty*,[169] and the *Bamako Convention on the Ban of the Import into Africa and the Control of Transboundary Movement and Management of Hazardous Wastes within Africa*.[170]

The core human rights treaty regimes and attendant governance systems will be familiar to many readers and arguably no discussion of human rights treaty regimes could be had without them. These are the bedrock of human rights law at the international and regional levels – in many instances building off each other to advance increasingly nuanced rights – that have become essential elements of how individuals throughout the world conceive of their

155 *United Nations Convention against Corruption* (2005).
156 *United Nations Convention against Transnational Organized Crime* (2003).
157 *Protocol to Prevent, Suppress and Punish Trafficking in Persons, Especially Women and Children Supplementing the United Nations Convention against Transnational Organized Crime* (2003).
158 *Protocol against the Smuggling of Migrants by Land, Sea and Air Supplementing the United Nations Convention against Transnational Organized Crime* (2004).
159 *Protocol against the Illicit Manufacturing of and Trafficking in Firearms, Their Parts and Components and Ammunitions Supplementing the United Nations Convention against Transnational Organized Crime* (2001).
160 *United Nations Convention against Illicit Traffic in Narcotic Drugs and Psychotropic Substances* (1990).
161 *Inter-American Convention against Corruption* (1997).
162 *African Union Convention on Preventing and Combating Corruption* (2003).
163 *Constitution of the World Health Organization* (1948).
164 *Constitution of the Food and Agriculture Organization* (1945).
165 *Treaty on the Prohibition of Nuclear Weapons* (2017) (not yet in force).
166 *Convention on Cluster Munitions* (2010).
167 *Convention on the Prohibition of the Development, Production, Stockpiling and Use of Chemical Weapons and on Their Destruction* (1992).
168 *Arms Trade Treaty* (2014).
169 *African Nuclear Weapon-Free-Zone Treaty* (2009).
170 *Bamako Convention on the Ban of the Import into Africa and the Control of Transboundary Movement and Management of Hazardous Wastes within Africa* (1998).

rights and duties in relation to the States. Further, these are treaty regimes and governance systems that have continued to evolve with new changes in and challenges to global society and the human rights issues it faces. As with the fundamental environmental treaty regimes, each of these treaties could itself be a book volume case study on governance mechanisms *per se*, and they are mentioned here in reference only to certain aspects which are directly relevant to the SDGs. However, especially in the context of the rights of the child, more of the specific hard law terms of each treaty regime are elaborated since they demonstrate the areas in which issues raised in the SDGs have been codified in human rights treaty regimes and are thus subject to internationalized governance systems. The choice to analyze a number of other social treaty regimes, including those with a specific criminal conduct focus or weapons focus, was made to demonstrate the diversity of treaty regimes and attendant governance systems existing in the social context. Additionally, given the COVID-19 pandemic and the issues it has raised in terms of global health governance and access to food, as well as food security, Chapter 3 addresses the specific ways in which the World Health Organization and Food and Agriculture Organization were created and empowered through treaty regimes as well as the methods through which their governance systems function. The treaties in this Chapter might seem to be a disparate collection yet under the surface are united in their largely social sector-oriented purposes and in the ways they connect with and entrench related SDGs and their targets.

In Chapter 4, economic regimes and associated governance systems are reviewed. Economic treaty regimes include a wide range of activities, interests and opportunities to craft governance systems. In this setting, it could be expected that various regimes and sectors share little in common in terms of governance systems and goals, however, the opposite is true. Regardless the differences in industry, function and form of governance system, there are core interconnections between the economic aspects of these entities and environmental and social aspects which make the regimes relatable to each other and to regimes set out in Chapters 2 and 3. Additionally, these interconnections demonstrate the ways in which these regimes can be directly connected to and entrench the SDGs.

Chapter 4 progresses by reviewing treaty regimes that are categorized into (1) trade regimes, (2) economic policy regimes, (3) banking and finance regimes and (4) industry focused regimes. It then provides an overview of the ways in which governance mechanisms contained in the treaties reviewed have responded to and been impacted by the COVID-19 pandemic as an indicator of the strengths and weaknesses of governance systems in the face of a global emergency. Finally, the chapter reviews discernible trends across economic treaty regimes and governance systems which can be used to understand how some SDGs and associated targets are already entrenched in these systems and how these systems may be used as a model for the achievement of the SDGs as long-term legal and policy instruments.

The treaties reviewed in Chapter 4 are the *General Agreement on Tariffs and Trade* (GATT),[171] the *Agreement Establishing the World Trade Organization* (*Marrakech Agreement*),[172] the *General Agreement on Trade in Services* (GATS),[173] the *Agreement on Agriculture*,[174] the *Revised Agreement on Government Procurement*,[175] the *Agreement on Import Licensing Procedures*,[176] the *Agreement on Safeguards*,[177] the *Agreement on the Application of Sanitary and Phytosanitary Measures*,[178] the *Agreement on Subsidies and Countervailing Measures*,[179] the *Agreement on Technical Barriers to Trade*,[180] *Agreement on Trade-Related Investment Measures* (TRIMS),[181] the *Marrakech Annex 2 on DSB*,[182] the *Agreement of Implementation of Article VI of the General Agreement on Tariffs and Trade 1994*,[183] the *Agreement on Implementation of Article VII of the GATT*,[184] the *Agreement on Pre-Shipment Inspection*,[185] *Agreement on Trade-Related Aspects of Intellectual Property Rights* (TRIPS),[186] the *OECD Guidelines for Multinational Enterprises*,[187] the *OECD Convention on Combatting Bribery of Foreign Public Officials in International Business Transactions*,[188] the *Treaty on Principles Governing the Activities of States in the Exploration and Use of Outer Space, Including the Moon and Other Celestial Bodies*,[189] the *Agreement on the Rescue of Astronauts, the Return of Astronauts and Return of Objects Launched into Outer Space*,[190] the *Convention on International Liability for Damage Caused by Space Objects*,[191] the *Agreement Governing the*

171 *General Agreement on Tariffs and Trade* (1947).
172 *Agreement Establishing the World Trade Organization* (1995).
173 *General Agreement on Trade in Services* (1995).
174 *Agreement on Agriculture* (1995).
175 *Revised Agreement on Government Procurement* (1995).
176 *Agreement on Import Licensing Procedures* (1995).
177 *Agreement on Safeguards* (1995).
178 *Agreement on the Application of Sanitary and Phytosanitary Measures* (1995).
179 *Agreement on Subsidies and Countervailing Measures* (1995).
180 *Agreement on Technical Barriers to Trade* (1995).
181 *Agreement on Trade-Related Investment Measures* (1995).
182 *Marrakech Annex 2 on DSB* (1995).
183 *Agreement of Implementation of Article VI of the General Agreement on Tariffs and Trade 1994* (1995).
184 *Agreement on Implementation of Article VII of the GATT* (1995).
185 *Agreement on Pre-shipment Inspection* (1995).
186 *Agreement on Trade-Related Aspects of Intellectual Property Rights* (1995).
187 *OECD Guidelines for Multinational Enterprises* (2011).
188 *OECD Convention on Combatting Bribery of Foreign Public Officials in International Business Transactions* (1999).
189 *Treaty on Principles Governing the Activities of States in the Exploration and Use of Outer Space, Including the Moon and Other Celestial Bodies* (1967).
190 *Agreement on the Rescue of Astronauts, the Return of Astronauts and Return of Objects Launched into Outer Space, United Nations* (1967).
191 *Convention on International Liability for Damage Caused by Space Objects* (1972).

Activities of States on the Moon and Other Celestial Bodies,[192] the *Convention on Registration of Objects Launched into Outer Space*,[193] the *International Bank for Reconstruction and Development Articles of Agreement*,[194] the *IFC Articles of Agreement*,[195] the *IDA Articles of Agreement*,[196] the *Convention Establishing the MIGA*,[197] the *IMF Articles of Agreement*,[198] the *Convention on the Determination of the Minimum Conditions for Access and Exploitation of Marine Resources within the Maritime Zones under Jurisdiction of the Member States of the Sub-Regional Fisheries Commission*,[199] the *Convention for the Establishment of an Inter-American Tropical Tuna Commission*,[200] the *Convention for the Conservation of Salmon in the North Atlantic Ocean*,[201] the *Convention on Future Multilateral Cooperation in North-East Atlantic Fisheries*,[202] the *Convention for the Conservation of Anadromous Stocks in the North Pacific Ocean*,[203] the *Northwest Atlantic Fisheries Convention*,[204] the *Convention on the Conservation and Management of Pollock Resources in the Central Bering Sea*,[205] the *Convention on the Conservation and Management of Fishery Resources in the South East Atlantic Ocean*,[206] the *Convention for the Conservation of Southern Bluefin Tuna*,[207] the *Convention on the Conservation and Management of Highly Migratory Fish Stocks in the Western and Central Pacific Ocean*,[208] the *International Renewable Energy Agency (IRENA)*,[209] the *Energy Charter Treaty*,[210] the *Convention of the African Energy Commission*,[211]

192 *Agreement Governing the Activities of States on the Moon and Other Celestial Bodies* (1984).
193 *Convention on Registration of Objects Launched into Outer Space* (1974).
194 *IBRD Articles of Agreement* (2012).
195 *IFC Articles of Agreement* (2020).
196 *IDA Articles of Agreement* (1960).
197 *Convention Establishing the MIGA* (1988).
198 *IMF Articles of Agreement* (1944).
199 *Convention on the Determination of the Minimum Conditions for Access and Exploitation of Marine Resources within the Maritime Zones under Jurisdiction of the Member States of the Sub-Regional Fisheries Commission* (2012).
200 *Convention for the Establishment of an Inter-American Tropical Tuna Commission* (1949).
201 *Convention for the Conservation of Salmon in the North Atlantic Ocean* (1983).
202 *Convention on Future Multilateral Cooperation in North-East Atlantic Fisheries* (1982).
203 *Convention for the Conservation of Anadromous Stocks in the North Pacific Ocean* (1993).
204 *Northwest Atlantic Fisheries Convention* (1949).
205 *Convention on the Conservation and Management of Pollock Resources in the Central Bering Sea* (1995).
206 *Convention on the Conservation and Management of Fishery Resources in the South East Atlantic Ocean* (2001).
207 *Convention for the Conservation of Southern Bluefin Tuna* (1994).
208 *Convention on the Conservation and Management of Highly Migratory Fish Stocks in the Western and Central Pacific Ocean* (1995).
209 *International Renewable Energy Agency* (*IRENA*) (2008).
210 *Energy Charter Treaty* (1991).
211 *Convention of the African Energy Commission* (2001).

the *Protocol on Energy in the SADC Region*,[212] the *Convention to Ban the Importation into Island Countries of Hazardous and Radioactive Wastes and to Control the Transboundary Movement and Management of Hazardous Wastes within the South Pacific Region* (*Waigani Convention*),[213] the *Basel Convention on the Control of Transboundary Movements of Hazardous Wastes and Their Disposal*,[214] the *Rotterdam Convention on Prior Informed Consent Procedure for Certain Hazardous Chemicals and Pesticides in International Trade*,[215] *International Tropical Timber Agreement*,[216] and the *Convention Establishing the Sustainable Tourism Zone of the Caribbean*.[217]

Some of these treaty regimes will also seem clear choices to many readers, notably those relating to the World Trade Organization, the World Bank Group and the International Monetary Fund. These are among the preeminent economic and trade treaty regimes in international law and serve as the foundation upon which many subsequent treaty regimes have been built. In the trade context, the WTO framework has also served to guide the boundaries of free trade agreements and regional trade agreements. At the same time, these treaty regimes continue to grow to meet the challenges of their specializations and their constituencies, including significant advancement in the governance realm. Indeed, the dispute settlement system of the WTO is increasingly used to address trade issues,[218] and the international banks have of late found themselves in an active role amidst efforts to address the short and long-term impacts of COVID-19 on society and economy alike.[219] As in the other chapters, each of these treaties could itself be a book volume case study on governance mechanisms *per se*, and they are mentioned here in reference only to certain aspects which are directly relevant to the SDGs. The choice to include a number of other treaty regimes, including those with a specific industry focus was made to demonstrate the diversity of treaty regimes and attendant governance systems existing in the economic context. Rather than assuming that the discussion should be bounded by

212 *Protocol on Energy in the SADC Region* (1996).

213 *Convention to Ban the Importation into Island Countries of Hazardous and Radioactive Wastes and to Control the Transboundary Movement and Management of Hazardous Wastes within the South Pacific Region* (2001).

214 *Basel Convention on the Control of Transboundary Movements of Hazardous Wastes and Their Disposal* (1992).

215 *Rotterdam Convention on Prior Informed Consent Procedure for Certain Hazardous Chemicals and Pesticides in International Trade* (2004).

216 *International Tropical Timber Agreement* (2006).

217 *Convention Establishing the Sustainable Tourism Zone of the Caribbean* (1994).

218 World Trade Organization, Dispute Settlement Body, available at https://www.wto.org/english/tratop_e/dispu_e/dispu_body_e.htm.

219 See World Bank Group, World Bank Group and COVID-19 (Coronavirus), available at https://www.worldbank.org/en/who-we-are/news/coronavirus-covid19; International Monetary Fund, IMF and COVID-19 (Coronavirus), available at https://www.imf.org/en/Topics/imf-and-covid19.

completely global treaty regimes or better-known treaty regimes, the aim is to highlight the breadth of such regimes and the lessons they can offer in connection with the SDGs. This is especially important in the context of various industries which are often difficult to regulate through an international treaty regime and governance system and yet are subject to effective regional or industry-sector focused treaty regimes.

Chapter 5 brings together the lessons of Chapters 2, 3 and 4 to analyze their potential impacts on and ties to the SDGs. There are a number of different arguments in the academic and policy-related literature regarding the status of the SDGs as purely hard law, purely soft law or a combination of the two, however, this Chapter offers an alternative understanding of this relationship. At the domestic level, it is the contention of the Chapter – and this book – that the SDGs reflect many aspects of national law and policy which either exist as suggestions rather than laws or are laws which suffer from enforcement and capacity gaps. At the international level, this book's central assertion is that the argument over whether the SDGs are soft or hard law is extraneous because they can be tied to existing treaty regimes and governance systems. In this way, the SDGs and their targets are perhaps best viewed as a high-level statement and policy tool that mirrors the international and national commitments already existing for States and the international community.

This conceptualization of the SDGs then allows States and non-State actors to use the SDGs as a consolidated statement of the most pressing and imperative international law treaty regimes and governance systems for the future. They thus incentivize compliance with their terms as well as the terms of the treaty regimes they reflect and can be entrenched and operationalized through the enforcement mechanisms which exist in these instruments. Through this lens, which views the SDGs not as an added layer of obligations but as a supplement to existing treaty regime and governance system-based obligations, it is then possible to conceive of a way for the SDGs to be accomplished even in the midst of a world that will forever be marked by the impacts of the COVID-19 pandemic. By understanding this as well as the ways in which the SDGs weave together various sectors to create a cross-cutting tapestry of governance systems and entrenchment vehicles, it is indeed possible to conceive of a successful system in which, as a matter of law and policy, no one is left behind.

Finally, Chapter 6 summarizes the key lessons and themes of the book, emphasizing the need to ensure that the SDGs are not lost in the process of adapting to the pandemic and the challenges which follow from it.

2 Environmental treaty regimes

Environmental treaty regimes are the first of the three genres of treaty regime discussed in this book since they represent the pillar with which sustainable development is perhaps most commonly associated. And, while environmental concerns in the Sustainable Development Goals (SDGs) tend to be clustered in SDGs 13, 14 and 15, in reality environmental issues are truly cross-cutting, playing a vital role in everything from food security concerns under SDG 2 to clean water under SDG 6 to renewable energy under SDG 7 to peace, justice and strong institutions under SDG 16. Indeed, as this Chapter demonstrates, environmental treaties are exceptionally diverse in context and content, scope and scale. They are united by the ways in which international law has shaped them through treaty regimes, and how these treaty regimes have established governance systems that allow them legitimacy and the ability to meet the current and future needs of their constituencies.

2.1 Generally focused regimes

While many environmental treaty regimes and attendant global governance mechanisms are geared toward addressing specific issues and targeted regions, significant regimes exist to regulate environmental issues at the global level. These regimes have national requirements and components, particularly in the context of climate change, yet are expressions of the global role and impacts of environmental concerns and, concomitantly, the impacts of national actions and schemes for pollution and related practices to impact on the global community.

In this context, the following treaty regimes are grouped together for analysis: the *United Nations Framework Convention on Climate Change* (UNFCCC) and the *Paris Agreement on Climate Change*/Katowice Outcomes[1]; the *Convention on Biological Diversity* (CBD) and *Nagoya* and *Cartagena*

1 *United Nations Framework Convention on Climate Change* (1992); *Paris Agreement on Climate Change* (2015); Katowice climate package (2018), available at https://unfccc.int/process-and-meetings/the-paris-agreement/katowice-climate-package.

Protocols[2]; the *United Nations Convention on the Law of the Sea* (UNCLOS)[3]; the *Antarctic Treaty*[4]; the *UNECE Convention on Environmental Impacts in the Transboundary Context* (*Espoo Convention*)[5]; and the *Regional Agreement on Access to Information, Public Participation and Justice in Environmental Matters in Latin America and the Caribbean* (*Escazu Convention*).[6] The inclusion of the *Antarctic Treaty* is in recognition of global interest in the environmental status and resources located within its territorial jurisdiction. Additionally, given the impact of the processes created under the *Espoo* and *Escazu Conventions* as guides for the international community, they are included in this discussion section.

2.1.1 *Treaty regime purposes and objectives*

State Parties to the 1992 UNFCCC emphasized that the Earth as a resource and entity is a common concern of humankind and that the impacts of greenhouse gases extend beyond pollution to causing existential issues at the global level.[7] In the UNFCCC there was a recognition that the state of knowledge regarding environmental threats is evolving and that the regime is an attempt to address this as a flexible framework that can accommodate new information and threats.[8] In recent years, scientific information has demonstrated that there is a severe and immediate threat to the sustainability of the climate and Earth as a resource based on the impacts of climate change and global warming.[9] With this in mind, the 2015 *Paris Agreement* builds on the UNFCCC structure to stress the importance of striving for warming at 1.5 degrees, and no more than 2 degrees Celsius, above pre-industrial levels.[10]

At the same time, it incorporates the concept of common but differentiated responsibilities for State Parties with varying development and capacity status,[11] noting the connection between this and the "protect[ion of] the climate system for the benefit of present and future generations of mankind."[12] Further, the UNFCCC makes clear that "the Parties have a

2 *Convention on Biological Diversity* (1992); *Nagoya Protocol on Access to Genetic Resources and the Fair and Equitable Sharing of Benefits Arising from Their Utilization to the Convention on Biological Diversity* (2010); *Cartagena Protocol on Biosafety to the Convention on Biological Diversity* (2003).
3 *United Nations Convention on the Law of the Sea* (1982).
4 *Antarctic Treaty* (1961).
5 *UNECE Convention on Environmental Impacts in the Transboundary Context* (1997).
6 *Regional Agreement in Access to Information, Public Participation and Justice in Environmental Matters in Latin America and the Caribbean* (2018).
7 UNFCCC, *supra* note 1 at preamble.
8 Ibid.
9 *Paris Agreement, supra* note 1 at art 2.
10 Ibid.
11 UNFCCC, *supra* note 1 at preamble.
12 Ibid. at art 3.

right to, and should, promote sustainable development"[13] and the *Paris Agreement* emphasizes the importance of economic and social factors, as well as sustainable development *per se*, in assessing and accomplishing the needs of the global environment.[14]

In creating the CBD, State Parties stressed the importance of biological resources found in various habitats as "life sustaining systems of the biosphere" and recognized that biological diversity is common heritage of mankind.[15] States established the CBD's objectives as "the conservation of biological diversity, the sustainable use of its components and the fair and equitable sharing of benefits arising out of the utilization of genetic resources, including by appropriate access to genetic resources and by appropriate transfer of relevant technologies."[16]

The *Nagoya Protocol* to the CBD highlights the inherent connections between genetic resources, food and agriculture and biological diversity.[17] As such, the *Nagoya Protocol*'s objective is to promote "the fair and equitable sharing of the benefits arising from the utilization of genetic resources, including by appropriate access to genetic resources and by appropriate transfer of relevant technologies, and by appropriate funding, thereby contributing to the conservation of biological diversity and the sustainable use of its components."[18] In creating the *Cartagena Protocol* to the CBD, the objective was "to contribute to ensuring an adequate level of protection in the field of the safe transfer, handling and use of living modified organisms resulting from modern biotechnology that may have adverse effects on the conservation and sustainable use of biological diversity, taking into account risks to human health, and specifically focusing on transboundary movements."[19]

State Parties adopted the *Antarctic Treaty* with the recognition "that it is in the interest of all mankind that Antarctica shall continue for ever to be used exclusively for peaceful purposes and shall not become the scene or object of international discord."[20] This is accompanied by the requirement that Antarctic territory not be used for military or nuclearization purposes, although this does not rule out the ability of military personnel to be in the area for legitimate scientific purposes.[21] Beyond the preservation of peace, the State Parties emphasized the importance of the area as a source of scientific value that should be retained as such.[22] Subsequently, the *Protocol on*

13 Ibid. at art 3(4).
14 See generally *Paris Agreement*, *supra* note 1.
15 CBD *supra* note 2 at preamble.
16 Ibid. at art 1.
17 *Nagoya Protocol*, *supra* note 2 at preamble.
18 Ibid. at art 1.
19 *Cartagena Protocol*, *supra* note 2 at art 1.
20 *Antarctic Treaty*, *supra* note 4 at preamble.
21 Ibid. at art I.
22 Ibid. at preamble.

Environmental Protection to the Antarctic Treaty was enacted based on the need to provide environmental protection measures for the entire region, including maintenance of peaceful purposes.[23]

In crafting the *Espoo Convention*, State Parties highlighted the essential connections between domestic and transboundary impacts and the need to coordinate them.[24] Subsequently, in 2003 the State Parties adopted the *Protocol on Strategic Environmental Assessment to the Espoo Convention* (*SEA Protocol*) "recognizing that strategic environmental assessment should have an important role in the preparation and adoption of plans, programmes and, to the extent appropriate, policies and legislation, and that wider application of the principles of Environmental Impact Assessments to plans, programmes, policies and legislation will further strengthen the systematic analysis of their significant environmental affects."[25] The *SEA Protocol* emphasizes health, climate and environmental concerns, as well as the importance of transparency in related policy and legislation.[26]

The State Parties to the *Escazu Convention* created this treaty regime while highlighting that environment, democracy, sustainable development and human rights are inherently intertwined, as is the need to include public access to the decision-making process and to protect justice and those who defend often underrepresented communities in the domestic legal system.[27] The elaborated objectives of the *Escazu Convention* are "full and effective implementation in Latin America and the Caribbean of the rights of access to environmental information, public participation in the environmental decision-making process and access to justice in environmental matters and the creation and strengthening of capacities and cooperation, contributing to the protection of the right of every person of present and future generations to live in a health environment and to sustainable development."[28]

2.1.2 *Governance mechanisms*

The main system for governance, including oversight and decision-making, in the majority of the treaty regimes discussed is the Conference of the Parties (CoP), comprised of representatives of all State Parties to the particular treaty system.[29] Using this system of governance, the CoPs are held at designated times – for example, annually for the UNFCCC and biennially for the CBD – and are often accompanied in practice by the use of intersessional

23 *Protocol on Environmental Protection to the Antarctic Treaty*, *supra* note 4 at preamble.
24 *Espoo Convention*, *supra* note 5 at preamble.
25 *Protocol on Strategic Environmental Assessment to the Espoo Convention*, *supra* note 5 at preamble.
26 Ibid. at preamble, arts 1, 3.
27 *Escazu Convention*, *supra* note 6 at preamble.
28 Ibid. at art 1.
29 UNFCCC, *supra* note 1 at art 7.

meetings and committee meetings to address issues which arise and to craft the agenda for the next CoP.[30]

The CoP is tasked with reviewing implementation of the UNFCCC, updating the terms and practices associated with the UNFCCC system to reflect new scientific knowledge and threats to national and international systems, facilitating the exchange of information between State Parties and those with expertise, issuing recommendations and decisions, creating subsidiary bodies and cooperating with non-State Party actors to facilitate knowledge dissemination.[31] For the duration of the *Kyoto Protocol*, the CoP was designated as the body to receive reports on implementation of its requirements at the national and international levels, particularly national steps toward meeting their emissions reduction targets.[32] Under the terms of the *Paris Agreement*, the CoP continues to serve as the decision-making body.[33]

Initially, the UNFCCC system established several technical committees and the *Kyoto Protocol* added to this structure. Many of the *Kyoto Protocol*-based entities remained in existence after the Protocol itself expired and ensure that functional governance systems for carbon markets remain in place. With the 2015 *Paris Agreement* and the associated 2018 Katowice Outcomes, the UNFCCC system became more nuanced in terms of committee governance structures.[34]

As part of the UNFCCC governance system, the Subsidiary Body for Scientific and Technological Advice (SBSTA) was established to share scientific updates and knowledge with the State Parties and the UNFCCC system generally, as well as assisting in technology transfer and addressing questioned posed to it by the CoP.[35] The Subsidiary Body for Implementation exists as an entity that assists the CoP with ascertaining the extent of compliance with the UNFCCC's terms at the State Party level.[36] Additionally, as part of the UNFCCC, the Financial Mechanism is established to assist in technology transfer and similar activities related to climate change, although this has subsequently been refined by the *Paris Agreement*.[37] The Financial Mechanism is currently operationalized through the Green Climate Fund and the Global Environment Facility.[38]

The *Kyoto Protocol* established the Clean Development Mechanism as the method of oversight and issuing of carbon credits where the projects for

30 *Kyoto Protocol of the United Nations Framework Convention on Climate Change* (1997) art 3.
31 UNFCCC, *supra* note 1 at art 7.
32 *Kyoto Protocol*, *supra* note 30 at art 8.
33 *Paris Agreement*, *supra* note 1 at art 6.
34 See generally ibid.
35 UNFCCC, *supra* note 1 at art 9.
36 Ibid. at art 10.
37 Ibid. at art 11.
38 See Katowice climate package, *supra* note 1 at 3/CMA.1.

which they were generated meet the established criteria.[39] In 2013, CoP19 established the Warsaw International Mechanism for Loss and Damage Associated with Climate Change (WIM). The WIM is part of the UNFCCC governance system under the supervision of a separate Executive Committee and holds independent meetings alongside the CoP.[40]

The *Paris Agreement* also established the Transparency Framework "to build mutual trust and confidence and to promote effective implementation, an enhanced transparency framework for action and support, with built-in flexibility which takes into account Parties' different capacities and builds upon collective experience."[41] Accordingly, State Parties are to provide information on commitment implementation and accomplishments through reporting requirements.[42] Further, the *Paris Agreement* establishes the Committee on Compliance as the oversight mechanism for various forms of reporting requirements, implementation of commitments and allegations of failure to fully comply with the obligations of the UNFCCC system.[43] This was provided additional operational parameters at CoP24 and CoP25, and will hold its first full meeting at CoP26.

The CBD CoP is tasked with reviewing the CBD's implementation at the national and international levels, issuing recommendations and updating policies and reviewing reports and other measures presented.[44] To assist in accomplishing the CBD, the Subsidiary Body on Scientific, Technical and Technological Advice (SBSTTA) was established.[45] The SBSTTA's designated responsibilities include providing scientific and technical advice and assistance, "identify[ing] innovative, efficient and state-of-the-art technologies and know-how relating to the conservation and sustainable use of biological diversity and advis[ing] on the ways and means of promoting development and/or transferring technologies," generating advice on cooperation and coordination and responding to specific questions relating to the subject matter of the CBD.[46] As part of the efforts to ensure a governance structure which is responsive to the needs of developed and developing State Parties, the CBD provides for financial mechanisms to protect and assist developing States in implementing the terms of the *Convention*.[47]

39 *Kyoto Protocol*, *supra* note 30 at art 12.

40 See UNFCCC, Warsaw International Mechanism for Loss and Damage Associated with Climate Change Impacts, available at https://unfccc.int/topics/adaptation-and-resilience/workstreams/loss-and-damage-ld/warsaw-international-mechanism-for-loss-and-damage-associated-with-climate-change-impacts-wim.

41 *Paris Agreement*, *supra* note 1 at art 13.

42 Ibid. at art 13.

43 Ibid. at art 15.

44 CBD, *supra* note 2 at art 23.

45 Ibid. at art 25.

46 Ibid.

47 Ibid. at art 21.

The *Nagoya Protocol* establishes a dedicated Meeting of the Parties (MoP) to serve as the decision-making entity for its implementation.[48] The *Nagoya Protocol* also establishes the Access and Benefit Sharing Clearing-House and Information-Sharing entity with the goal of facilitating the exchange of information and transparency between State Parties.[49] Should the MoP deem them necessary, subsidiary bodies and organs can be established within the *Nagoya Protocol* structure.[50]

The decision-making entity for the *Cartagena Protocol* is also the MoP, which is convened during the CBD CoP and serves oversight, review and policy-making functions.[51] Should the MoP deem it necessary, subsidiary bodies may be created.[52] Similar to the *Nagoya Protocol*, the *Cartagena Protocol* designates the Biosafety Clearing-House as the clearing-house mechanism to be used by State Parties for information sharing.[53] The *Cartagena Protocol* also designates the CBD financial mechanism as the its financial mechanism.[54]

The primary decision-making entity in the *Antarctic Treaty*'s governance system is the Conference of the Parties. Under the *Treaty*'s terms, the CoP has the authority to address matters relating to the "use of Antarctica for peaceful purposes only; facilitation of scientific research in Antarctica; facilitation of international scientific cooperation in Antarctica; facilitation of the exercise of the rights of inspection; questions relating to the exercise of jurisdiction in Antarctica; [and] preservation and conservation of living resources in Antarctica."[55] The *Protocol on Environmental Protection to the Antarctic Treaty* establishes the Committee for Environmental Protection, comprised of representatives from all State Parties.[56] The Committee is charged with providing advice and guidance for *Treaty* implementation, including whether the *Treaty* should be updated to reflect changes in environmental issues, reviewing the functioning of environmental impact assessments and requirements, reviewing and recommending methods to minimize and mitigate environmental impacts, creating environmental inspection requirements and assessing the environmental condition of the region.[57]

Under the *Espoo Convention*, the Meeting of the Parties is established as the decision-making entity.[58] This includes reviewing the methodology

48 *Nagoya Protocol*, *supra* note 2 at art 26.
49 Ibid. at art 14.
50 Ibid. at art 27.
51 *Cartagena Protocol*, *supra* note 2 at art 29.
52 Ibid. at art 30.
53 Ibid. at art 20.
54 Ibid. at art 28.
55 *Antarctic Treaty*, *supra* note 4 at art IX.
56 *Protocol on Environmental Protection to the Antarctic Treaty*, *supra* note 4 at art 11.
57 Ibid. at art 12.
58 *Espoo Convention*, *supra* note 5 at art 11.

and conduct of environmental impact assessments by State Parties, facilitating sharing of information relating to environmental impact assessment practices, generating dialogue and cooperation between State Parties and reviewing the need for amendments, protocols or other updates to the *Espoo Convention*.[59] The *Escazu Convention* establishes the Conference of the Parties as the decision-making entity for governance purposes. With this in mind, the CoP is empowered to review and generate information, adopt decisions and recommendations, provide oversight and guidance on implementation of the *Convention* and, where appropriate, adopt amendments and protocols.[60] To support the implementation of the *Convention* and information available to the CoP, a Committee to Support Implementation and Compliance is also established as a consultative entity.[61]

In a somewhat different system, the primary governance mechanism for UNCLOS is the International Seabed Authority, comprised of the Assembly, the Council, the Secretariat, the Enterprise and subsidiary bodies as deemed appropriate.[62] The Assembly functions as the equivalent general membership entity and is empowered with oversight and monitoring authority as well as the ability to create recommendations and to elect the Secretary General.[63] The Council functions as the UN Security Council equivalent in many respects, and is authorized to supervise and coordinate implementation of UNCLOS, propose Secretary General candidates, establish subsidiary organs of the Authority, conclude agreements with the UN and other organizations, generate reports and oversee both the Economic Planning Commission and the Legal and Technical Commission.[64] Additionally, the Enterprise carries out and oversees Area-based activities relating to resource exploration and exploitation, as well as "transporting, processing and marketing of minerals received from the Area."[65]

To facilitate the administrative and bureaucratic functions of these treaty regimes, all have established Secretariat systems. Some of these, such as the UNFCCC, CBD and UNCLOS Secretariats, are complex and highly sophisticated entities tasked with coordination of a variety of functions and sectors.[66] In other instances, namely in the *Espoo Convention* and the *Escazu Convention*, the Secretariat function is served by an affiliated organizational Secretariat body. Further, the Secretariat function for the *Antarctic Treaty*

59 Ibid.
60 *Escazu Convention*, *supra* note 6 at art 15.
61 Ibid. at art 18.
62 UNCLOS, *supra* note 3 at arts 156–158.
63 Ibid. at art 160.
64 Ibid. at arts 161–162.
65 Ibid. at art 170.
66 UNFCCC, *supra* note 1 at art 8.

is not defined in the original treaty regime and was instead adopted through a CoP decision in 2003.[67]

2.1.3 *Dispute settlement mechanisms*

Generally, across the environmental treaty regimes and the other regimes addressed throughout this book contain efforts to address disputes between State Parties or between a State Party and the treaty regime system in a peaceful and less formalized setting where possible. This is logical in the context of efforts at using global governance to undermine more violent means of addressing conflicts and disagreements. Where this is not possible, the various governance systems have generated different alternatives and methods of bringing about dispute settlement and resolution. It must be remembered that certain issues, such as compliance in the UNFCCC system, are to be handled by committee as an internal matter.

Disputes between State Parties to the UNFCCC are to be addressed by negotiation or other forms of peaceful settlement where possible.[68] Should these efforts fail the matter may be referred to the International Court of Justice (ICJ) or an arbitral body as the Parties to the dispute agree.[69] To address disputes relating to the CBD, the first step is to seek a negotiated settlement.[70] As a second step there is recourse to good offices, conciliation and other peaceful methods through third-party assistance and, finally, the third step is to submit the matter to the ICJ or to binding arbitration as agreed by the Parties.[71]

Disputes arising under the *Antarctic Treaty* regime are first to be addressed through consultations and negotiations or other agreed upon attempts at peaceful settlement.[72] Following these efforts, a dispute can be referred to the ICJ for final determinations.[73] Similarly, disputes arising under the *Espoo Convention* are to be handled through negotiations or other agreed means, including referral to the ICJ or the convening of an arbitral panel where appropriate.[74] Disputes arising under the *Escazu Convention* are to be settled by any methods agreed upon by the Parties involved.[75]

Generally, under UNCLOS, disputes between State Parties or between a State Party and the Authority or the Enterprise or between the Authority and private entities are under the jurisdiction of the Seabed Disputes Chamber of

67 See Antarctic Treaty Secretariat, available at https://www.ats.aq/e/secretariat.html.
68 UNFCCC, *supra* note 1 at art 14.
69 Ibid.
70 CBD, *supra* note 2 at art 27.
71 Ibid.
72 UNFCCC, *supra* note 1 at art 14.
73 *Antarctic Treaty, supra* note 4 at art XI.
74 *Espoo Convention, supra* note 5 at art 15.
75 Ibid. at art 19.

the International Tribunal on the Law of the Sea (ITLOS).[76] Included in this system is the ability of the Seabed Disputes Chamber to issue advisory opinions where requested.[77] For matters not relating to seabed issues, the first step of dispute settlement is the obligation to attempt to peacefully and mutually resolve an issue.[78] If this fails to be effective, conciliation by the Authority or with the assistance of other State Parties is provided for in UNCLOS.[79] Finally, disputes may be brought to ITLOS, the ICJ or an ad hoc or specially convened arbitral tribunal as agreed upon by the State Parties involved in the dispute.[80] Where disputes arise in relation to an Exclusive Economic Zone (EEZ), UNCLOS provides that these issues "should be resolved on the basis of equity and in the light of all the relevant circumstances, taking into account the respective importance of the interests involved to the Parties as well as to the international community as a whole."[81]

2.1.4 *Hard law elements in governance systems*

State Parties to the UNFCCC agree to implement a reporting system for emissions, mitigation plans, adaptation plans, sustainable management systems and other methods of compliance with the terms of the treaty.[82] This has been updated by the Nationally Determined Contribution (NDC) reporting requirements under the *Paris Agreement* and Katowice Outcomes, which establish a reporting system and subject non-filing State Parties to the jurisdiction of the Paris Agreement Committee on Compliance.[83] Additionally, the UNFCCC established commitment levels which are tied to the development status of the State Party, as created and updated in Annexes, with the most robust commitment requirements placed on highly developed States which are in the position to address climate change concerns and have, in many cases, benefitted in development status by contributing to climate change and environmental degradation.[84] These commitments were first amplified in the *Kyoto Protocol to the UNFCCC*, which also established the internationally accepted structures for national and regional carbon markets and trading systems as well as methods for generating additional credits through accepted projects.[85]

76 UNCLOS, *supra* note 3 at arts 186–187.
77 Ibid. at art 191.
78 Ibid. at art 279.
79 Ibid. at art 284.
80 Ibid. at art 287.
81 Ibid. at art 59.
82 Ibid. at art 4.
83 *Paris Agreement*, *supra* note 1 at art 3.
84 UNFCCC, *supra* note 1 at art 4(2).
85 See *Kyoto Protocol*, *supra* note 30.

Under the CBD, States have obligations to create and report on national strategies, plans and programs for implementing the regime as well as to update existing strategies as appropriate. These obligations include incorporating "conservation and sustainable use of biological diversity into relevant sectoral or cross-sectoral plans, programmes and policies."[86] In addition, States are to create identification and monitoring requirements as a matter of national law and practice, including *in situ* and *ex situ* conservation of biological diversity.[87] Relatedly, States are to provide for research, education and training on biological diversity issues at all levels, in a variety of economic sectors and for society as a whole.[88] Additionally, States are under an obligation to implement laws, rules and policies for the protection of genetic resources and access to genetic resources, as well as for access to and transfer of technology.[89] Further, States must cooperate with each other for the implementation of the CBD and its protocols.[90] This includes the exchange of information and knowledge on topics related to the CBD and for cooperation in the fields of technical knowledge and science.[91]

Under the terms of the *Nagoya Protocol*, States are to "take measures ... with the aim of ensuring that traditional knowledge associated with genetic resources that is held by the indigenous and local communities is accessed with the prior and informed consent or approval and involvement of these indigenous and local communities, and that mutually agreed terms have been established."[92] The *Nagoya Protocol* requires State Parties to implement laws and rules related to fair and equitable benefit-sharing, especially for related traditional knowledge, as well as related to access to genetic resources, including prior informed consent elements.[93] Additionally, there are obligations for States to operationalize special considerations to encourage conservation, biodiverse resources and potential emergencies to animal and human health.[94] To facilitate the sharing of information, States are to create national focal points and designated national authorities.[95] Further, there is an obligation for States to cooperate and promote capacity and capacity-building in the interests of developing States and SIDS[96] and for technology transfer and collaboration.[97]

86 CBD, *supra* note 2 at art 6.
87 Ibid. at arts 7–9.
88 Ibid. at arts 12–13.
89 Ibid. at arts 15–16.
90 Ibid. at art 5.
91 Ibid. at arts 17–18.
92 *Nagoya Protocol*, *supra* note 2 at art 7; see also ibid. at art 12.
93 Ibid. at arts 4–5, 15–16.
94 Ibid. at art 8.
95 Ibid. at art 13.
96 Ibid. at art 22.
97 Ibid. at art 23.

State Parties to the *Cartagena Protocol* are required to implement its terms as a matter of law and through policy, including provisions relating to import and export notification for transboundary movement of living organisms.[98] Further, the *Cartagena Protocol* contains an obligation for States to implement procedures for living organisms intended for direct use as food or feed or for processing, as well as for the handling, transportation, packaging and identification of living organisms.[99] Concomitantly, States must adopt penalties for illegal transboundary movements of living organisms.[100] In conjunction with these disclosure obligations, States are required to implement risk assessment and risk management plans for activities involving living organisms.[101] State Parties to the *Cartagena Protocol* assume an obligation to ensure public awareness and public participation in planning and decision-making that involves living organisms, and also to entrench capacity promotion and capacity-building.[102] At the international information sharing and coordination level, States have the obligation to designate competent national authorities and national focal points to serve as liaisons under the *Protocol*.[103]

Under the *Antarctic Treaty*, there is a strict prohibition on nuclear explosions in the Antarctic and on disposing of radioactive wastes in the area.[104] In the subsequent *Protocol*, the State Parties established the protection of the region and associated ecosystems as environmental principles underlying its terms and "shall be fundamental considerations in the planning of conduct of all activities in the *Antarctic Treaty* area."[105] This includes requirements for States operating in the region to limit the potential adverse effects stemming from their activities and to ensure that activities do not cause harm to natural resources, species or the historical and biological value of the area,[106] as well as a prohibition on non-research related mineral resource-based activities.[107] As part of these requirements, States are obligated to cooperate with each other for the implementation and in terms of information sharing.[108] States are also obligated to create and implement emergency response actions for environmental issues where appropriate.[109]

Under the *Espoo Convention*, States have obligations to "take all appropriate and effective measures to prevent, reduce and control significant adverse

98 *Cartagena Protocol*, *supra* note 2 at arts 2, 8.
99 Ibid. at arts 11, 18.
100 Ibid. at art 25.
101 Ibid. at arts 15–16.
102 Ibid. at arts 22–23.
103 Ibid. at art 19.
104 *Antarctic Treaty*, *supra* note 4 at art V.
105 *Protocol on Environmental Protection to the Antarctic Treaty*, *supra* note 4 at art 3.
106 Ibid.
107 Ibid. at art 7.
108 Ibid. at art 6.
109 Ibid. at art 15.

transboundary environmental impact from proposed activities."[110] To implement this, States are required to entrench laws and rules for environmental impact assessments that ensure public information and participation.[111] As a corollary, States are to notify others when there is a project with potential environmental implications, including other States that could be effected.[112] Once environmental impact assessment documents have been generated, States are under an obligation to share information and enter into consultations with affected communities or States, especially regarding transboundary impacts and measures that can be undertaken to minimize the potential impacts.[113] Included in this is the responsibility to, at the very least, share potential alternatives to the proposed activities and mutual assistance elements.[114] When a final decision has been made regarding the environmental impact assessment and the feasibility of the proposed activity, States are required to share this information with affected States, including the rationale for the decision.[115]

Under the terms of the *SEA Protocol to the Espoo Convention*, States are obligated to carry out SEAs in a number of situations and sectors, including "agriculture, forestry, fisheries, energy, industry including mining, transport, regional development, waste management, water management, telecommunications, tourism, town and country planning or land use, and which set the framework for future development and consent."[116] To implement this, as an initial matter States must conduct project screenings to determine whether a SEA is necessary.[117] Where a SEA is deemed necessary, States must create an environmental report as part of the SEA and include consideration of the interests of the public, along with public participation and transboundary consultations when there is a likelihood of significant impact.[118] These initial procedural requirements are supplemented by continuing requirements to create and oversee monitoring systems for SEAs, especially in the transboundary context.[119]

Under the *Escazu Convention*, State Parties assume an obligation to implement national laws and rules that make allowances for all constituencies to participate throughout environmental impact assessment and similar processes.[120] Relatedly, there are State obligations regarding the generation and dissemination of environmental information, ensuring public participation

110 *Espoo Convention*, *supra* note 5 at art 2.
111 Ibid. at art 2.
112 Ibid. at arts 2, 3.
113 Ibid. at art 5.
114 Ibid.
115 Ibid. at art 6.
116 *Protocol on Strategic Environmental Assessment to the Espoo Convention*, *supra* note 5 at art 4.
117 Ibid. at art 5.
118 Ibid. at arts 7–10.
119 Ibid. at art 12.
120 *Escazu Convention*, *supra* note 6 at art 4.

in environmental decision-making processes at all levels, guaranteeing access to justice in environmental matters and cooperating with other State Parties.[121]

As a general matter, UNCLOS establishes hard law requirements and tenets for States and the international community in relation to regulation of national maritime resources and international waters.[122] These requirements span a significant set of topics and sectors, ranging from national and international waters and resource rights to fishing and fleet requirements to the designation of exploration and extraction rights and abilities.[123]

2.1.5 *Soft law elements in governance systems*

State Parties to the UNFCCC agree to assist developing States with the promotion of education and training at all levels in regard to climate change, its dangers and its causes.[124] Additionally, many aspects of the *Paris Agreement* are accompanied by soft law requirements, such as commitments to carbon neutrality by 2050, increased ambition efforts to assist in this, capacity-building in norm generation and fulfilment of legal and normative requirements and the involvement of additional voices that are often excluded from discussions at the highest levels of international law, such as those from Indigenous communities, women, children, those with disabilities and those in climate vulnerable areas.[125]

Under the CBD, States are to include biological diversity and conservation into impact assessments, as well as determining and minimizing diverse impacts and ensuring that national emergencies are included in biodiversity planning.[126] The *Nagoya Protocol* establishes the need for *in situ* cooperation between State Parties[127] and also for the creation of national codes of conduct, guidelines, standards and best practices for the operationalization of the Protocol and related CBD terms.[128]

The *Antarctic Treaty* establishes State Party ability to share scientific research and knowledge, including information on planned scientific programmes, exchange of scientific personnel and sharing of observations.[129] The *Escazu Convention* provides for State options regarding implementing capacity-building opportunities.[130]

121 Ibid. at arts 6–9, 11.
122 See generally UNCLOS, *supra* note 3.
123 See generally ibid.
124 UNFCCC, *supra* note 1 at art 6.
125 See generally *Paris Agreement*, *supra* note 1.
126 CBD, *supra* note 2 at art 14.
127 *Nagoya Protocol*, *supra* note 2 at art 11.
128 Ibid. at art 20.
129 *Antarctic Treaty*, *supra* note 4 at art III.
130 *Escazu Convention*, *supra* note 5 at art 10.

2.2 Pollution-based regimes

Regulation of pollution at the international and regional level is perhaps the most commonly thought of form of treaty regime in the context of international law and environmental regimes. Indeed, the UNFCCC itself is at heart an attempt to regulate pollution, although it has taken on a larger scope and governance system since its 1992 inception. The treaty regimes reviewed in this section are directly tied to the concept of international regulation for pollution and pollutant-generating activities as a matter of law and, at the level of implementation, are highly intertwined with the use of regulatory activities to ensure that legal regimes are given effect at all levels and across all sectors. In this way, they represent governance regimes that bridge between aspiration and implementation.

In this context, the following treaty regimes are grouped together under the rubric of air pollution regimes for analysis: the *Stockholm Convention on Persistent Organic Pollutants*[131]; the *Convention for the Protection of the Ozone Layer* (*Vienna Convention*)[132]; the *Montreal Protocol on Substances That Deplete the Ozone Layer*[133]; and the *UNECE Convention on Long-Range Transboundary Air Pollution.*[134] Additionally, the maritime pollution regimes addressed in this context are the *UNECE Convention on the Protection and Use of Transboundary Watercourses and International Lakes,*[135] the *UNECE European Agreement on Main Inland Waterways of International Importance,*[136] the *Agreement on Cooperation on Marine Oil Pollution Preparedness and Response in the Arctic,*[137] the *Convention on the Protection of the Rhine,*[138] the *Agreement on the Nile River Basin Cooperation Framework*[139] and the *Convention on the Protection of the Black Sea against Pollution.*[140]

2.2.1 *Treaty regime purposes and objectives*

State Parties to the *Stockholm Convention* stressed the need for such a regime due to the transboundary nature of Persistent Organic Pollutants (PoPs), specifically in terms of impacts on migratory species, human and animal

131 *Stockholm Convention on Persistent Organic Pollutants* (2004).
132 *Convention for the Protection of the Ozone Layer* (1988).
133 *Montreal Protocol on Substances That Deplete the Ozone Layer* (1989).
134 *UNECE Convention on Long-Range Transboundary Air Pollution* (1981).
135 *UNECE Convention on the Protection and Use of Transboundary Watercourses and International Lakes* (1996).
136 *UNECE European Agreement on Main Inland Waterways of International Importance* (2015).
137 *Agreement on Cooperation on Marine Oil Pollution Preparedness and Response in the Arctic* (2013).
138 *Convention on the Protection of the Rhine* (1963).
139 *Agreement on the Nile River Basin Cooperative Framework* (2010).
140 *Convention on the Protection of the Black Sea against Pollution* (1994).

health and water and soil resources.[141] In crafting the *Montreal Protocol*, the State Parties stressed that ozone depletion issues are global issues and have a particularly damaging dynamic for developing countries.[142]

In creating the *Vienna Convention*, the State Parties highlighted the inherent threat posed to humans and the environment by air pollution and the transboundary spread of pollution.[143] While setting out the protections and requirements of the *Convention*, the State Parties articulated the fundamental principles "to protect man and his environment against air pollution and … to endeavor to limit, as far as possible, gradually reduce and prevent air pollution including long-range transboundary air pollution."[144] Following the *Vienna Convention*'s adoption, several protocols were enacted regarding the governance of specific PoPs and compounds, each of which has similar provisions relating to information sharing and pollution reduction.[145] The governance structures for these protocols parallel and use the same organs as in the *Vienna Convention*.[146] In creating the *European Agreement on Main Inland Waterways of International Importance* (1996), State Parties stressed the need for the regime because of greater maritime traffic in the area linked to trade and the concomitant ecological impacts as well as trade impacts.[147] As a result, the *Agreement* sets out the scope of covered European networks of waterways.[148]

The State Parties to the *Agreement on Cooperation on Marine Oil Pollution Preparedness and Response in the Arctic* ensured that the terms contain a particular focus on Indigenous communities and concerns in the regions as well as protecting natural resources, shipping lanes and maritime commerce.[149] Reflecting these concerns, the objective of the *Agreement* is "to strengthen cooperation, coordination and mutual assistance among the Parties on oil pollution preparedness and response in the Arctic in order to protect the marine environment from pollution by oil."[150]

141 *Stockholm Convention*, *supra* note 131 at preamble.
142 *Montreal Protocol*, *supra* note 133 at preamble.
143 *UNECE 1979 Convention on Long-Range Transboundary Air Pollution*, *supra* note 134 at preamble.
144 Ibid. at art 2.
145 See *Protocol Concerning the Control of Emissions of Volatile Organic Compounds or their Transboundary Fluxes; Protocol on the Reduction of Sulphur Emissions or their Transboundary Fluxes by at least 30 per cent; Protocol on Long-term financing of the cooperative programme for monitoring and evaluation of the long-range transmission of air pollution in Europe; Protocol to abate acidification, eutrophication and ground-level ozone; Protocol concerning the control of emissions of nitrogen oxides or their transboundary fluxes; Protocol on further reduction of Sulphur emissions.*
146 See ibid.
147 *UNECE—European Agreement on Main Inland Waterways of International Importance*, *supra* note 136 at preamble.
148 Ibid. at art 1.
149 *Agreement on Cooperation on Marine Oil Pollution Preparedness and Response in the Arctic*, *supra* note 137 at preamble.
150 Ibid. at art 1.

In adopting the *Convention on the Protection of the Rhine*, the State Parties noted the importance of using a comprehensive approach for the protection of the Rhine, including the riverbanks and surrounding areas, as a natural and commercial resource.[151] State Parties to the *Agreement on the Nile River Basin Cooperation Framework* highlighted the environmental and natural resource importance of the Nile River Basin, including the role of sustainable development.[152] Specifically, the Nile River Basin is to be "protected, used, conserved and developed" using the principles of cooperation, sustainable development, subsidiarity, equitable and reasonable utilization, prevention of significant harm, the right of Nile Basin States to use water within their territories, protection and conservation, information concerning planned measures, community of interest, exchange of data and information, environmental impact assessments and audits, peaceful resolution of disputes, waters as a finite and vulnerable resource, water as having social and economic value and water security.[153]

2.2.2 *Governance mechanisms*

The Conference of the Parties is the primary decision-making entity for the *Stockholm Convention*, with authority including the ability to perform oversight, compliance and policy-generating functions, as well as the ability to operationalize the PoPs Review Committee.[154] Under the terms of the *Stockholm Convention*, there is a periodic requirement for the CoP to review the effectiveness of the treaty and the need to evaluate areas of potential updates.[155] To assist with this, the CoP must establish non-compliance and assessment of mechanisms[156] and facilitate interchange between developed and developing countries.[157]

The *Vienna Convention* establishes the Conference of the Parties as the primary decision-making entity for governance purposes.[158] This includes oversight, compliance and policy-issuing capabilities that are tailored to a focus on ozone depletion and related issues, such as law and policy harmonization given transboundary nature of the issue.[159] In the *Convention on Long-Range Transboundary Air Pollution* governance system, the Executive Body, comprised of State Party representatives, serves the decision-making function, including reviewing the *Convention*'s implementation, the need to

151 *Convention on the Protection of the Rhine, supra* note 138 at preamble.
152 *Agreement on the Nile River Basin Cooperation Framework, supra* note 139 at preamble.
153 Ibid. at art 3.
154 *Stockholm Convention, supra* note 131 at art 19.
155 Ibid. at art 16.
156 Ibid. at art 17.
157 *Montreal Protocol, supra* note 133 at art 10.
158 *Vienna Convention, supra* note 132 at art 6.
159 Ibid.

generate amendments and updates to the treaty as appropriate and to liaise with other States and international organizations.[160]

The Meeting of the Parties is established as the decision-making entity for the *Convention on the Protection and Use of Transboundary Watercourses and International Lakes* and is charged with reviewing methods and concerns regarding watercourses that are to be assessed in the transboundary context, exchanging and cooperating on relevant information and practices and engaging with other States and international organizations.[161] The primary means of decision-making under the *Agreement on Cooperation on Marine Oil Pollution Preparedness and Response* is the Meeting of the Parties, which is to be held regularly in order to make decisions and through mechanisms used by the Arctic Council.[162] The primary decision-making entity in the *Convention on the Protection of the Black Sea against Pollution*'s governance system is the Commission on the Protection of the Black Sea against Pollution, which is vested with policy and oversight capacities.[163] A MoP with limited review and oversight jurisdiction is also created.[164]

The primary governance and decision-making apparatus for the *Convention on the Protection of the Rhine* is the Commission, which is tasked with oversight, recommendation and policy promulgation and creating a coordinated system for warning on issues related to the Rhine.[165] Additionally, the Commission serves as the coordinating entity with other State Parties and international organizations.[166] The overarching governance mechanism for the *Agreement on the Nile River Basin Cooperation Framework* is the Nile River Basin Commission, which is comprised of the Conference of Heads of State and Government, the Council of Ministers, the Technical Advisory Committee, the Security Advisory Committee and the Secretariat.[167] The Conference of Heads of State and Government functions as the highest organ in this system and provides guidance as needed.[168] The Council of Ministers is comprised of ministers with water-related portfolios and provides technical expertise as well as making decisions.[169] The Technical Advisory Committee creates programs and policies of the Council and the Organization, makes recommendations to the Council,

160 *UNECE 1979 Convention on Long-Range Transboundary Air Pollution*, *supra* note 134 at art 10.

161 *UNECE Convention on the Protection and Use of Transboundary Watercourses and International Lakes*, *supra* note 135 at art 17.

162 *Agreement on Cooperation on Marine Oil Pollution Preparedness and Response in the Arctic*, *supra* note 137 at art 14.

163 *Convention on the Protection of the Black Sea against Pollution*, *supra* note 140 at art XVII.

164 Ibid. at art XIX.

165 *Convention on the Protection of the Rhine*, *supra* note 138 at arts 6, 8.

166 Ibid. at art 14.

167 *Agreement on the Nile River Basin Cooperation Framework*, *supra* note 139 at art 15.

168 Ibid. at art 21.

169 Ibid. at arts 22–23.

creates appropriate working groups and provides technical assistance as needed.[170] Further, the Council has the ability to create additional Sectoral Advisory Committees at its discretion.[171]

In terms of administrative oversight and bureaucratic functions, there is a divergence between treaty regimes such as the *Stockholm Convention* and *Montreal Protocol*, which have their own dedicated Secretariat structures[172] and the *Vienna Convention*, which is served by the UNEP Secretariat.[173] Further, implementation of the *European Agreement on Main Inland Waterways of International Importance*'s governance is intended to be conducted by the UNECE and its Executive Secretariat.[174]

2.2.3 *Dispute settlement mechanisms*

Under the *Stockholm Convention*, disputes settlement is to begin with attempts at negotiation or the use of other peaceful means.[175] The second step is for the matter to be referred to the ICJ or a specially convened arbitral tribunal, however, if progress is not made after a year from this referral a conciliation commission is to be assembled under the auspices of the *Stockholm Convention*.[176]

Disputes arising in connection with the *Convention on Long-Range Transboundary Air Pollution* are to be settled through negotiation or other peaceful methods agreed on by the Parties to the matter.[177] Similarly, under the *Agreement on Cooperation on Marine Oil Pollution Preparedness and Response in the Arctic*, disputes are to be settled through direct consultations,[178] as are disputes arising under the *Convention on the Protection of the Black Sea against Pollution*. Disputes arising under the *Convention on the Protection and Use of Transboundary Watercourses and International Lakes* are to be settled through negotiation or other agreed upon means where possible.[179] Where

170 Ibid. at art 26.

171 Ibid. at art 28.

172 *Stockholm Convention*, *supra* note 131 at art 20; *Montreal Protocol*, *supra* note 133 at art 12; *Convention on the Protection of the Rhine*, *supra* note 138 at art 12; *Agreement on the Nile River Basin Cooperation Framework*, *supra* note 139 at art 30.

173 *Vienna Convention*, *supra* note 132 at art 7; *UNECE 1979 Convention on Long-Range Transboundary Air Pollution*, *supra* note 134 at art 11; *UNECE Convention on the Protection and Use of Transboundary Watercourses and International Lakes*, *supra* note 135 at art 19.

174 *UNECE—European Agreement on Main Inland Waterways of International Importance*, *supra* note 136.

175 *Stockholm Convention*, *supra* note 131 at art 18.

176 Ibid.

177 *UNECE 1979 Convention on Long-Range Transboundary Air Pollution*, *supra* note 134 at art 13.

178 *Agreement on Cooperation on Marine Oil Pollution Preparedness and Response in the Arctic*, *supra* note 137 at art 18.

179 *UNECE Convention on the Protection and Use of Transboundary Watercourses and International Lakes*, *supra* note 135 at art 22.

additional intervention is necessary, the dispute may be referred to the ICJ or to an arbitral panel.[180] A similar system is used by the *Vienna Convention*, although a middle step exists which involves recourse to third-party interventions, largely through conciliation, to attempt a settlement.[181]

The initial phase of addressing disputes under the *European Agreement on Main Inland Waterways of International Importance* is through arbitration.[182] If required, in the second phase the UN Secretary General may appoint a designated arbitrator to issue a binding decision.[183] Disputes arising under the *Convention on the Protection of the Rhine* are to be addressed first through negotiations and other attempts at peaceful resolution, and then through arbitration as agreed upon by the Parties.[184] Disputes arising in connection with the *Agreement on the Nile River Basin Cooperation Framework* are first to be addressed through attempts at peace settlement between the Parties.[185] Should it be necessary, it is then possible for the Parties to request assistance from the Council.[186]

2.2.4 *Hard law elements in governance systems*

Under the terms of the *Stockholm Convention*, State Parties have the obligation to take legal and regulatory measures to prohibit releases of PoPs as the result of intentional production and use.[187] Should there be exemptions granted at the national level, these must be placed on a State registry and transmitted to the Stockholm Convention Secretariat.[188] Further, States are obligated to take legal and regulatory measures to prohibit and make restricted releases of PoPs from stockpiles and wastes.[189] States are also under an obligation to expand and implement capacities to engage in public information campaigns, public awareness and public education efforts related to PoPs and associated issues.[190] At the compliance level, States must provide information on implementation plans for the *Convention*'s terms as well as reporting requirements to the Secretariat, including providing updates as required.[191]

180 Ibid. at art 22.
181 *Vienna Convention*, *supra* note 132 at art 11.
182 *UNECE—European Agreement on Main Inland Waterways of International Importance*, *supra* note 136 at art 10.
183 Ibid.
184 *Convention on the Protection of the Rhine*, *supra* note 138 at art 16.
185 *Agreement on the Nile River Basin Cooperation Framework*, *supra* note 139 at art 34.
186 Ibid.
187 *Stockholm Convention*, *supra* note 131 at arts 3, 5.
188 Ibid. at art 4.
189 Ibid. at art 6.
190 Ibid. at art 10.
191 Ibid. at arts 7–9, 15.

Under the terms of the *Vienna Convention*, State Parties have general obligations "to protect human health and the environment against adverse effects resulting or likely to result from human activities which modify or are likely to modify the ozone layer."[192] These obligations include collaboration and cooperation on scientific understandings of the threat posed by ozone depletion, creation of commensurate laws, rules and policies and cooperation with other organizations as necessary to meet the *Vienna Convention*'s goals.[193] At the national level, States are obligated to "facilitate and encourage" legal, scientific and technical exchanges with each other and with Convention-related bodies, as well as to assist developing States in the generation of relevant laws, science and technology.[194] States must also provide compliance reports to the *Vienna Convention* bodies on a periodic basis and be subject to review processes.[195]

Under the *Montreal Protocol*, State Parties are required to implement bans on the importation of banned and restricted substances which are linked to depletion of the ozone layer,[196] and must engage in periodic reporting to the Secretariat regarding these actions.[197] Additionally, State Parties are to cooperate with each other regarding research, development, public awareness and exchange of information relating to efforts to ban the designated substances.[198] State Parties to the *Convention on Long-Range Transboundary Air Pollution* are obligated to share information on air pollution, consult, engage in research and monitoring and create evolving strategies to address pollution and associated issues, as well as policies and efforts undertaken to address these issues.[199] In instances where there is a risk or occurrence of qualifying air pollution discharge, State Parties are under an obligation to disclose this and consult with impacted States.[200]

Under the terms of the *Convention on the Protection and Use of Transboundary Watercourses and International Lakes*, States are required to "take all appropriate measures to prevent, control and reduce any transboundary impact," including waters that are likely to have a transboundary impact.[201] As part of these requirements, States must review and protect ecological status and conservation, and ensure that waters are "used in a reasonable and equitable way, taking into particular account their

192 *Vienna Convention, supra* note 132 at art 2.
193 Ibid. at art 2, 3.
194 Ibid. at art 4.
195 Ibid. at art 5.
196 *Montreal Protocol, supra* note 133 at art 4.
197 Ibid. at art 6.
198 Ibid. at art 9.
199 *UNECE 1979 Convention on Long-Range Transboundary Air Pollution, supra* note 134 at arts 3, 4, 7.
200 Ibid. at art 5.
201 *UNECE Convention on the Protection and Use of Transboundary Watercourses and International Lakes, supra* note 135 at art 2.

transboundary character, in the case of activities which cause or are likely to cause transboundary impact."[202] These measures are to be taken using the precautionary approach and the polluter pays principle, as are the laws, rules and policies enacted to effect this goal.[203] States are also under obligations to cooperate on research and development for prevention, control and reduction of environment and related damage with potential for transboundary effects, including at the bi-lateral and multi-lateral levels.[204] This involves efforts at joint monitoring and assessment regarding pollution and transboundary impacts as well as obligations for Riparian States to create and implement warning systems and provide mutual assistance.[205]

Pursuant to the terms of the *European Agreement on Main Inland Waterways of International Importance*, States must "establish national action plans and/or bilateral or multinational agreements, such as international treaties, guidelines, memorandum of understanding, joint studies, or any other similar arrangements, aimed at elimination of existing bottlenecks and completion of missing linkings in the networks."[206] State Parties to the *Agreement on Cooperation on Marine Oil Pollution Preparedness and Response in the Arctic* are obligated to "maintain a national system for reporting promptly and effectively to oil pollution incidents," including elements of concern relating to environment and ecology in protected areas.[207] Further requirements involve having equipment available and in-place in order to mitigate oil spills in conjunction with private industries.[208] States must also designate competent national authorities and contact points for *Agreement* implementation, notify *Agreement* bodies and State Parties in the event of an oil spill and continuously monitor for oil pollution within its territory.[209] This is part of a larger obligation for States to engage in cooperation and coordination for information exchange.[210]

In the *Convention on the Protection of the Rhine*, State Parties assume obligations to ensure the protection of the Rhine ecosystem through sustainable development, protection of species in the area, conservation and environmentally sound usages and attempts at safe implementation of dredging activities.[211] In fulfilling these elements of the *Convention*, States are obliged to use core elements of sustainable development law and principles, such

202 Ibid.
203 Ibid. at arts 2, 3.
204 Ibid. at arts 5–6, 10.
205 Ibid. at arts 11, 14–15.
206 *UNECE—European Agreement on Main Inland Waterways of International Importance*, *supra* note 136 at art 2.
207 *Agreement on Cooperation on Marine Oil Pollution Preparedness and Response in the Arctic*, *supra* note 137 at art 4.
208 Ibid. at art 4.
209 Ibid. at arts 5–7.
210 Ibid. at art 12.
211 *Convention on the Protection of the Rhine*, *supra* note 138 at art 3.

as the precautionary principle and the polluter pays principle.[212] State Parties to the *Agreement on the Nile River Basin Cooperation Framework* have obligations not to cause significant harm to the resource and to "protect, conserve and, where necessary, rehabilitate the Nile River Basin and its ecosystems."[213] Further, States are required to communicate emerging situations and threats to the Nile River Basin and to protect the River and associated areas from harm during armed conflict.[214]

Overall, State Parties to the *Convention on the Protection of the Black Sea against Pollution* emphasized the ecological importance of the Black Sea region.[215] To achieve this, States agree to create and implement laws, policies and regulations that work to "prevent, reduce and control" pollution,[216] especially from hazardous substances, land-based sources, ships and vessels, by dumping from various sources and in emerging situations.[217] States have heightened responsibilities to prevent pollution stemming from activities on the Continental shelf and also through atmospheric sources.[218] The legal and regulatory measures adopted by State Parties must also include protections for marine living resources and in transboundary contexts.[219] Together, States have the obligation to create and implement scientific and technical cooperation and monitoring systems.[220]

2.2.5 *Soft law elements in governance systems*

The *Stockholm Convention* provides for State abilities regarding research, development and monitoring of PoPs and their impacts, as well as the ability to engage in technical assistance and technological transfer.[221] States also have the ability to provide financial resources and mechanisms for assistance in implementing the terms of the *Stockholm Convention*.[222]

Under the *Convention on Long-Range Transboundary Air Pollution*, State Parties have the ability to agree on the need to implement and develop cooperation programmes for monitoring and evaluation of the long-range transmission of air pollution in Europe.[223] Further, in the *Agreement on Cooperation on Marine Oil Pollution Preparedness and Response in the*

212 Ibid. at art 4.
213 *Agreement on the Nile River Basin Cooperation Framework*, *supra* note 139 at arts 5–6.
214 Ibid. at arts 12–13.
215 *Convention on the Protection of the Black Sea against Pollution*, *supra* note 140 at preamble.
216 Ibid. at art V.
217 Ibid. at art VI–X.
218 Ibid. at arts XI–XII.
219 Ibid. at arts III–XIV.
220 Ibid. at art XV.
221 *Stockholm Convention*, *supra* note 131 at arts 11–12.
222 Ibid. at art 13.
223 *UNECE 1979 Convention on Long-Range Transboundary Air Pollution*, *supra* note 134 at art 9.

Arctic, State Parties have the ability to request assistance from other States in the event of an incident or oil spill.[224] States also have the ability to engage in a joint review of oil pollution incident response operations and to engage in joint training exercises for oil spill response.[225]

2.3 Species and wildlife regimes

If pollution prevention is one of the quintessential aspects of the perceived underpinnings for global governance mechanisms that promote environmental regimes, species protections are a concomitant concern. While the regimes discussed in this section are, more often than not, concerned with a particular species or habitat that is circumscribed within an area or region, they are discussed separately from the geographically focused regimes set out below since the primary goal of their governance systems is species and natural resource specific rather than specific regional protection.

In this context, the following treaty regimes are grouped together for analysis: the *Convention on Migratory Species of Wild Animals*[226]; the *Agreement on the Conservation of Gorillas and Their Habitats*[227]; the *Agreement on the Conservation of Albatrosses and Petrels*[228]; the *Agreement on the Conservation of African-Eurasian Migratory Birds*[229]; the *Agreement on the Conservation of Populations of European Bats*[230]; the *Convention on the International Trade in Endangered Species*[231]; the *International Plant Protection Convention*[232]; the *Convention on Wetlands of International Importance Especially as Waterfowl Habitats (Ramsar Convention)*[233]; the *Convention on the Conservation of European Wildlife and Natural Habitats*[234]; the *Agreement on the Conservation of Cetaceans of the Black Sea, Mediterranean Sea and Contiguous Atlantic Area*[235]; the *Inter-American Convention for the Protection and Conservation of Sea Turtles*[236]; the *Treaty on the Conservation and Sustainable Management of Forest Ecosystems in Central Africa and to Establish the Central African*

224 *Agreement on Cooperation on Marine Oil Pollution Preparedness and Response in the Arctic*, *supra* note 137 at art 8.
225 Ibid. at arts 11, 13.
226 *Convention on Migratory Species of Wild Animals* (1979).
227 *Agreement on the Conservation of Gorillas and Their Habitats* (2007).
228 *Agreement on the Conservation of Albatrosses and Petrels* (2004).
229 *Agreement on the Conservation of African-Eurasian Migratory Birds* (1999).
230 *Agreement on the Conservation of Populations of European Bats* (1994).
231 *Convention on the International Trade in Endangered Species* (1975).
232 *International Plant Protection Convention* (1952).
233 *Convention on Wetlands of International Importance Especially as Waterfowl Habitats* (1975).
234 *Convention on the Conservation of European Wildlife and Natural Habitats* (1979).
235 *Agreement on the Conservation of Cetaceans of the Black Sea, Mediterranean Sea and Contiguous Atlantic Area* (1996).
236 *Inter-American Convention for the Protection and Conservation of Sea Turtles* (2001).

Forests Commission[237]; and the *Convention for the Conservation of Antarctic Seals*.[238]

2.3.1 *Treaty regime purposes and objectives*

State Parties to the *Convention on the Conservation of Migratory Species of Wild Animals* (CMS) noted current and future generations' needs to interact with wildlife and wild animals, as well as special concerns regarding migratory species and the need for concerted conservation efforts at national and regional levels for these species.[239] With this in mind, States "acknowledge the importance of migratory species being conserved and of Range States agreeing to take action to this end wherever possible and appropriate, paying special attention to migratory species the status of which is unfavorable, and taking individually or in cooperation appropriate and necessary steps to conserve such species or their habitat."[240]

In creating the *Agreement on the Conservation of Gorillas and Their Habitats*, State Parties stressed that it was an outgrowth of the legal and governance regime established in the *Convention on Migratory Species*' CoP decision on the need to address gorilla protection as a specific entity.[241] Against this backdrop, the *Agreement* provides that States "shall take coordinated measures to maintain gorillas in a favorable conservation status or to restore them to such a status."[242] In creating the *Agreement on the Conservation of African-Eurasian Migratory Waterbirds*, State Parties noted the direct connection with the CMS regime and highlighted the importance of migratory waterbirds for current and future generations, including sustainable development and sustainable use.[243] The *Agreement on the Conservation of Populations of European Bats* stresses that it is created as an outgrowth of the CMS regime and in response to threats facing bats in regional Range States and non-Range States.[244]

In creating the CITES regime, the State Parties stressed the inherent value of wildlife to humanity and to ecosystems.[245] At the same time, they noted that, although States and people are often in the best position to know the needs of wildlife, international cooperation is essential for achieving full

237 *Treaty on the Conservation and Sustainable Management of Forest Ecosystems in Central Africa and to Establish the Central African Forests Commission* (2005).

238 *Convention for the Conservation of Antarctic Seals* (1972).

239 *Convention on the Conservation of Migratory Species of Wild Animals, supra* note 226 at preamble.

240 Ibid. Animals at art II.

241 *Agreement on the Conservation of Gorillas and Their Habitats, supra* note 227 at preamble.

242 Ibid. at art II.

243 *Agreement on the Conservation of African-Eurasian Migratory Waterbirds, supra* note 229 at preamble.

244 *Agreement on the Conservation of Populations of European Bats, supra* note 230 at preamble.

245 CITES, *supra* note 231 at preamble.

protections.[246] The *International Plant Protection Convention* was created by State Parties to emphasize the need to correlate protection of plants with protection of human health, animal health and the environment.[247]

Under the *Agreement on the Conservation of Cetaceans of the Black Sea, Mediterranean Sea and Contiguous Atlantic Area*, the regional community of States inherently "recogniz[es] that cetaceans are an integral part of the marine ecosystem which must be conserved for the benefit of present and future generations, and that their conservation is a common concern."[248] State Parties to the *Inter-American Convention for the Protection and Conservation of Sea Turtles* recognized the critical importance of sea turtles to the habitats and ecosystems in which they are located as a foundation matter of the *Convention*.[249] At the same time, the State Parties recognized the existing and emerging threats posed to the continued vitality of the species unless further action was taken.[250] This is reflected in the core objectives of the *Convention* "to promote the protection, conservation and recovery of sea turtle populations and of the habitats on which they depend, based on the best available scientific evidence, taking into account the environmental, socioeconomic and cultural characteristics of the Parties."[251]

The State Parties to the *Convention for the Conservation of Antarctic Seals* highlight the vulnerability of Antarctic seals and the need to conserve them and their habitats, and also emphasize the need to improve the state of scientific knowledge in these areas.[252] The State Parties to the *Agreement on the Conservation of Albatrosses and Petrels* created it as an outgrowth of commitments under the CMS regime.[253] The *Agreement* establishes the importance of the albatross and petrel populations generally, as well as their habitats and associated biodiversity, and the real and potential threats posed to them by human activities.[254] This background informs the objective of the *Agreement* to promote an increased in the conservation status of albatrosses and petrels and to ensure that their protection and the protection of their habitats is accomplished using the precautionary principle.[255]

246 Ibid.

247 *International Plant Protection Convention*, *supra* note 232 at preamble.

248 *Agreement on the Conservation of Cetaceans of the Black Sea, Mediterranean Sea and Contiguous Atlantic Area*, *supra* note 235 at preamble.

249 *Inter-American Convention for the Protection and Conservation of Sea Turtles*, *supra* note 136 at preamble.

250 Ibid.

251 Ibid. at art II.

252 *Convention for the Conservation of Antarctic Seals*, *supra* note 238 at preamble.

253 *Agreement on the Conservation of Albatrosses and Petrels*, *supra* note 228 at preamble.

254 Ibid.

255 Ibid. at art II.

2.3.2 *Governance mechanisms*

The principal decision-making entity under the CMS is the Conference of the Parties, which is convened at least every three years.[256] The CoP is tasked with reviewing the status of migratory species and conservation progress internationally and in State Parties, generating recommendations and guidance in implementation of the *Convention* and providing comments and responses to reports and other documents received.[257] A secondary governing entity within the CMS structure is the Scientific Council, which provides technical and scientific information and guidance to the Secretariat and CoP, makes recommendations regarding cooperation and coordination for research and species management and generates findings and suggestions for review by the CoP.[258]

The *Agreement on the Conservation of Gorillas and Their Habitats* establishes the Meeting of the Parties as the primary decision-making entity, to meet at least every three years.[259] Included in the MoP's functions are reviewing and making changes to regulations and restrictions on gorillas and their habitats, reviewing progress in the implementation of the *Agreement*'s terms and reporting on them, drafting proposals to the *Agreement*'s texts and ratifying them and creating subsidiary bodies as necessary.[260] The functions of the MoP are assisted by the Technical Committee, which provides reports and expert opinions on various topics, provides scientific and technical research and may make recommendations to the MoP.[261]

The *Agreement on the Conservation of Cetaceans of the Black Sea, Mediterranean Sea and Contiguous Atlantic Area* established the Meeting of the Parties as the decision-making body.[262] The MoP's functions include reviewing new and available information and scientific data on cetaceans, reviewing progress made toward and issues in implementation of the *Agreement*, generating recommendations, amendments and protocols relating to the *Agreement*, creating an annual report and reviewing the work of the various committees.[263] In addition, the MoP elects the members of the Bureau, an expert entity for the provision of guidance relating to *Agreement*-related policy and budgeting, serving intersessional functions as needed and representing the treaty regime at the international organization level.[264] Under

256 *Convention on the Conservation of Migratory Species of Wild Animals*, *supra* note 226 at art VII.
257 Ibid.
258 Ibid. at art VIII.
259 *Agreement on the Conservation of Gorillas and Their Habitats*, *supra* note 227 at art V.
260 Ibid. at art V.
261 Ibid. at art VI.
262 *Agreement on the Conservation of Cetaceans of the Black Sea, Mediterranean Sea and Contiguous Atlantic Area*, *supra* note 235 at art III.
263 Ibid.
264 Ibid. at art VI.

the *Agreement*, a Scientific Committee of experts in cetacean conservation is created to provide advisory functions to the MoP and all other *Agreement*-based organizations.[265] These types of advisory functions include advice and technical knowledge, advice relating to guidelines and mechanisms for researching and reporting information related to cetacean conservation.[266] In addition, the *Agreement* establishes a series of sub-regional Co-ordination Units, which are to facilitate implementation in the designated sub-regions, gather and review pertinent information and produce of reports and other documents.[267] The primary governance system established in the *Agreement on the Conservation of Populations of European Bats* is the Meeting of the Parties, which has the ability to generate findings and recommendations as well as to create committees and subsidiary bodies as deemed necessary.[268]

CITES established the Conference of the Parties as the primary decision-making entity, which is scheduled to meet every three years.[269] Critical tasks of the CoP include reviewing and providing guidance on new trends and issues in fields related to the treaty regime and its implementation, making policy decisions, treaty amendments and guidelines and reviewing implementation of the treaty as well as additional policy instruments.[270] Administrative functions are to be carried out by the UNEP Secretariat, which is designated as the entity to serve secretariat functions for CITES.[271] In this function, a mechanism for the Secretariat to receive and transmit allegations regarding issues of species transportation and State responses, investigations and determinations of the need for remedial action.[272] Subsequently, three specialized committees were created to oversee the implementation of CITES – the Standing Committee, the Animals Committee and the Plants Committee.[273] These were created under the auspices of various CoPs and have their own sets of procedure for meeting, typically during the CoP, as well as for addressing and generating recommendations based on their portfolios and issues referred to them.[274]

Much of the governance for the *Convention on the Conservation of European Wildlife and Natural Habitats* is done in the confines of the European Union's governance structure. However, a dedicated Standing Committee is created under the terms of the *Convention* in order to review the application of the *Convention*'s terms, make recommendations regarding

265 Ibid. at art VII.
266 Ibid.
267 Ibid. at art V.
268 *Agreement on the Conservation of Populations of European Bats*, *supra* note 230 at art V.
269 CITES, *supra* note 231 at art XI.
270 Ibid.
271 Ibid. at art XII.
272 Ibid. at art XIII.
273 CITES, available at https://www.cites.org/.
274 Ibid.

its application and on how to best inform the public of its contents and make proposals regarding future methods of implementation.[275] The *Agreement on the Conservation of Albatrosses and Petrels* stipulates that the Meeting of the Parties is to serve as the primary decision-making entity within the governance system.[276] The essential functions of the MoP are reviewing reports and other information submitted, reviewing that conservation and scientific status of albatrosses and petrels, reviewing the accomplishments of and challenges facing achieving the *Agreement*'s objectives, generating annual reports and adopting amendments or other changes to the Agreement.[277] Additionally, an Advisory Committee is created to provide expert advice to both the MoP and the Secretariat.[278] Areas of expertise for the Advisory Committee include science and technology, aspects of creating standard taxonomies for conservation of albatrosses and petrels, implementation recommendations and generation of indicators and other measures to gauge the success of conservation efforts.[279]

The main decision-making entity for the *Inter-American Convention for the Protection and Conservation of Sea Turtles* is the Meeting of the Parties, which must convene at least every three years and is tasked with review and oversight of national and international implementation, as well as gathering and generating information on the scientific and conservation status of sea turtles and their habitats.[280] There are two additional entities, the Consultative Committee of Experts and the Scientific Committee, which provide information and governance support under the *Agreement* structure. The Consultative Committee of Experts consists of State representatives as well as representatives from the scientific community, private sector and non-governmental organizations.[281] It serves to review and analyze reports and information on sea turtles, request and evaluate information received from States and generate reports and findings.[282] The Scientific Committee is tasked with providing scientific and technical information to State Parties, the MoP, the Secretariat and the Consultative Committee of Experts.[283]

Under the *Treaty on the Conservation and Sustainable Management of Forest Ecosystems in Central Africa and to Establish the Central African Forests Commission*, the highest decision-making entity is the Summit of the

275 *Convention on the Conservation of European Wildlife and Natural Habitats, supra* note 234 at arts 13–14.

276 *Agreement on the Conservation of Albatrosses and Petrels, supra* note 228 at art VIII.

277 Ibid.

278 Ibid. at art IX.

279 Ibid.

280 *Inter-American Convention for the Protection and Conservation of Sea Turtles, supra* note 236 at art V.

281 Ibid. at art VII.

282 Ibid.

283 Ibid. at art VIII.

Heads of State and Government.[284] Additionally, the Council of Ministers functions as the organ that is responsible for making some decisions, coordinating and overseeing the implementation of the *Treaty* and information received from State Parties.[285]

A significant element of the *International Plant Protection Convention*'s governance system exists under the auspices of the Food and Agriculture Organization (FAO), including the Secretariat, which is appointed by the Director-General of the FAO.[286] The key governance body for the *Convention* is the Committee on Phytosanitary Measures, which is empowered to review plant protections and the need for new national and international laws, rules and regulations, to generate new rules and standards relating to international plant protection, assist in dispute settlement, create subsidiary bodies as necessary, facilitate cooperation between State Parties and with international organizations and make recommendations for implementing the *Convention*.[287] The primary governance system established under the *Ramsar Convention* is the Conference of the Parties, which functions as the primary oversight, recommendation and guidance generating entity.[288] Administrative and bureaucratic functions relating to the *Ramsar Convention* are exercised through the IUCN.[289]

The *Convention for the Conservation of Antarctic Seals* is somewhat unique in that it operates on consensus and does not use the strict governance systems which as associated with standard treat regimes. In the system adopted by the *Convention*, State Parties are provided with a series of areas in which they may make decisions and update the terms of the treaty. Crucially, the *Convention* allows States to periodically update and/or amend it in terms of the species of seals covered, protections to be afforded to them and the handling of unprotected species, as well as the methodology to be used for review and assessment of *Convention* terms.[290]

The *Agreement on the Conservation of African-Eurasian Migratory Waterbirds* establishes the Meeting of the Parties as the primary decision-making authority for its governance system.[291] In this capacity, it is tasked with reviewing potential changes to the *Agreement* and methods of enforcement, reviewing reports and other information and undertaking budgeting

284 *Treaty on the Conservation and Sustainable Management of Forest Ecosystems in Central Africa and to Establish the Central African Forests Commission*, *supra* note 237 at art 7.

285 Ibid. at art 10.

286 *International Plant Protection Convention*, *supra* note 232 at art XII.

287 Ibid. at art XI.

288 *Convention on Wetlands of International Importance Especially as Waterfowl Habitats*, *supra* note 233 at art 6.

289 Ibid. at art 8.

290 *Convention for the Conservation of Antarctic Seals*, *supra* note 238 at art 3.

291 *Agreement on the Conservation of African-Eurasian Migratory Waterbirds*, *supra* note 239 at art VI.

and finance functions.[292] Additionally, the MoP is charged with creating the Action Plan as a binding instrument that States are to implement with the aid of Conservation Guidelines also established by the MoP and expert bodies.[293] To assist in this and in the generation of technical recommendations, a Technical Committee exists as part of the *Agreement*'s governance structure.[294]

Except as noted above, the treaty regimes in this section have established separate Secretariats, which focus on providing administrative and bureaucratic structures to the State Parties, CoPs and committees which exist within the governance systems of the regimes.[295]

2.3.3 *Dispute settlement mechanisms*

Should disputes arise in the context of CITES, the first step is to attempt settlement through peaceful methods, including negotiations.[296] The second step, if required, is to seek resolution through arbitration, preferably at the Permanent Court of Arbitration.[297] Similar provisions exist in the CMS,[298] *Agreement on the Conservation of Gorillas and Their Habitats*[299] and *Agreement on the Conservation of African-Eurasian Migratory Waterbirds.*[300] Under the *Agreement on the Conservation of Populations of European Bats*, the sole referenced mechanism for addressing disputes is through negotiation.[301]

Disputes arising in connection with the *Agreement on the Conservation of Cetaceans of the Black Sea, Mediterranean Sea and Contiguous Atlantic Area* are to be addressed first through negotiation or third-party mediation, and then arbitration or judicial settlement as agreed by the Parties.[302] The

292 Ibid.

293 Ibid at art IV.

294 Ibid. at art VII.

295 See *Agreement on the Conservation of Cetaceans of the Black Sea, Mediterranean Sea and Contiguous Atlantic Area, supra* note 235 at art IV; *Convention on the Conservation of Migratory Species of Wild Animals, supra* note 226 at art IX; *Agreement on the Conservation of Gorillas and Their Habitats, supra* note 227 at art VII; *Inter-American Convention for the Protection and Conservation of Sea Turtles, supra* note 236 at art VI; *Convention on Wetlands of International Importance Especially as Waterfowl Habitats, supra* note 233 at art 8; *Convention for the Conservation of Antarctic Seals, supra* note 238 at art 7; *Agreement on the Conservation of Albatrosses and Petrels, supra* note 228 at art X; *Agreement on the Conservation of African-Eurasian Migratory Waterbirds, supra* note 229 at art VIII.

296 CITES, *supra* note 231 at art XVIII.

297 Ibid.

298 *Convention on the Conservation of Migratory Species of Wild Animals, supra* note 226 at art XIII.

299 *Agreement on the Conservation of Gorillas and Their Habitats, supra* note 227 at art XII.

300 *Agreement on the Conservation of African-Eurasian Migratory Waterbirds, supra* note 229 at art XII.

301 *Agreement on the Conservation of Populations of European Bats, supra* note 230 at art IX.

302 *Agreement on the Conservation of Cetaceans of the Black Sea, Mediterranean Sea and Contiguous Atlantic Area, supra* note 235 at art XII.

Convention on the Conservation of European Wildlife and Natural Habitats provides that disputes are first to go to the Standing Committee, which is tasked with attempting the facilitation of a settlement.[303] Following this, the dispute would go to arbitration under a system designated at the agreement of the Parties and then, if necessary, to the EC as a whole.[304]

In the event of disputes relating to the *Inter-American Convention for the Protection and Conservation of Sea Turtles* and its implementation, there is a designated two-step settlement process.[305] At the first step is the attempt to settle the issue through peaceful means, such as negotiations.[306] Should it be required, the second step is international arbitration through the UNCLOS system.[307] Disputes arising under the *International Plant Protection Convention* are first to be addressed through attempts at negotiations. The Director-General of the FAO has the ability to convene a panel of experts to create a binding outcome to the dispute should initial attempts at negotiations fail.

Should a dispute arise in connection with the *Agreement on the Conservation of Albatrosses and Petrels*, the first step is to convene consultations with the Chair of the Advisory Committee for attempts at a peaceful, mediated settlement.[308] The second step, if necessary, is referral of the matter to a specifically created technical arbitration panel.[309]

2.3.4 *Hard law elements in governance systems*

Under the terms of the CMS, State Parties agree to designate endangered migratory species and to create allowances for when and how they may be removed from their territories.[310] There are additional protection regimes established in instances where the species in question is not yet endangered but is in a position where it could be without further conservation and management plans.[311]

Under the *Agreement on the Conservation of Gorillas and Their Habitats*, State Parties have a number of legal and governance requirements in terms of management and conservation of gorilla populations and habitats. Specifically, these include identifying, protecting and restoring gorilla habitats, ensuring that gorilla habitats are protected across Range States

303 *Convention on the Conservation of European Wildlife and Natural Habitats*, *supra* note 234 at art 18.
304 Ibid.
305 *Inter-American Convention for the Protection and Conservation of Sea Turtles*, *supra* note 236 at art XVI.
306 Ibid.
307 Ibid.
308 *Agreement on the Conservation of Albatrosses and Petrels*, *supra* note 228 at art XIV.
309 Ibid.
310 *Convention on the Conservation of Migratory Species of Wild Animals*, *supra* note 226 at art III.
311 Ibid. at art IV.

and ensuring habitat sustainability, coordinating with other States and the private sector to prevent poaching, assisting the capacity of law enforcement and the judiciary in handling issues relating to gorilla protection and conservation, preventing human activities that threaten or harm gorillas and their habitats, cooperating in emergencies, including human-generated emergencies, which have the potential to impact gorillas and their habitats, harmonizing national laws, rules and policies, conducting scientific research and engaging in public awareness and education campaigns.[312] To coordinate these activities, liaise with other State Parties and the *Agreement* regime and share information, States are required to designate an authority for implementation and monitoring of *Agreement* terms.[313] States are also required to designate a specific national focal point and establish funding to assist in implementation at the national level.[314]

The *Agreement on the Conservation of Cetaceans of the Black Sea, Mediterranean Sea and Contiguous Atlantic Area* provides for conservation and requires States to coordinate conservation and species preservation efforts, ban purposeful takings of cetaceans and create and implement laws and rules to actualize the *Agreement*, notably including the precautionary principle.[315] The specific legal actions to be addressed are the assessment and management of human-cetacean interactions, habitat protection measures, engagement in research and monitoring activities for the species, engagement in capacity-building efforts and generation of protections for emerging situations.[316]

CITES provides for the creation of an appendix of species "threatened with extinction which are or may be affected by trade" and that are to be subject to strict trade regulations.[317] There are additional provisions for the designation of species which, while threatened, do not face as immediate a threat.[318] Finally, there is a third appendix provision in CITES which is to be comprised of species designated by State Parties as being in need of protection to avoid further damage due to trade.[319] In relation to these prohibition on trade in species, States are required to agree on and provide information regarding when and how exportation in the limited capacities allowed through the appendices might occur, notably through State approval for import, export and re-export.[320] To ensure that these terms are complied

312 *Agreement on the Conservation of Gorillas and Their Habitats*, *supra* note 227 at art III.
313 Ibid. at art IV.
314 Ibid.
315 *Agreement on the Conservation of Cetaceans of the Black Sea, Mediterranean Sea and Contiguous Atlantic Area*, *supra* note 235 at art II.
316 Ibid.
317 CITES, *supra* note 231 at art II.
318 Ibid. at appx. II.
319 Ibid. at appx. III.
320 Ibid. at arts III, IV, V.

with, CITES requires States to create permitting and certification systems to be used in connection with exports and imports.[321]

In recognition of the importance of species protections, CITES State Parties agree to take measures to criminalize the trade in protected species under the treaty regime, establish a system for the confiscation of illegally traded wildlife and the potential for its repatriation, impose a strict record-keeping system for legitimate imports and exports of species as well as permits and certificates issued and generate State-based reports to CITES.[322] For information sharing and liaison purposes, States are required to designate at least one coordinating management and scientific authority within their jurisdictions.[323] Through decisions of various CoPs, the reporting requirements for State Parties has been expanded to include as generalized report as well as a report on illegal trade and on implementation.[324]

Under the terms of the *Convention on the Conservation of European Wildlife and Natural Habitats*, State Parties agree to "take requisite measures to maintain the population of wild flora and fauna at, or adapt it to, a level which corresponds in particular to ecological, scientific and cultural regulations, while taking account of economic and recreational requirements and the needs of sub-species, varieties or forms at risk locally."[325] As a result, States have an obligation to implement these undertakings in national law, policies, plans and programming.[326] This obligation extends to implementing laws and rules that protect species habitats and ecosystems, including those used by migratory species and migratory species themselves.[327]

Pursuant to the terms of the *Inter-American Convention for the Protection and Conservation of Sea Turtles*, State Parties undertake obligations to ensure that land and maritime protection laws and rules are created and implemented for the benefit of sea turtle populations, and that conservation and recovery of sea turtles is entrenched as a matter of law and policy at the national level.[328] Through the terms of the *Treaty on the Conservation and Sustainable Management of Forest Ecosystems in Central Africa and to Establish the Central African Forests Commission*, State Parties undertake to include conservation and sustainable management of forests in national environmental laws and plans, harmonize regional and international standards of forestry policies, translate forestry issues into related sectors,

321 Ibid. at art VI.
322 Ibid. at art VII.
323 Ibid at art IX.
324 CITES website, *supra* note 237.
325 *Convention on the Conservation of European Wildlife and Natural Habitats*, *supra* note 234 at art 2.
326 Ibid. at arts 3, 5–7.
327 Ibid. at arts 4, 10.
328 *Inter-American Convention for the Protection and Conservation of Sea Turtles*, *supra* note 236 at art IV.

provide financial and assistance measures for sustainable forestry and taxation planning, create transborder protections and implementation systems, create mechanisms to address logging and poaching and create certification and documentation systems regarding forestry practices and products.[329]

State Parties adopted the *International Plant Protection Convention* "with the purpose of securing common and effective action to prevent the spread and introduction of pests, plants and plant products, and to promote appropriate measures for their control."[330] In order to accomplish this, States are required to create legal and regulatory regimes that reflect and entrench the purposes of the *Convention* within the national framework.[331] This is accompanied by State obligations to pass national legislation and policy related to plan protection and phytosanitary regulation, to create and utilize phytosanitary certification systems and to create regulations for importation and trans-shipment of plants, plant products and similar products.[332]

Under the terms of the *Ramsar Convention*, States must designate wetlands for the List of Wetlands of International Importance based on the necessary criteria established at the international levels and generate planning rules.[333] Further, States are obliged to determine methods to protect wetlands and associated natural resources and to coordinate and cooperate with other State Parties.[334]

Pursuant to the *Convention for the Conservation of Antarctic Seals*, State Parties are required to enact laws and rules to prohibit capture and killing of seals, especially through State Party flagships and related activities.[335] Additionally, there are obligations for State Parties to exchange information with other Parties and to share scientific information and advice as relevant to the Convention.[336]

2.4 Geographically focused regimes

Finally, there are the treaty regimes which focus on protecting the entirety of a regional area from a variety of threats and potential environmental damage. The majority of these treaty regimes establish governance mechanisms for the regulation of an especially valuable transboundary natural resource – such as a river or sea – which serves as an economic or cultural

329 *Treaty on the Conservation and Sustainable Management of Forest Ecosystems in Central Africa and to Establish the Central African Forests Commission*, *supra* note 237 at art 1.

330 *International Plant Protection Convention*, *supra* note 232 at art I.

331 Ibid.

332 Ibid. at arts IV, V, VII.

333 *Convention on Wetlands of International Importance Especially as Waterfowl Habitats*, *supra* note 233 at arts 2, 3.

334 Ibid. at arts 4, 5.

335 *Convention for the Conservation of Antarctic Seals*, *supra* note 238 at art 2.

336 Ibid. at art 5.

resource as well. In essence, these are more focused versions of the general treaties discussed above in that they focus on a particular area and a set of environmental concerns to it, although with a wide lens and wide-ranging governance mechanisms.

In this context, the following treaty regimes are grouped together for analysis: the *Kuwait Regional Convention for Co-Operation on the Protection of the Marine Environment from Pollution*,[337] the *Convention for the Protection, Management and Development of the Marine and Coastal Environment of the Eastern African States* (*Nairobi Convention*),[338] the *Convention for Co-Operation in the Protection and Development of the Marine and Coastal Environment of the West and Central African Region* (*Abidjan Convention*),[339] the *Convention for the Protection of the Natural Resources and Environment of the South Pacific Region and Related Protocols*,[340] the *Convention on the Conservation of Antarctic Marine Living Resources*,[341] the *Convention for the Protection of the Marine Environment of the North-East Atlantic* (OSPAR *Convention*),[342] the *Convention on the Protection of the Marine Environment of the Baltic Sea Area* (*Helsinki Convention*),[343] the *Convention for the Protection and Development of the Marine Environment of the Wider Caribbean Region* (*Cartagena Convention*),[344] the *Convention for the Protection of the Marine Environment and the Coastal Region of the Mediterranean and Its Protocols* (*Barcelona Convention*),[345] the *Convention for the Protection of the Marine Environment and Coastal Area of the South-East Pacific*,[346] *Framework Agreement on the Sava River Basin*,[347] the *Agreement on the Cooperation for the Sustainable Development of the Mekong River Basin*[348] and *Regional*

337 *Kuwait Regional Convention for Co-Operation on the Protection of the Marine Environment from Pollution* (1978).

338 *Convention for the Protection, Management and Development of the Marine and Coastal Environment of the Eastern African States* (1996).

339 *Convention for Co-Operation in the Protection and Development of the Marine and Coastal Environment of the West and Central African Region* (1984).

340 *Convention for the Protection of the Natural Resources and Environment of the South Pacific Region and Related Protocols* (1986).

341 *Convention on the Conservation of Antarctic Marine Living Resources* (1982).

342 *Convention for the Protection of the Marine Environment of the North-East Atlantic* (1992).

343 *Convention on the Protection of the Marine Environment of the Baltic Sea Area* (1992).

344 *Convention for the Protection and Development of the Marine Environment of the Wider Caribbean Region* (1986).

345 *Convention for the Protection of the Marine Environment and the Coastal Region of the Mediterranean and Its Protocols* (1976).

346 *Convention for the Protection of the Marine Environment and Coastal Area of the South-East Pacific* (1981).

347 *Framework Agreement on the Sava River Basin* (2004).

348 *Agreement on the Cooperation for the Sustainable Development of the Mekong River Basin* (1995).

Convention for the Conservation of the Red Sea and Gulf of Aden Environment (Jeddah Convention).[349]

Given the specific remit and parameters of these treaty regimes, a discussion of their purposes and objectives is not necessary or particularly insightful, although these regimes do tend to stress the importance of the area and the resource to the wider region and the global community.

2.4.1 *Governance mechanisms*

The *Jeddah Convention* establishes the Regional Organization for the Conservation of the Red Sea and Gulf of Aden Environment as the overarching governance and implementation entity.[350] The Organization is comprised of the Council for all States, the General Secretariat and the Committee for the Settlement of Disputes.[351] Within this structure, the Council is tasked with reviewing the implementation of the *Convention* and associated protocols, recommending amendments to the *Convention* when deemed appropriate, entering into agreements with other States and with international organizations, establishing subsidiary bodies within the structure as necessary, reviewing the state of the marine environment, generating reports and other forms of evaluations and attempting to act as a source of dispute settlement in certain circumstances.[352]

Under the terms of the *Barcelona Convention*, a Conference of the Parties is established and required to meet at least once every two years.[353] As part of this function, the States, acting as the CoP are required to review activities and accomplishments during the period between CoPs, review State reports generated in advance of the CoP, create amendments or protocols to the *Convention* where deemed appropriate, establish and oversee working groups to specialize in emerging topics and to undertake research or other activities to further the goals of the *Convention* and the Parties.[354] The reporting requirements for States include information on legal and regulatory measures taken for compliance, effectiveness of and issues in implementing *Convention*-based obligations and the overall effectiveness of the system created to implement the *Convention* at the national level.[355] The *Protocol concerning Specifically Protected Areas and Biological Diversity in the Mediterranean* creates a designated Organization and Centre to

349 *Regional Convention for the Conservation of the Red Sea and Gulf of Aden Environment* (1982).
350 Ibid. at XII.
351 Ibid.
352 Ibid. at art XVII.
353 *Barcelona Convention*, *supra* note 345 at art 18.
354 Ibid.
355 Ibid. at art 26.

implement its terms, and requires that State Parties designate National Focal Points for information sharing and policy coordination.[356]

Decision-making in the *Cartagena Convention* context is conducted by the Meeting of the Parties, which must occur at least once every two years. The MoP is empowered to assess the environmental situation in the territorial area subject to the *Convention*'s terms, review reports and other materials submitted from a variety of sources, generate reports, recommendations and amendments or protocols where appropriate, establish topic or sector-specific working groups and foster cooperation between State Parties and international organizations.[357] Further, the *Protocol* establishes the Science and Technical Advisory Committee as an entity within the overall structure of the *Cartagena Convention* system.[358]

The primary decision-making and policy generating entity in the *Helsinki Convention* governance system is the Baltic Marine Environmental Protection Committee.[359] The Committee is charged with oversight of the *Convention*'s implementation, making recommendations and defining pollution control criteria as well objectives for pollution reduction, reviewing the requisite reports from State Parties and supporting cooperation with international organizations and other relevant entities.[360] Further, the Committee is delegated essential Secretariat functions.[361] An additional element of the governance system is the Commission on Science and Technology.[362]

Under the system established through OSPAR, the Commission exists as the primary decision-making entity.[363] In this role, the Commission is vested with the ability to supervise implementation of OSPAR's terms, create new subsidiary bodies as deemed necessary to the functioning of OSPAR, adopt appropriate amendments or changes to the OSPAR system and conduct reviews of the ways in which OSPAR is implemented at the national level as a matter of law.[364] Decisions made by the Commission are deemed to be binding on State Parties after a designated period of time.[365]

Comprised of State Parties to the *Convention on the Conservation of Antarctic Marine Living Resources* as well as regional integration organizations where appropriate, the Commission for the Conservation of Antarctic Marine Living Resources is established as the primary decision-making

356 See *Protocol concerning Specifically Protected Areas and Biological Diversity in the Mediterranean*, *supra* note 345 at arts 24–25.

357 *Cartagena Convention*, *supra* note 344 at art 16.

358 *Protocol Concerning Specially Protected Areas and Wildlife*, *supra* note 344 at art 20.

359 *Helsinki Convention*, *supra* note 343 at art 19.

360 Ibid. at art 20.

361 Ibid. at art 21.

362 Ibid. at art 24.

363 OSPAR, *supra* note 342 at art 10.

364 Ibid. at art 10.

365 Ibid. at art 13.

entity for the treaty regime.[366] The Commission's core functions involve facilitating research and scientific studies in the region, data gathering and sharing between the State Parties, coordinating catch levels for various species in the Antarctic, determining the conservation needs and effectiveness of responses in the region, creating and revising responsive conservation measures as needed, liaising with the Scientific Committee and taking decisions which become legally binding on the Parties after 180 days.[367] The Scientific Committee for the Conservation of Antarctic Marine Living Resources functions as a specialized and consultative body.[368]

There are two primary elements of governance systems existing under the *Convention for the Protection of the Natural Resources and Environment of the South Pacific Region and Related Protocols*' structure – the Meeting of the Parties and the Secretariat. The MoP is convened at least every two years and is charged with the oversight and coordination of implementation for Convention terms and related national activities.[369] The primary governance organ within the *Convention for the Protection of the Marine Environment and Coastal Area of the South-East Pacific* system is the Conference of the Parties, which meets at least every two years.[370] The CoP's functions include assessing the state of the *Convention*'s implementation and the need for potential amendments and protocols, reviewing the environmental impact assessment procedures and laws adopted at the national level and reviewing the reports from States as well as other sources.[371]

To implement the *Abidjan Convention*, a Conference of the Parties is established with the requirement to serve as the primary decision-making entity, meeting at least every two years.[372] The CoP serves to provide review and oversight functions, make recommendations regarding the implementation of terms and intentions in the *Abidjan Convention* as well as instances where it is important to adopt amendments, create working groups as appropriate and to specifically conduct reviews of the state of pollution and the environment in the area.[373] The *Nairobi Convention* establishes the Conference of the Parties as the decision-making entity in the organizational structure.[374] It is an entity charged with reviewing reports and other information generated in relation to the *Convention*, adopting reports, protocols and amendments to

366 *Convention on the Conservation of Antarctic Marine Living Resources*, *supra* note 341 at art VII.

367 Ibid. at art IX.

368 Ibid. at art XIV.

369 *Convention for the Protection of the Natural Resources and Environment of the South Pacific Region and Related Protocols*, *supra* note 340 at art 22.

370 Ibid. at art 12.

371 Ibid. at arts 12, 14.

372 *Abidjan Convention*, *supra* note 339 at art 17.

373 Ibid.

374 *Nairobi Convention*, *supra* note 338 at art 17.

the *Convention* text, establishing working groups as appropriate and creating assessments of pollution and the environment in the *Convention* Area.[375]

Under the *Framework Agreement on the Sava River Basin*, the primary decision-making body is the Meeting of the Parties, which is convened biennially and serves as a source of oversight, compliance and recommendations for future actions.[376] Additionally, the International Sava River Basin Commission serves to provide safe navigation information and policy as well as to provide financial assistance in implementing the *Framework Agreement*.[377] Pursuant to the *Agreement on the Cooperation for the Sustainable Development of the Mekong River Basin*, the institutional structure to be used is centered on the Mekong River Commission, which is comprised of the Council, the Joint Committee and the Secretariat.[378] Decision-making capacities are vested in the Council, which has oversight and policy generating authority.[379] The Joint Committee is vested with the ability to implement the Council's established priorities, create the Mekong development plan, obtain and analyze data regarding the Mekong and address issues of dispute management.[380]

Typically, the administrative and bureaucratic functions of the governance mechanisms created in these treaty regimes are conducted by a separate and dedicated Secretariat structure.[381] There are several exceptions to this, notably that the administrative function of the *Cartagena Convention* is vested in the UNEP Secretariat,[382] as is the case for the *Abidjan Convention*[383] and the *Nairobi Convention*.[384]

2.4.2 *Dispute settlement mechanisms*

Under the *Jeddah Convention*, the first step in attempting to resolve disputes between State Parties is to encourage the use of peaceful settlement between

375 Ibid.
376 *Framework Agreement on the Sava River Basin*, *supra* note 347 at art 14.
377 Ibid. at art 15.
378 *Agreement on the Cooperation for the Sustainable Development of the Mekong River Basin*, *supra* note 348 at arts 7–8.
379 Ibid. at art 18.
380 Ibid. at art 24.
381 See *Jeddah Convention*, *supra* note 349 at art XIX; OSPAR, *supra* note 342 at art 12; *Convention on the Conservation of Antarctic Marine Living Resources*, *supra* note 341 at art XVII; *Convention for the Protection of the Marine Environment and Coastal Area of the South-East Pacific*, *supra* note 346 at art 13; *Framework Agreement on the Sava River Basin*, *supra* note 347 at art 18; *Agreement on the Cooperation for the Sustainable Development of the Mekong River Basin*, *supra* note 348 at arts 28–30.
382 *Cartagena Convention*, *supra* note 344 at art 15.
383 *Abidjan Convention*, *supra* note 339 at art 16.
384 *Nairobi Convention*, *supra* note 338 at art 16.

the States themselves.[385] Should this prove unsuccessful, the next step is to refer the dispute to the Council for review and consideration.[386] Finally, a dispute can be referred to the Committee for the Settlement of Disputes for a disposition.[387] Dispute settlement under the terms of the *Kuwait Convention* centers first on attempts at negotiation and peaceful settlement, with recourse to the Judicial Commission for the Settlement of Disputes as the final arbiter if necessary.[388]

Dispute settlement under the *Barcelona Convention* is a two-step system. The first step in this process is for State Parties to seek peaceful settlement and, should this fail, States agree to arbitration through a mechanism established under the auspices of the *Convention*.[389] Under the *Protocol for the Protection of the Mediterranean Sea against Pollution from Land-Based Sources and Activities to the Barcelona Convention*, the dispute settlement system is somewhat refined to require attempts at conciliation efforts first, followed by submission to and recommendations from the Barcelona CoP if no settlement can be reached.[390]

Where disputes arise under the *Cartagena Convention*, they are to be settled through negotiation or other similar means to the extent possible.[391] Should this not be possible, the dispute is to be submitted to an ad hoc arbitral entity established under the terms of protocols to the *Convention*.[392] Disputes arising between OSPAR State Parties are to be settled through mediation or other peaceful efforts where at all possible.[393] As a secondary option, State Parties may request the creation of an ad hoc arbitral panel convened under the aegis of OSPAR to hear and issue a determination on the issues.[394] Similar provisions exist in the *Convention on the Conservation of Antarctic Marine Living Resources*,[395] the *Convention for the Protection of the Natural Resources and Environment of the South Pacific Region and Related Protocols*,[396] the *Abidjan Convention*[397] and the *Nairobi Convention*.[398]

385 *Jeddah Convention*, *supra* note 349 at art XXIV.
386 Ibid.
387 Ibid.
388 *Kuwait Regional Convention for Co-Operation on the Protection of the Marine Environment from Pollution*, *supra* note 337 at art XXV.
389 *Barcelona Convention*, *supra* note—at art 28.
390 See *Protocol for the Protection of the Mediterranean Sea against Pollution from Land-Based Sources and Activities*, *supra* note 345 at art 12.
391 *Cartagena Convention*, *supra* note 344 at art 23.
392 Ibid.
393 OSPAR, *supra* note 342 at art 32.
394 Ibid.
395 *Convention on the Conservation of Antarctic Marine Living Resources*, *supra* note 341 at arts XVII, XXV.
396 *Convention for the Protection of the Natural Resources and Environment of the South Pacific Region and Related Protocols*, *supra* note 340 at art 26.
397 *Abidjan Convention*, *supra* note 339 at art 24.
398 *Nairobi Convention*, *supra* note 338 at art 24.

Disputes arising between State Parties relating to the *Helsinki Convention* are to be handled, where possible, through negotiation and peaceful means.[399] If this is unsuccessful, the next step is for the intervention of the Committee through the provision of good offices or mediation.[400] Where both steps are unsuccessful to generate a resolution, the Parties may take the matter to the ICJ for resolution or to an ad hoc arbitral tribunal generated through the *Convention* system.[401]

Disputes connected with the *Framework Agreement on the Sava River Basin* are to be addressed through negotiations between the Parties as a first step.[402] The second step in the dispute settlement system is the intervention of third parties to mediate the dispute.[403] As a final step, the dispute may be submitted to a separately created fact-finding expert committee for a decision.[404] Disputes arising under the *Agreement on the Cooperation for the Sustainable Development of the Mekong River Basin* are first brought to the Mekong Basin Commission for attempts at facilitating settlement.[405] Should this not be possible, the dispute then is referred to the collective of State Party governments for resolution by consensus if possible.[406]

2.4.3 *Hard law elements in governance systems*

As a matter of hard law, the *Jeddah Convention* requires State Parties to implement measures for environmental protection within their territories and within the jurisdiction of the treaty terms, "including the prevention, abatement and combating of marine pollution."[407] To further this, States are required to enact national laws and rules to implement elements of the *Convention*'s terms.[408] The *Jeddah Convention* expressly requires that States implement laws and rules relating to a number of topic areas, such as pollution from ships and related sources, dumping-based pollution and pollution stemming from exploration and exploitation activities in the territorial area under control, including from activities relating to the seabed.[409] Additionally, the *Jeddah Convention* contains cooperation requirements for

399 *Helsinki Convention, supra* note 343 at art 26.
400 Ibid.
401 Ibid.
402 *Framework Agreement on the Sava River Basin, supra* note 347 at art 22.
403 Ibid.
404 Ibid.
405 *Agreement on the Cooperation for the Sustainable Development of the Mekong River Basin, supra* note 348 at art 34.
406 Ibid. at art 35.
407 *Jeddah Convention, supra* note 349 at art II.
408 Ibid.
409 Ibid. at arts IV, XXIII.

the coordination of responses to pollution-based emergencies and in scientific fields such as research, monitoring and assessment.[410]

Under the *Barcelona Convention*, State Parties have hard law obligations to prevent pollution from ships, pollution caused by dumping from ships and aircraft or by incineration at sea, pollution resulting from exploration and exploitation of the continental shelf and the seabed and its subsoil, pollution from land-based sources, pollution resulting from the transboundary movements of hazardous wastes and their disposal and cooperation duties between the State Parties for dealing with pollution-related emergencies.[411] Further, State Parties to the *Convention* are required to protect all biodiversity, as well as ecosystems, flora and fauna species and threatened and rare species.[412] To solidify these undertakings, the States are under obligations to adopt national legislation codifying the *Barcelona Convention* and any subsequent protocols.[413] In accordance with this, the States are under an obligation to provide the public with information and to ensure public participation and involvement in decision-making processes that are related to the matters provided for in the *Barcelona Convention*.[414]

Subsequent protocols to the *Barcelona Convention* have established more detailed hard law requirements for addressing pollution by dumping from ships and aircraft or by incineration at sea,[415] pollution from ships and especially during emergencies[416] and pollution from land-based sources and activities.[417] Under the *Protocol concerning Specifically Protected Areas and Biological Diversity in the Mediterranean*, State Parties have hard law obligations regarding the creation of protection measures for designated areas,[418] cooperation between States where a specially protected area of importance to the Mediterranean is that crosses borders is to be created,[419] implementation of national laws and mechanisms for the protection and conservation of the specially protected areas[420] and creation of national guidelines and common regional criteria for designated territories.[421] Additionally, this

410 Ibid. at arts IX, X.

411 *Barcelona Convention*, *supra* note 345 at arts 5–9, 11.

412 Ibid. at art 10.

413 Ibid. at art 14.

414 Ibid. at art 15.

415 See *Protocol for the Prevention and Elimination of Pollution of the Mediterranean Sea by Dumping from Ships and Aircraft or Incineration at Sea*, *supra* note 345.

416 *Protocol Concerning Cooperation in Preventing Pollution from Ships and, in Cases of Emergency, Combatting Pollution of the Mediterranean Sea*, *supra* note 345.

417 See *Protocol for the Protection of the Mediterranean Sea against Pollution from Land-Based Sources and Activities*, *supra* note 345.

418 See *Protocol Concerning Specifically Protected Areas and Biological Diversity in the Mediterranean*, *supra* note 345 at arts 6–7.

419 See ibid. at art 8.

420 See ibid. at arts 11–13.

421 See ibid. at arts 16–17.

Protocol binds States to integrate traditional activities and communities into the review process for the creation of specially designated areas, along with sharing of information on the proposal to create these areas with the public, encouraging public participation in and public awareness of the process.[422]

The *Protocol for the Protection of the Mediterranean Sea against Pollution Resulting from Exploration and Exploitation on the Continental Shelf and the Seabed and Its Soil* establishes hard law requirements for States to follow in terms of combatting pollution.[423] This includes an express provision that "all activities in the *Protocol* Area, including erection on site of installations, shall be subject to the prior written authorization for exploration or exploitation from the competent authority," which must in turn review the compliance of the proposed activity with international standards and national requirements before allowing it to continue.[424] The *Protocol* contains a sanction requirement for State Parties to implement in the event of a breach of the authorization procedure.[425] Further, it requires the use of hard law standards regarding various forms of potential pollutant regulation and entrenchment as a matter of law.[426] Relatedly, there are legal and regulatory measures which States must take regarding installations that could cause pollution, such as pipelines, and the generation of contingency plans in the event of spills.[427] In a similar vein, the States are required to make private entities operating in their jurisdictions subject to reporting and oversight elements and to establish provisions for reporting and oversight of transboundary pollution issues.[428] Similar requirements are established in the *Protocol on the Prevention of Pollution of the Mediterranean Sea by Transboundary Movements of Hazardous Wastes and Their Disposal*.[429]

The *Protocol on Integrated Coastal Zone Management in the Mediterranean* establishes the objectives of facilitating sustainable development in the area by protecting coastal environments and landscapes, ensuring sustainable development of natural resources in the area, preserving the integrity of coastal systems, reducing harms from climate change and balancing public

422 See ibid. at arts 18–19.

423 *Protocol for the Protection of the Mediterranean Sea against Pollution Resulting from Exploration and Exploitation on the Continental Shelf and the Seabed and Its Soil*, *supra* note 345 at arts 3, 5–6.

424 Ibid. at art 4.

425 Ibid. at art 7. This includes the requirement that "Parties shall impose a general obligation upon operators to use the best available, environmentally effective and economically appropriate techniques and to observe internationally accepted standards regarding wastes, as well as the use, storage and discharge of harmful or noxious substances or materials, with a view to monitoring the risk of pollution." Ibid. at art 8.

426 Ibid. at arts 10–13.

427 Ibid. at arts 15–16.

428 See ibid. at arts 17–19, 23, 26, 28.

429 *Protocol on the Prevention of Pollution of the Mediterranean Sea by Transboundary Movements of Hazardous Wastes and Their Disposal*, *supra* note 345 at arts 4–6.

and private concerns over development and preservation.[430] As part of this, the States are required to enact and implement laws and rules for the protection and sustainable use of the coastal zone and associated resources, including cultural heritage of the region.[431] Further, States are required to implement national measures for monitoring and oversight of the *Protocol*'s terms, environmental impact assessments, hazards to the coastal area and coordination for emergency responses.[432]

Under the terms of the *Cartagena Convention*, State Parties are required to "prevent, reduce and control" pollution from ships, as the result of dumping of wastes, from land-based sources, from sea-bed related activities and from airborne activities and sources.[433] Additionally, the *Convention* requires State Parties to ensure that environmental impact assessments are conducted in instances of potential and/or actual pollution to protected areas.[434]

In the *Protocol Concerning Specially Protected Areas and Wildlife*, State Parties are required to implement sustainable use and preservation of wildlife in the Caribbean region as well as their ecosystems.[435] Under the *Protocol*, there is a requirement for States to establish protected areas as necessary and to include considerations involving the short-term and long-term viability of the designation, the impact on the local community and the involvement of cultural and historical values.[436] Recognizing the need for national law and rules to implement the *Protocol*'s terms and the need to ensure that the immediate impacts of these measures do not cause unintended consequences, the *Protocol* provides for phasing in the legal aspects relating to species and habitats.[437] The *Protocol* also provides national legislation to identify and protect endangered and other species in the covered area, as well as to address issues such as invasive species and the introduction of genetically modified organisms.[438] Additionally, the *Protocol* contains hard law requirements for States to provide publicity, information and public awareness and education relating to protected areas and associated species.[439]

The *Protocol Concerning Co-Operation in Combating Oil Spills in the Wider Caribbean Region* creates hard law requirements for State Parties to cooperate in order to prevent and remediate oil spills, especially in coastal

430 *Protocol on Integrated Coastal Zone Management in the Mediterranean*, *supra* note 345 at art 5.
431 Ibid. at arts 7–14.
432 Ibid. at arts 17–19, 22–24.
433 *Cartagena Convention*, *supra* note 344 at arts 5–9.
434 Ibid. at art 12.
435 *Protocol Concerning Specially Protected Areas and Wildlife to the Cartagena Convention*, *supra* note 344 at art 3.
436 Ibid. at art 4.
437 Ibid. at arts 5–6.
438 Ibid. at arts 10, 12.
439 Ibid. at art 16.

islands.[440] As part of this requirement, States must have response plans in place, including capacity planning and legislative updates where necessary.[441] In conjunction with this, the *Protocol* requires State cooperation to effect information exchanges regarding laws, rules and other ways to implement its terms.[442] Further, there are requirements that States create communication and reporting systems at the national and international level for oil spills and that States render mutual assistance during an oil spill when requested by another State.[443]

Additionally, the *Protocol Concerning Pollution from Land-Based Sources and Activities* contains hard law requirements for State Parties to implement laws and rules to "prevent, reduce and control" pollution from land-based sources and to report on how these laws are entrenched in national systems.[444] Included in this *Protocol* is the requirement for States to implement monitoring and assessment programs at the national level and use environmental impact assessments in this context.[445] Further, there are hard law requirements for the development of national public awareness and education campaigns for land-based pollution and its potential impacts[446] and the designation of national focal points for liaising with other State Parties as well as fielding questions from States and from the international system as a whole.[447]

At its core, the *Helsinki Convention* is comprised of a system of hard law obligations undertaken by State Parties, as is demonstrated by early provisions requiring that States "take all appropriate legislative, administrative or other relevant measures to prevent and eliminate pollution in order to promote the ecological restoration of the Baltic Sea Area and the preservation of its ecological balance."[448] As part of this, States are required to incorporate the precautionary principle, the polluter pays principle and measures to verify levels of pollution within their legal regimes relating to sectors covered by the *Helsinki Convention*.[449] In relation to this, there are requirements that States provide information on potential development, health and safety impacts of a project to the public.[450] State Parties to the *Helsinki Convention* assume hard law obligations to prevent pollution of the Baltic Sea and surrounding resources from sources including land-based

440 *Protocol Concerning Co-Operation in Combating Oil Spills in the Wider Caribbean Region*, *supra* note 344 at art 3.

441 Ibid.

442 Ibid. at art 4.

443 Ibid. at arts 5–6.

444 *Protocol Concerning Pollution from Land-Based Sources and Activities*, *supra* note 344 at arts III, XII.

445 Ibid. at arts VI, VII.

446 Ibid. at art XI.

447 Ibid. at art XIII.

448 *Helsinki Convention*, *supra* note 343 at art 3.

449 Ibid. at art 3.

450 Ibid. at art 17.

pollution, airborne pollution, pollution from ships, pollution from dumping activities and pollution stemming from incineration within the protected Area.[451] There is a concomitant obligation for States to ensure that pollution does not occur during exploration and exploitation of the seabed area.[452] When States undertake an environmental impact assessment for an activity that might have transnational impacts or impact the entirety of the *Helsinki Convention* Area, there is a requirement that all potentially impacted States be informed and involved in the EIA process.[453] Along the continuum of obligations is the requirement that a State notify other impacted States and the *Helsinki Convention* apparatus in the event of an incident in its jurisdiction that is likely to cause pollution.[454]

Under the terms of OSPAR, State Parties have hard law obligations to prevent and address pollution from land-based sources, from dumping or incineration and offshore sources.[455] States also have a number of other obligations, including to engage in consultations with other State Parties where there is the potential for transboundary pollution due to an existing or potential activity.[456] As a general matter, *State Parties to the Convention for the Protection of the Natural Resources and Environment of the South Pacific Region and Related Protocols* are required to "prevent, reduce and control pollution" in the covered area.[457] This includes specific, binding requirements relating to pollution from vessels, land-based sources, seabed activities, air pollution and the disposal of wastes, particularly toxic and hazardous wastes and nuclear devices.[458] Additionally, there are hard law requirements for States relating to national creation and protection of specially protected areas and the protection of wild flora and fauna[459] and to scientific and technical cooperation between State Parties.[460]

Under the terms of the *Abidjan Convention*, State Parties are obligated to "prevent, reduce, combat and control pollution in the Convention Area and to ensure sound environmental management of natural resources using for this purpose the best possible means for their disposal and in accordance with their capabilities."[461] To accomplish this, States must use and adapt their laws and rules to include terms that entrench these international

451 Ibid. at arts 6, 8, 11.
452 Ibid. at art 12.
453 Ibid. at art 7.
454 Ibid. at art 13.
455 OSPAR, *supra* note 342 at arts 3–5.
456 Ibid. at art 21.
457 *Convention for the Protection of the Natural Resources and Environment of the South Pacific Region and Related Protocols, supra* note 340 at art 5.
458 Ibid. at arts 6–12.
459 Ibid. at art 14.
460 Ibid. at art 17.
461 *Abidjan Convention, supra* note 339 at art 4.

obligations.[462] Essential elements include regulations and prohibitions for pollution from ships and vessels, dumping wastes from ships and aircrafts, land-based sources, activities relating to the exploration and exploitation of the seabed in the *Abidjan Convention* Area and through the atmosphere.[463] Further, there are hard law obligations for States to address and abate pollution from activities of mankind, notably land reclamation and coastal engineering.[464] To ensure that these protections exist for particularly important areas, States have requirements to create specially protected areas as a matter of national law.[465] States are also required to incorporate pollution of *Abidjan Convention* areas under their jurisdictions in to the analysis conducted as part of environmental impact assessments for the purposes of evaluating proposed activities.[466] At the international level, there are hard obligations for States to inform others when there is the potential for transboundary pollution due to an emergency as well as a requirement to cooperate with each other regarding science and technology.[467]

From the outset, State Parties to the *Nairobi Convention* assume hard law obligations to "prevent, reduce and combat pollution of the *Convention* Area and to ensure sound environmental management of natural resources, using for this purpose the best practicable means at their disposal, and in accordance with their capabilities."[468] To effect these obligations as a matter of law, States are required to prevent and regulate pollution from ships and vessels, dumping into the *Nairobi Convention* Area, land-based sources, seabed activities and air-based pollution.[469] In addition, States are required to "take all appropriate measures to prevent, reduce and combat environmental damage in the *Convention* Area, in particular the destruction of marine and coastal ecosystems, caused by engineering activities such as land reclamation and dredging."[470] Relatedly, States must include marine pollution and related impacts in national environmental impact assessments.[471] At the international level, the *Nairobi Convention* requires State Parties to cooperate with each other in terms of information regarding emergency and potential emergency situations and scientific and technical capacity.[472]

State Parties to the *Kuwait Convention* have obligations including the generation and implementation of laws, rules and policies, to "prevent,

462 Ibid. at art 4.
463 Ibid. at arts 5–9.
464 Ibid. at art 10.
465 Ibid. at art 11.
466 Ibid. at art 13.
467 Ibid. at arts 12, 14.
468 *Nairobi Convention*, *supra* note 338 at art 4.
469 Ibid.at arts 5–9.
470 Ibid. at art 12.
471 Ibid. at art 13.
472 Ibid. at arts 11, 14.

abate and combat pollution of the maritime environment in the Sea area."[473] This includes requirements to enact laws relating to pollution from ships, dumping from ships and aircraft, land-based sources, human activities – including land reclamation and dredging – and pollution resulting from exploitation and exploration of the bed of the terrestrial sea and the sub-soil on the continental shelf.[474] The *Convention*'s terms also require States to incorporate *Kuwait Convention*-based pollution issues into national environmental impact assessment laws and rules.[475] Additionally, States are required to cooperate in information sharing and technical assistance in times of emergency and in scientific and technical knowledge.[476]

State Parties to the *Convention for the Protection of the Marine Environment and Coastal Area of the South-East Pacific* have the obligation "to prevent, reduce and control pollution of the marine environment and coastal area of the South-East Pacific and to ensure appropriate environmental management of natural resources," including legal and regulatory undertakings at the national level.[477] The specifically articulated forms of pollution to be prevented and addressed include from ships and other vessels, land-based sources, the atmosphere, dumping of wastes and "any other installation and devices operating in the marine environment."[478] In order to implement these forms of regulation, the *Convention* provides for the inclusion of marine pollution control and evaluation in environmental impact assessments.[479] At the international level, the *Convention* provides that States will notify each other in the event of an emergency relating to pollution, and that State Parties create a joint pollution monitoring program or set of programs for the region.[480] The *Convention* also provides for State Party scientific and technical cooperation and knowledge sharing.[481]

Information and data-sharing regarding the status of the Sava River is an obligation for State Parties to the *Framework Agreement on the Sava River Basin*.[482] Further, States are required to create early warning and related systems for extraordinary impacts on the Sava and associated bodies.[483]

473 *Kuwait Regional Convention for Co-Operation on the Protection of the Marine Environment from Pollution*, *supra* note 337 at art III.
474 Ibid. at arts IV–VIII.
475 Ibid. at art XI.
476 Ibid. at arts IX, X.
477 *Convention for the Protection of the Marine Environment and Coastal Area of the South-East Pacific*, *supra* note 346 at art 3(1).
478 Ibid. at art 4.
479 Ibid. at art 8.
480 Ibid. at arts 6–7.
481 Ibid. at art 10.
482 *Framework Agreement on the Sava River Basin*, *supra* note 347 at art 4.
483 Ibid. at art 13.

States have an obligation to create joint plans and development strategies for the Sava provided they are consistent with applicable EU laws.[484]

2.4.4 *Soft law elements in governance systems*

Under the terms of the *Jeddah Convention*, State Parties are to cooperate in the creation of standards and best practices for the implementation of the treaty terms and intent.[485] The *Convention* further provides elements to be taken into consideration by States when creating and implementing assessment and management systems for pollution and environmental impacts.[486] This includes the generation of standards to be used for planning purposes as well as allowing for the sharing of potential environmental impacts between States likely to be impacted by activities or proposed activities.[487]

The *Barcelona Convention*'s terms regarding monitoring of joint programs and a variety of forms of scientific and technical cooperation activities are rooted in soft law recommendations rather than hard law requirements.[488] Several of the subsequent protocols to the *Barcelona Convention* also establish soft law elements regarding information exchange and dissemination, contingency planning and combatting of potential issues relating to pollution,[489] establishment of specially protected areas and requirements for these areas when they cut across several jurisdictions[490] and integration of coastal zone management in the Mediterranean region.[491]

The *Convention for the Protection of the Natural Resources and Environment of the South Pacific Region and Related Protocols* contains wide-ranging soft law provisions regarding the creation of agreements with other States and organizations to promote protection, development and management of marine and coastal resources.[492] Soft law elements also exist in relation to the conduct of environmental impact assessment development and implementation within State Parties.[493]

The *Agreement on the Cooperation for the Sustainable Development of the Mekong River Basin* is a largely soft law and cooperative agreement "in all fields of sustainable development, utilization, management and

484 Ibid. at art 2.

485 *Jeddah Convention, supra* note 349 at art II.

486 Ibid. at art XI.

487 Ibid.

488 *Barcelona Convention, supra* note 345 at arts 12–13.

489 See *Protocol Concerning Cooperation in Preventing Pollution from Ships and, in Cases of Emergency, Combatting Pollution of the Mediterranean Sea, supra* note 345.

490 See *Protocol concerning Specifically Protected Areas and Biological Diversity in the Mediterranean, supra* note—at art 5.

491 *Protocol on Integrated Coastal Zone Management in the Mediterranean, supra* note 345.

492 *Convention for the Protection of the Natural Resources and Environment of the South Pacific Region and Related Protocols, supra* note 340 at art 4.

493 Ibid. at art 16.

conservation of the water and related sources of the Mekong River Basin, including ... irrigation, hydro-power, navigation, flood control, fisheries, timber floating, recreation and tourism, in an manner to optimize the multiple-use and mutual benefits of all riparians and to minimize the harmful effects that might result from natural occurrences and man-made activities."[494] To further these commitments, State Parties agree to cooperate on projects, policies and plans, including those to protect the environmental and ecological balance of the Mekong while also preserving the sovereign equality and territorial integrity of the States involved.[495]

2.5 Pandemic responses

From a governance perspective, perhaps the most immediately impactful response of several treaty regimes to the COVID-19 pandemic was to postpone their scheduled 2020 CoPs to 2021, as planned at the time of writing, along with postponing their intersessional meetings. The first occurrence of this was in the CBD context, where the regularly scheduled SBSSTA meetings for May 2020 were postponed several times and the scheduled CoP in October 2020 in Kunming, China was postponed to May 2021.[496] Similarly, the UNFCCC intersessional meetings were postponed to the fall of 2020 and CoP26, scheduled for November 2020 in Glasgow, was postponed by a full year.[497] Beyond scheduling difficulties, these responses, which are necessary from the public health and security perspectives, have slowed the momentum of State Parties toward meaningful short-term and long-term environmental commitments and changes. While adaptive to the needs of the international community that comprises their constituencies, the decisions of the treaty bodies highlight an inherent weakness in the current governance system in terms of the ability to make critical decisions in the context of a CoP structure that is intended to function as an in-person, negotiation-centered entity.

At the same time, the pressures to "build back better" across the world highlight the need to balance a quick economic recovery with one that is sustainable and advances climate related concerns as well as financial needs of national citizenries and the international community. In this context, the UNFCCC Secretariat and governance authorities have turned their

494 *Agreement on the Cooperation for the Sustainable Development of the Mekong River Basin*, *supra* note 348 at art 1.

495 Ibid. at arts 2–7.

496 Convention on Biological Diversity, Meeting documents: Fifteenth Conference of the Parties to the Convention on Biological Diversity, available at https://www.cbd.int/meetings/COP-15; Convention on Biological Diversity, Meeting documents: Twenty-fourth Meeting of the SBSTTA, available at https://www.cbd.int/meetings/SBSTTA-24.

497 UNFCCC, COP26 Postponed, available at https://unfccc.int/news/cop26-postponed.

attention toward providing guidance and support to State Parties attempting to implement a green recovery.[498]

Additionally, recognizing the importance of operationalizing the Committee on Compliance, which is first scheduled to formally sit during CoP26, the UNFCCC convened the members of the Committee to elect a leadership structure and begin working on procedural elements by using a series of virtual meetings and technologies.[499] Despite the pandemic, the UNFCCC has not suspended the NDC filing requirements for State Parties, although it can be expected that many States will file later in the cycle or require updates in the future based on the emerging pandemic and post-pandemic realities. This poses a challenge to the current NDC timing structures and the overall targets for 2050 as established in the *Paris Agreement*, although it also offers lessons which can be incorporated into the global stocktaking process to take place following submission of the complement of NDCs. Further, as has been highlighted across international and national communities, the COVID-19 pandemic demonstrates the threats posed by climate change and inattentiveness to the need to prepare for it in ways that could be useful in framing the discussions and momentum at CoP26, where a number of issues were held over following CoP25 in Madrid in 2019.

Similarly, the CBD must postpone decisions regarding the Post-2020 Global Biodiversity Framework, which was intended for debate and finalization during the Kunming CoP. Unlike the UNFCCC situation, in which the ability to postpone the CoP by a year will result in a potential lack of momentum but not a significant gap in policy and future governance development, a gap will exist since the current Aichi Biodiversity Targets were not intended for operationalization after 2020.[500] Thus, there is a governance gap which has not been addressed through the treaty regime-based system and highlights an area of concern for the CBD as well as other treaty regimes. It should, however, be noted that many of the working groups and committees established within the CBD structure have continued to produce reports and meet virtually, allowing some of the substantive organizational work to continue.

Additionally, the COVID-19 pandemic has resulted in questions regarding whether and how to ensure that the *Nagoya Protocol* is adequately implemented and incentivized to prevent future outbreaks from the public health perspective while continuing to foster biological diversity and

498 UNFCCC, An Economic Recovery that Builds a Greener Future, available at https://unfccc.int/news/an-economic-recovery-that-builds-a-greener-future; UNFCCC, Call to Action for a Climate Resilient Recovery from COVID-19, available at https://unfccc.int/news/call-to-action-for-a-climate-resilient-recovery-from-covid-19.

499 See UNFCCC, Compliance Committee bodies page, available at https://unfccc.int/compliance-committee-bodies-page.

500 CBD, Post-2020 Biological Diversity Framework, available at https://www.cbd.int/recommendations/wg2020/?m=wg2020-02.

development.[501] Not only does this represent a threat to the validity and functionality of international and national law made pursuant to the *Nagoya Protocol*, but it also creates a governance and oversight issue, which the CBD CoP and *Nagoya Protocol* MoP will have to address in the immediate and long-term.

Further, it is important to note two other CoP-related issues occurring in 2019 that highlight the need to focus on how governance systems are structured in the environmental context and global governance mechanisms as a whole, especially for the SDGs. First, CITES CoP18 had been scheduled to take place in May 2019 in Columbo, Sri Lanka, however these plans, along with many lives, were shattered by the 2019 terrorist bombing in the city.[502] This resulted in the postponement of the CoP by several months and its relocation to Geneva.[503] While at the practical level important decisions were made, especially regarding species protection and the designation of such species as pangolin as being particularly endangered, it did prevent the participation of and interchange with members of civil society groups which have increasingly been used in CoPs across multiple environmental treaty regimes as sources of information. Second, UNFCCC CoP25 had been scheduled to occur in Santiago, Chile in December 2019, after the initial designation of Brazil as the host State was cancelled by the then-newly elected Brazilian President, Jair Bolsonaro.[504] Governmental, academic and non-governmental organizations in Chile embraced this as part of a platform to emphasize national laws on climate-related issues as well as push for additional reform. However, the escalation of protests over public transportation fares in October 2019 resulted in significant rioting and social unrest which caused in the Chilean government to announce that it could not prioritize holding and securing the CoP.[505] By the first week of November, Spain was designated as the new host for the 2019 CoP, with Madrid rapidly preparing for over 30,000 CoP attendees by early December.[506] This resulted in a somewhat disjointed, though well-meaning, effort for the Chilean and Spanish governments to nominally share the CoP presidency and attempt to guide the negotiations, although neither was in a position to completely do so.

501 See WHO, Public Health Implications of Implementation of the Nagoya Protocol, available at https://www.who.int/activities/public-health-implications-of-implementation-of-the-nagoya-protocol.

502 CITES, Notification to the Parties: Eighteenth meeting of the Conference of the Parties, New dates and venue (12 June 2019).

503 Ibid.

504 See UNFCCC, Statement on COP25 Host, available at https://unfccc.int/news/statement-on-cop25-host.

505 Ernesto Londono & Somini Sengupta, Chile, Rocked by Unrest, Withdraws from Hosting Climate and Trade Summits, NY Times, available at https://www.nytimes.com/2019/10/30/world/americas/chile-cop25-apec.html.

506 Matt McGrath, Climate change: Spain offers to host COP25 in Madrid (31 October 2020), BBC, available at https://www.bbc.com/news/science-environment-50255460.

Other treaty regimes have similarly opted to conduct virtual meetings and exchanges of information for intersessional purposes in addition to cancelling or postponing their 2020 CoPs and MoPs.[507] Further, where appropriate, entities such as the CoP and Secretariat of the *Convention on the Protection and Use of Transboundary Watercourses and International Lakes* have begun to collaborate the other international organizations, notably the World Health Organization, to assist in conservation-based supply of water to those in the region who are in need of it during the pandemic lockdowns and restrictions on water shipments.[508] Emphasizing the role of zoonotic diseases in current and future pandemic spread, the *CMS* regime has undertaken significant research studies to highlight the importance of studying these issues and understanding them in context.[509]

The International Plant Protection Convention Secretariat has used the pandemic as a lens through which is discuss five identified critical issues for current and future plant health and human health, specifically: (1) Overview on General Impacts and Mitigation Strategies for pandemics and emergencies, (2) Impacts on Food Security and Mitigation Strategies for pandemics and emergencies, (3) Impacts on Safe Trade and Mitigation Strategies for pandemics and emergencies, (4) Impacts on Quarantine staff's Health and Mitigation Strategies for pandemics and emergencies and (5) Communication, Partnership and Solidarity.[510] In so doing, the Secretariat can be seen as proactive in beginning the process of understanding the threats posed by the pandemic to the areas under its jurisdiction and how the pandemic will impact on national and international commitments. At the same time, this indicates a reformulation of current and future policy in a way that is forced rather than the result of measured planning and interventions from impacted constituencies. It is likely that the International Plant Protection Convention Secretariat will not be the only treaty regime-based governance system to enact such reactive policies and plans in the coming period.

507 See Secretariat of the Antarctic Treaty, Next steps following cancellation of ATCM XLIII-CEP XXII in Finland (12 June 2020), available at https://www.ats.aq/devph/en/news/179; Basel, Rotterdam and Stockholm Conventions, Impact of COVID-19 on BRS meetings (9 December 2020), available at http://www.brsmeas.org/Implementation/MediaResources/NewsFeatures/COVID19Communication/tabid/8372/language/en-US/Default.aspx; UNECE, COVID-19: the role of the Water Convention and the Protocol on Water and Health, available at https://www.unece.org/environmental-policy/conventions/water/covid-19-the-role-of-the-water-convention-and-the-protocol-on-water-and-health.html; OSPAR Commission, OSPAR Countries Make Collective Decision to Postpone Ministerial Meeting (3 April 2020), available at https://www.ospar.org/news/ospar-countries-make-collective-decision-to-postpone-ministerial-meeting.

508 See UNECE, COVID-19: the role of the Water Convention and the Protocol on Water and Health, *supra* note 507.

509 CMS, COVID-19 & Migratory Species (29 October 2020), available at https://www.cms.int/en/news/covid19-wildlife.

510 FAO, Plant Health & COVID-19, available at https://www.ippc.int/en/covid-19/.

2.6 Trends and summaries

This Chapter has surveyed treaty regimes and concomitant governance mechanisms across a range of topics relating to environmental, biodiversity and climate change concerns. It found that there are significant trends within and across regime classifications that relate to global governance issues and correlate to the SDGs as a whole as well as to particular elements of the SDGs, such as those found in SDGs 13, 14, 15 and 16.

From the outset, it must be noted that a number of the treaty regimes discussed designate environmental threats as common concerns of humankind, thus extending the reach of their governance systems from purely environmental to issues such as sustainable development and human rights. This can be seen in the incorporation of sustainable development, sustainable use and management of resources and principles of sustainable development such as the precautionary principle and the polluter pays principle, as fundamental purposes of treaty regime-based governance regimes. Further, and connecting to SDG 16, there is a recurrent emphasis on environmental preservation as being tied to peace and the advancement of scientific and cultural knowledge, accompanied by prohibitions on harmful conduct, including militarization of sensitive areas and the protection of sensitive areas in the event of national or regional conflict.

Transparency is a vital trend in the treaty regimes and governance systems discussed in this Chapter. At the public level, inclusion of requirements for State Parties to engage in public awareness, public education and public participation where there are decisions which will cause impact represents a significant effort to use global governance systems to ensure the protection of individual and community rights. This works in tandem with requirements for national and, in certain instances, transboundary environmental impact assessments requirements in treaty regimes which are overseen by governance mechanisms. These measures are intended to assess the environmental damage and threat at the national level – often with a focus on traditional and Indigenous communities – as well as the transboundary level where there is a likelihood that the proposed activity would have a cross-border impact. In this context, the other State has the ability to receive information, comment on the plans and receive the final decision regarding the proposed activity.

Many of these treaty regimes also require that risk assessments or risk measures be created for the purposes of sharing transparent information and understandings with all potentially impacted States. Further, many of these treaties, especially those involve maritime resources, require State Parties to share information on real and potential emergencies with the governance system and other State Parties which could be affected, for example through an oil spill. In this way, there are several levels of global oversight included in the governance planning for activities which have the ability to cause lasting environmental damage and undermine the foundational principles enshrined in many environmental treaty regimes.

Overall, there are significant trends and similarities in the creation of governance systems across environmental treaty regimes. Generally, there will be a decision-making entity that is either a CoP or MoP, allowing the State Parties to come together to issue decisions and to engage in negotiations on the most pressing issues facing the regime at the time. Successive iterations of CoPs at the UNFCCC and CBD level have demonstrated the ability of this system to generate results that are responsive to the needs of the international community in the face of evolving information to environmental threats, albeit more slowly than some might hope. The ability to create committees and other advisory entities as part of the governance system for treaty regimes is a significant and shared ability which ensures that these structures are able to receive and make decisions informed by expertise that is, in theory, removed from many of the political concerns found in the CoP process. Similarly, the use of reporting requirements and oversight, monitoring and compliance systems – whether a dedicated Committee on Compliance as used by the UNFCCC under the *Paris Agreement* or a CoP-based review – ensures that transparency is maintained in the international system.

At the same time, the tiered and escalating approach used by most environmental treaty regimes and governance systems discussed in the face of disputes demonstrates the need to balance governance concerns at the international level with the national sovereignty rights that form the bedrock of international law. Each level in this process allows States to engage in their own forms of diplomatic settlement while at the same time ensuring that there is an organizational structure for these disputes to use rather than threatening to undermine the entirety of the treaty regime. Further, by seeking to settle these disputes within the governance system established under the treaty regime, there is a discernible attempt to ensure that they are solved by States or arbitrators with knowledge in the issues involved rather than through a more generalized system.

The terms of the treaty regimes tend to emphasize the interlinkages between environmental and economic concerns as a potential source of strength and solidity in terms of generating a consolidated and holistic means to addressing these concerns. This is reflected in the financing mechanisms created through many treaty regimes and included in governance systems as well as efforts to increase capacity and to ensure that certain areas of particular ecological value are designated as such and exempted from commercialization.

At the core of each treaty regime and governance system discussed in this chapter is the recognition of environmental issues as touching on many sectors and practices but having a wide-ranging impact that requires both general and specific legal and governance systems and responses to having lasting impact.

3 Social treaty regimes

Social treaty regimes represent a spectrum of legal and governance concerns, as has been highlighted by the COVID-19 pandemic's impacts on health practice and governance as well as on nearly all aspects of the core international human rights system. The connections between social treaty regimes, governance systems and the Sustainable Development Goals (SDGs) are similarly wide-ranging, although the justice and rule of law issues governed by many of the treaty regimes discussed below suggest that SDG 16 is the more all-encompassing SDG in terms of reflecting and furthering the social treaty regimes.

3.1 Core human rights regimes

A plethora of treaty regimes which touch on aspects of human rights concerns and law across international and regional systems exist in the international system. However, within this, there is a fundamental core of treaty regimes which form the crux of the ways in which modern international law and the international community conceives of human rights. These treaties generally stem from the *Universal Declaration on Human Rights*, a non-binding statement of the beliefs and goals of a global community seeking to recover from the horrors of World War II is a bedrock on which human rights are both internationalized and individualized as law and governance systems.

In this context, the following treaty regimes are grouped together for analysis: the *International Covenant on Civil and Political Rights* (ICCPR),[1] the *International Covenant on Economic, Social and Cultural Rights* (ICESCR),[2] the *Convention on the Rights of the Child* (CRC),[3] the *International Convention on the Protocol of the Rights of all Migrant Workers and Members of Their*

1 *International Covenant on Civil and Political Rights* (1976).

2 *International Covenant on Economic, Social and Cultural Rights* (1976).

3 *Convention on the Rights of the Child* (1989).

Families,[4] the *International Convention on the Elimination of All Forms of Racial Discrimination* (CERD),[5] the *Convention on the Elimination of All Forms of Discrimination against Women* (CEDAW),[6] the *Convention against Torture and Other Cruel, Inhuman and Degrading Treatment or Punishment* (CAT)[7] and the *International Convention on the Protection of All Persons from Enforced Disappearance*.[8]

Additionally, several regional human rights treaty regimes have come to the forefront of entrenching human rights within their jurisdictions and expanding them to meet the special needs and experiences of their constituencies. These treaty regimes are the *American Convention on Human Rights*[9] and the *African Charter on Human Rights and Peoples' Rights*.[10]

3.1.1 *Treaty regime purposes and objectives*

In adopting the CRC, State Parties acknowledged that children have a special status in addition to that granted in existing human rights law and that their rights are essential for current and future generations.[11] Subsequent to the CRC, State Parties adopted several thematic protocols which reflect issues that have emerged, namely the *Optional Protocol to the Convention on the Rights of the Child on the Sale of Children, Child Prostitution and Child Pornography*[12] and the *Optional Protocol to the Convention on the Rights of the Child on the Involvement of Children in Armed Conflict*.[13]

In adopting the *Convention on Migrant Workers*, the State Parties recognized the special situation of migrant workers and their families as a duality that necessitates special protections.[14] The State Parties to CERD emphasized that each of the treaties in international law provides protections but that there are still needs which warrant a dedicated national and international apparatus to address racial discrimination.[15] The *Convention on*

4 *International Convention on the Protocol of the Rights of all Migrant Workers and Members of Their Families* (1990).
5 *International Convention on the Elimination of All Forms of Racial Discrimination* (1969).
6 *Convention on the Elimination of All Forms of Discrimination against Women* (1981).
7 *Convention against Torture and Other Cruel, Inhuman and Degrading Treatment or Punishment* (1978).
8 *International Convention on the Protection of All Persons from Enforced Disappearance* (2010).
9 *American Convention on Human Rights (1969).*
10 *African Charter on Human Rights and Peoples' Rights (1981).*
11 CRC, *supra* note 3 at preamble.
12 *Optional Protocol to the Convention on the Rights of the Child on the Sale of Children, Child Prostitution and Child Pornography*, *supra* note 3.
13 *Optional Protocol to the Convention on the Rights of the Child on the Involvement of Children in Armed Conflict*, *supra* note 3.
14 *International Convention on the Protocol of the Rights of all Migrant Workers and Members of Their Families*, *supra* note 4 at preamble.
15 *International Convention on the Elimination of All Forms of Racial Discrimination*, *supra* note 5 at preamble.

the Elimination of All Forms of Discrimination against Women reflects the commitment of State Parties to specialized protections for women as a matter of law, rules and society and to acknowledging societal damage suffered by all sectors and genders as a result of gender discrimination.[16] In establishing the *International Convention on the Protection of All Persons from Enforced Disappearance*, the State Parties emphasized that disappearances are a crime against humanity that also have lasting impacts on victims' families and society, resulting in human rights impacts for current and future generations.[17]

In the Inter-American human rights system, the *American Convention on Human Rights* is the foundational statement of State Party commitments and responsibilities. Through the *American Convention*, States recognize that importance of human rights in the international and Americas context as well as the need to entrench human rights in the legal and societal mechanisms used at the national level.[18] The terms of the *American Convention* were strengthened and modernized in the *Additional Protocol to the American Convention on Human Rights in the Area of Economic, Social and Cultural Rights*.[19]

The Inter-American Human Rights system created through the *American Convention* and the *Protocol* has been expanded to include claims regarding the violation of other Inter-American human rights treaties. For this reason, when discussing governance mechanisms, a complete understanding of the Inter-American system can be established by noting the intersection of these treaty regimes. At the core of the treaty regimes in this context are the *Inter-American Convention against Racism, Racial Discrimination and Related Forms of Intolerance*,[20] *Inter-American Convention on Protecting the Human Rights of Older Persons*,[21] *Inter-American Convention on the Elimination of all Forms of Discrimination against Persons with Disabilities*,[22] *Inter-American Convention to Prevent and Punish Torture* (CAT),[23] *Inter-American Convention on Forced Disappearance of Persons*,[24] and *Inter-American Convention on the Prevention, Punishment and Eradication of Violence against Women*.[25] These

16 CEDAW, *supra* note 6 at preamble.

17 *International Convention on the Protection of All Persons from Enforced Disappearance*, *supra* note 8 at preamble.

18 *American Convention on Human Rights*, *supra* note 9 at preamble.

19 See *Additional Protocol to the American Convention on Human Rights in the Area of Economic, Social and Cultural Rights* ("Protocol of San Salvador"), *supra* note 9.

20 *Inter-American Convention against Racism, Racial Discrimination and Related Forms of Intolerance* (2013).

21 *Inter-American Convention on Protecting the Human Rights of Older Persons* (2015).

22 *Inter-American Convention on the Elimination of all Forms of Discrimination against Persons with Disabilities* (1999).

23 *Inter-American Convention to Prevent and Punish Torture* (1987).

24 *Inter-American Convention on Forced Disappearance of Persons* (1996).

25 *Inter-American Convention on the Prevention, Punishment and Eradication of Violence against Women* ("Convention of Belam do Para") (1994).

instruments have increasingly been invoked by complainants and used for findings against States at the Inter-American Commission on Human Rights and Inter-American Court of Human Rights levels.

State Parties to the *African (Banjul) Charter on Human Rights and Peoples' Rights* noted the need to include peoples' rights as a quintessential part of constructing a human rights system and governance mechanism for the region.[26] Subsequent to the Charter, the *African Charter on the Rights and Welfare of the Child* was adopted and forms an important area of jurisdiction for the human rights system in Africa, including the African Commission and Court of Human and Peoples' Rights.[27]

3.1.2 *Governance mechanisms*

Governance of the ICCPR system is vested in the Human Rights Committee, which reviews submissions by State Parties on a rotating basis and is empowered to produce reports and findings as well as General Comments on specific thematic issues.[28] The Committee may liaise with States directly as well as with international organizations and other relevant entities.[29] Similarly, governance of the ICESCR system is vested in the Committee on Economic, Social and Cultural Rights, which reviews State Party submissions on a rotating basis and generates findings as well as General Comments on specific issues.[30] The Committee has the ability to liaise with States, international organizations and non-State actors as appropriate in the circumstances.[31]

The governance and oversight function for the CRC is vested in the Committee on the Rights of the Child, which reviews reports submitted by State Parties on a rotating basis every 5 years and is empowered to produce reports and findings as well as General Comments on specific thematic issues.[32] The Committee is also able to liaise with States directly as well as with international organizations and other relevant entities.[33] Similar requirements and abilities exist for the Committee on the Protection of the Rights of All Migrant Workers and Members of Their Families[34] and the Committee on the Elimination of Racial Discrimination.[35]

26 *African (Banjul) Charter on Human Rights and Peoples' Rights*, *supra* note 10 at preamble.
27 *African Charter on the Rights and Welfare of the Child* (1990).
28 ICCPR, *supra* note 1 at arts 28, 40.
29 Ibid. at arts 28, 40.
30 ICESCR, *supra* note 2 at arts 16–17.
31 Ibid. at arts 16–17.
32 *Convention on the Rights of the Child*, *supra* note 3 at arts 43–44.
33 Ibid. at art 45.
34 *International Convention on the Protocol of the Rights of all Migrant Workers and Members of Their Families*, *supra* note 4 at arts 72, 73.
35 *International Convention on the Elimination of All Forms of Racial Discrimination*, *supra* note 5 at arts 8–9.

Governance of the CEDAW system is vested in the Committee on the Elimination of Discrimination against Women, which reviews reports submitted by State Parties on a rotating basis every 4 years and is empowered to produce reports and findings as well as General Comments on specific thematic issues.[36] The Committee on the Elimination of Discrimination against Women is also able to liaise with States directly as well as with international organizations and other relevant entities.[37] Similar requirements and abilities exist for the Committee against Torture,[38] as well as the Committee on Enforced Disappearances, which operates on a biennial reporting cycle.[39]

In order to achieve the goals and requirements of the *American Convention* and *Protocol*, a dual level system of governance and dispute resolution was established.[40] The first level is the Inter-American Commission on Human Rights, consisting of members elected by the Organization of American States (OAS) and assisted by the OAS General Secretary, who serves as the Commission Secretary.[41] A dedicated administration and bureaucracy has emerged in the form of the Inter-American Commission itself.[42] The Inter-American Commission is charged with generating recommendations and norms relating to human rights practices and controversies in the region, receiving and hearing complaints from State Parties or individuals and communities regarding allegations of violations of the treaty regimes by other State Parties, fortifying the position and use of human rights in the region and issuing communications and reports on a variety of related topics.[43] Over time, the complaint function in particular has grown exponentially and the Inter-American Commission routinely addresses hundreds of these filings in a year.[44]

Should a complaint be brought and settled, or where the Inter-American Commission issues a finding of wrong-doing by a State Party which then acts to implement the Commission's findings and recommendations for remedying the violation, the matter is typically considered concluded.[45] However, in instances where there is a persistent failure of the State to implement the Inter-American Commission's findings and recommendations, where there is a particularly compelling issue or threat to the complainant or where an advisory opinion has been requested, jurisdiction shifts to the Inter-American Court of Human Rights.[46] The Inter-American Court has

36 CEDAW, *supra* note 6 at arts 17–18.
37 Ibid. at art 17.
38 CAT, *supra* note 7 at art 17, 19.
39 *International Convention on the Protection of All Persons from Enforced Disappearance*, *supra* note 8 at arts 26–27, 29.
40 *American Convention on Human Rights*, *supra* note 9 at art 3.
41 Ibid. at art 35.
42 Ibid.
43 Ibid. at Ch VII.
44 Ibid.
45 Ibid.
46 Ibid. at Ch VIII.

the ability to issue judicial decisions that are binding on the State(s) at issue, including comprehensive remedies that can extend to efforts to make entire communities whole and acknowledge the harms suffered as well as the ability to craft remedies for individual harms.[47]

Additionally, some of the treaty regimes used in the Inter-American human rights system include a separate Conference of the Parties (CoP) to address governance and implementation questions related solely to their specific sectors.[48] Further, specialized committees of experts are created under several treaties Inter-American treaties in order to conduct a parallel yet non-dispute-based system of compliance review, oversight and recommendation making.[49]

Initially, the African Charter established the African Commission on Human and Peoples' Rights in order to conduct research, education and outreach on human rights issues in Africa, assist national and subnational governments in creating and implementing laws, principles and rules that implement the Charter and cooperate with other international organizations.[50] The African Commission was further empowered to receive and issue findings regarding compliance-related complaints from either a State Party against another State Party or individuals or peoples against a State Party.[51] This system has been updated to follow the model used for the Inter-American human rights system in the sense that the African Court of Human and Peoples' Rights has been established to serve similar juridical functions to those of the Inter-American Court of Human Rights. At the same time, the African Commission serves a similar gatekeeper function as in the Inter-American system.

Further, under the African Charter on the Rights and Welfare of the Child, the African Committee of Experts on the Rights and Welfare of the Child is tasked with information gathering and sharing, creating principles and rules to assist in its implementation and monitoring the implementation of the Charter.[52] This includes a requirement for State Parties to provide compliance reports every two years.[53]

3.1.3 *Dispute settlement mechanisms*

A formalized process through which the Human Rights Committee may address complaints regarding the actions of a State Party either from other States or from individual citizens is established in the *Optional Protocol*

47 Ibid.

48 See *Inter-American Convention on Protecting the Human Rights of Older Persons*, *supra* note 21 at arts 33–34.

49 Ibid. at art 35; *Inter-American Convention on the Elimination of all Forms of Discrimination against Persons with Disabilities*, *supra* note 22 at art VI.

50 *African (Banjul) Charter on Human Rights and Peoples' Rights*, *supra* note 10 at arts 30, 41, 45.

51 Ibid. at arts 46–59.

52 Ibid. at arts 40–42.

53 Ibid. at art 43.

to the ICCPR.[54] Specifically, the *Protocol* establishes rules of admissibility, standing to bring a complaint, exhaustion of available remedies, communication of complaints, attempts at friendly settlement, response and inquiry procedures and reporting of decisions as well as the authority to make them.[55] Similar protocols have been used to establish a complaints review system under the auspices of the Committee on Economic, Social and Cultural Rights,[56] the Committee on the Rights of the Child,[57] the Committee on the Elimination of Discrimination against Women[58] and the Committee on Enforced Disappearances.[59]

A formalized process through which the Committee on the Protection of the Rights of All Migrant Workers and Members of Their Families may address complaints regarding the actions of a State Party either from other States or from individual citizens is established in the *Migrant Workers Convention*.[60] In some instances, especially in recently enacted treaty regimes, these procedures have been incorporated into the main text, allowing for more immediate operationalization. For instance, the *Migrant Workers Convention* directly establishes rules of admissibility, standing to bring a complaint, exhaustion of available remedies, communication of complaints, attempts at friendly settlement, response and inquiry procedures and reporting of decisions, as well as the authority to make them.[61] Similar processes have been established under the auspices of the Committee on the Elimination of Racial Discrimination[62] and the Committee against Torture.[63]

3.1.4 *Hard law elements in governance systems*

Under the ICCPR, the State Parties are required to recognize and respect the inherent right to self-determination of peoples,[64] the need for non-discrimination in law along with the need to grant a remedy where a fundamental freedom has been violated[65] and the equality of genders in all

54 *Optional Protocol to the ICCPR, supra* note 1.
55 Ibid.
56 *Optional Protocol to the ICESCR, supra* note 2.
57 *Optional Protocol to the Convention on the Rights of the Child on a Communications Procedure, supra* note 3.
58 *Optional Protocol to the CEDAW, supra* note 6.
59 *International Convention on the Protection of All Persons from Enforced Disappearance, supra* note 8 at arts 30–31.
60 *International Convention on the Protection of the Rights of all Migrant Workers and Members of Their Families, supra* note 4 at art 77.
61 Ibid.
62 *International Convention on the Elimination of All Forms of Racial Discrimination, supra* note 5 at arts 11–14.
63 CAT, *supra* note 7 at arts 20–22.
64 ICCPR, *supra* note 1 at art 1.
65 Ibid. at art 2.

rights established under the Covenant.[66] In furtherance of this, the ICCPR establishes a number of individual rights and freedoms that are to be guaranteed to citizens of all State Parties.[67]

Many of the initial protections and rights guaranteed under the ICCPR, such as the right to self-determination, are also contained in the ICESCR.[68] State Parties are further required to recognize and enforce employment rights and working conditions,[69] individual and collective rights to form trade union and engage in strikes,[70] the right to adequate food, clothing, housing and freedom from hunger,[71] the "right of everyone to the enjoyment of the highest available standard of physical and mental harm,"[72] the rights to education at different levels, for all and especially for girls and including vocational and technical training[73] and the right to cultural life and scientific benefits from it.[74]

The CRC establishes a number of areas in which State Parties are obligated to ensure legal identity, rights and capacities for children are recognized and included as a matter of law, policy and practice.[75] Such rights and duties are truly generational, with the immediate goal of protection and allowing children to enjoy basic rights and the long-term goal of creating the next generation of citizens and leaders. These protections include respecting the rights of the child without discrimination based on status or identity,[76] the use of the best interests of the child standard as a matter of law,[77] the right of the child to life, survival and development,[78] the right of the child to be registered at birth and the concomitant right of the child to a name,[79] the obligation to combat child trafficking and educate parents on the issue,[80] the obligation to respect and incorporate the evolving capacities of the child in relation to issues which impact the child,[81] the rights of the child to freedom of thought, conscience and religion,[82] the rights of the child to freedom of association and peaceful assembly,[83] the obligation of States

66 Ibid. at art 3.
67 Ibid. at arts 6–27.
68 Ibid. at arts 1–3.
69 Ibid. at arts 6–7.
70 Ibid. at art 8.
71 Ibid. at art 9.
72 Ibid. at art 12.
73 Ibid. at art 13.
74 Ibid. at art 15.
75 See generally *Convention on the Rights of the Child*, *supra* note 3 at art 4.
76 Ibid. at art 2.
77 Ibid. at art 3.
78 Ibid. at art 6.
79 Ibid. at art 7.
80 Ibid. at art 11.
81 Ibid. at art 12.
82 Ibid. at art 14.
83 Ibid. at art 15.

to ensure that children are protected from violence and abuse,[84] the obligations of States toward children seeking refugee status in their jurisdiction,[85] the obligation of States to protect children with disabilities,[86] the obligation of States to implement the right of the child to "enjoyment of the highest attainable standard of health,"[87] the right of the child to social security and social insurance,[88] the right to the child to education,[89] the right of the child to employment and protection against exploitation in employment,[90] the obligation of the State to protect children from narcotics, sexual abuse and sexual exploitation,[91] the obligation to provide children with trial rights and procedural rights during detention[92] and the obligation to implement international humanitarian law rights for children.[93]

The essential human rights of migrant workers are established throughout the *Migrant Workers Convention*,[94] and State Parties are obliged to "ensure that migrant workers are not deprived of any rights" by virtue of their status.[95] This includes the right to be fairly paid and to be protected from illegal working or other conditions.[96] Additionally, the rights of migrant workers' families are set out as an integral part of the Convention,[97] and States are required to ensure that these family members are protected by social security when they qualify and that family members of migrant workers have access to education.[98] Together, migrant workers and their families are subject to a number of protections from the States in which they are working, the ability to maintain and practice their cultural identity,[99] protections from illegal and clandestine measures to keep migrant workers in irregular situations,[100] and assisting in ensuring that their rights are maintained when they return to their home States.[101]

Under CERD, State Parties have the obligation to ensure that racially discriminatory laws, rules and policies are rescinded and not subsequently

84 Ibid. at arts 19–20.
85 Ibid. at art 22.
86 Ibid. at art 23.
87 Ibid. at art 24.
88 Ibid. at art 26.
89 Ibid. at art 28.
90 Ibid. at art 32.
91 Ibid. at arts 33, 34.
92 Ibid. at arts 37, 40.
93 Ibid. at arts 38–39.
94 *International Convention on the Protocol of the Rights of all Migrant Workers and Members of Their Families*, *supra* note 4 at arts 9–25.
95 Ibid. at art 25.
96 Ibid.
97 Ibid. at arts 28–63.
98 Ibid. at arts 27, 45.
99 Ibid. at art 31.
100 Ibid. at arts 68–69.
101 Ibid. at art 67.

enacted,[102] as well as ensuring that there is an effort to make law and society integrated.[103] States are required to prohibit and make illegal racist propaganda, organizations and dissemination of racist messages, and "shall not permit public authorities or public institutions, national or local, to promote or incite racial discrimination."[104] Further, States are required to enact laws and rules which guarantee non-discrimination in law and justice, security of the person, enjoyment of civil and political rights, enjoyment of economics, social and cultural rights and rights of access to public spaces.[105] In conjunction with this, States are obligated to ensure that there are judicial and other remedies available for addressing claims of racial discrimination and to address and remediate racial discrimination and prejudice in the education, culture and information sectors.[106]

Pursuant to CEDAW, "State Parties condemn discrimination against women in all its forms, agree to pursue by all appropriate means and without delay" to create policies that eliminate discrimination against women.[107] These means include gender equality in national constitutions, implementing laws and rules to prohibit discrimination against women, ensuring equal access to courts, especially for discrimination claims, ensuring that public actors do not engage in discrimination against women and adapting laws and rules in national jurisdiction to remove measures that are discriminatory against women.[108] In line with this, State Parties are required to create laws and rules relating to equality of access and use of rights,[109] maternity protections and non-discrimination,[110] non-discrimination in terms of access to education and family roles,[111] prohibitions on the trafficking and prostitution of women,[112] rights of women to vote and participate in public life,[113] non-discrimination in citizenship and nationality rights,[114] equality in employment and career opportunities,[115] non-discrimination in healthcare,[116] special rights and protections for rural women,[117] equality in

102 *International Convention on the Elimination of All Forms of Racial Discrimination*, *supra* note 5 at art 2.
103 Ibid.
104 Ibid. at art 4.
105 Ibid. at art 5.
106 Ibid. at arts 6–7.
107 CEDAW, *supra* note 6 at art 2.
108 Ibid. at art 2.
109 Ibid. at art 3.
110 Ibid. at art 4.
111 Ibid. at art 5.
112 Ibid. at art 6.
113 Ibid. at art 7.
114 Ibid. at art 9.
115 Ibid. at arts 10–11.
116 Ibid. at art 12.
117 Ibid. at art 14.

contracting and civil proceedings[118] and equality in marriage and family rights.[119]

Under CAT, State Parties have the obligation to "take effective legislative, administrative, judicial or other measures to prevent acts of torture," as well as prohibiting the use of war as a justification for committing acts of torture and doing away with the command responsibility exception.[120] With this as context, the State Parties are required to make acts of torture illegal,[121] ensure that non-refoulement is applied as a matter of law,[122] create and implement laws and procedures for detention and trial of those accused of torture,[123] cooperate with each other in criminal proceedings investigating torture claims,[124] provide a safe system for those who report torture through official channels,[125] assist victims of torture,[126] and ensure that evidence obtained under torture is excluded for official use.[127]

Through the *Convention on Enforced Disappearances*, State Parties are obligated to investigate enforced disappearances and State involvement in them,[128] criminalize enforced disappearances regardless the actors responsible,[129] create punishments for those found guilty of it,[130] enact criminal procedures for enforced disappearances,[131] ensure availability of judicial and other procedures connected with deprivations of liberty, including allowances of visitors[132] and prevent the taking of children from their families along with the concealment of true identity from the victims of child disappearances.[133]

Generally, the *American Convention on Human Rights* contains a litany of human rights recognitions for individuals and communities within the Americas as a region as well as for State Parties to recognize and incorporate into their legal, regulatory and societal systems.[134] A key example of this is in the context of gender rights and equality, where there is a

118 Ibid. at art 15.
119 Ibid. at art 16.
120 CAT, *supra* note 7 at art 2.
121 Ibid. at art 4.
122 Ibid. at art 3.
123 Ibid. at art 6.
124 Ibid. at art 9.
125 Ibid. at art 13.
126 Ibid. at art 14.
127 Ibid. at art 15.
128 *International Convention on the Protection of All Persons from Enforced Disappearance, supra* note 8 at art 3.
129 Ibid. at art 4.
130 Ibid. at arts 6–7.
131 Ibid. at arts 10, 12.
132 Ibid. at art 17.
133 Ibid. at art 25.
134 *American Convention on Human Rights, supra* note 9 at arts 3–25.

requirement for States to recognize these rights and include them as a matter of constitutional as well as statutory law.[135]

Essential rights guaranteed and owed to citizens of State Parties to the *African Charter* are set forth as core elements of the treaty regime.[136] In this context, States are obligated to provide education and information relating to *African Charter* rights and freedoms to all citizens,[137] to guarantee judicial and court-based independence and to create institutions to ensure and promote the independence of the judicial branch.[138] Additionally, the *African Charter* establishes the duties of individuals under the *Charter* to each other and their States as a matter of law and civil responsibility.[139]

3.2 Criminal regimes

The link between certain types of crimes – especially those which undermine the political and social fabric of a State or give some actors seeming impunity – and human rights issues is well established. Many of these criminal activities are facially more economic in scope, yet their application serves to impact not only the economic stability of the State but also the ability of individuals and communities to access services and participate equitably in society.

In this context, the following treaty regimes are grouped together for analysis: the *United Nations Convention against Corruption* (UNCAC);[140] the *United Nations Convention against Transnational Organized Crime*[141] and its *Protocol to Prevent, Suppress and Punish Trafficking in Persons, Especially Women and Children,*[142] *Protocol against the Smuggling of Migrants by Land, Sea and Air*[143] and *Protocol against the Illicit Manufacturing of and Trafficking in Firearms, Their Parts and Components and Ammunitions;*[144] the *United Nations Convention against Illicit Traffic in Narcotic Drugs and Psychotropic*

135 Ibid. at art 1.

136 *African (Banjul) Charter on Human Rights and Peoples' Rights*, *supra* note 10 at arts 3–24.

137 Ibid. at art 25.

138 Ibid. at art 26.

139 Ibid. at arts 27–29.

140 *United Nations Convention against Corruption* (2005).

141 *United Nations Convention against Transnational Organized Crime* (2003).

142 *Protocol to Prevent, Suppress and Punish Trafficking in Persons, Especially Women and Children Supplementing the United Nations Convention against Transnational Organized Crime* (2003).

143 *Protocol against the Smuggling of Migrants by Land, Sea and Air supplementing the United Nations Convention against Transnational Organized Crime* (2004).

144 *Protocol against the Illicit Manufacturing of and Trafficking in Firearms, Their Parts and Components and Ammunitions supplementing the United Nations Convention against Transnational Organized Crime* (2001).

Substances;[145] the *Inter-American Convention against Corruption*;[146] and the *African Union Convention on Preventing and Combating Corruption*.[147]

3.2.1 *Treaty regime purposes and objectives*

The State Parties to the UNCAC emphasize that corruption poses a threat to all aspects of society, including fostering crime and criminal conduct.[148] The purpose of the UNCAC is "to promote and strengthen measures to prevent and combat corruption more effectively and efficiently,"[149] as well as to include international cooperation and assistance mechanisms in national plans and laws, and "to promote integrity, accountability and proper management of public affairs and public property."[150]

Initially, the *United Nations Convention against Transnational Organized Crime* was enacted "to prevent and combat transnational organized crime more effectively."[151] Over time, the *Convention*'s scope has been expanded to include the *Protocol to Prevent, Suppress and Punish Trafficking in Persons, Especially Women and Children*,[152] *Protocol against the Smuggling of Migrants by Land, Sea and Air*[153] and *Protocol against the Illicit Manufacturing of and Trafficking in Firearms, Their Parts and Components and Ammunitions*.[154] The *UN Convention against Illicit Traffic in Narcotic Drugs and Psychotropic Substances* reflects the concerns of State Parties over the rise in the use of these substances and the threats posed to human health and welfare, leading to larger societal issues, including child drug use.[155] Further, State Parties expressed their concerns regarding the connections between illicit traffic in these substances and organized crime networks which undermines stability and the rule of law.[156]

145 *United Nations Convention against Illicit Traffic in Narcotic Drugs and Psychotropic Substances* (1990).

146 *Inter-American Convention against Corruption* (1997).

147 *African Union Convention on Preventing and Combating Corruption* (2003).

148 *UN Convention against Corruption, supra* note 140 at preamble.

149 Ibid. at art 1.

150 Ibid.

151 *UN Convention against Transnational Organized Crime, supra* note 141 at art 1.

152 *Protocol to Prevent, Suppress and Punish Trafficking in Persons, Especially Women and Children supplementing the United Nations Convention against Transnational Organized Crime, supra* note 142.

153 *Protocol against the Smuggling of Migrants by Land, Sea and Air supplementing the United Nations Convention against Transnational Organized Crime, supra* note 143.

154 *Protocol against the Illicit Manufacturing of and Trafficking in Firearms, Their Parts and Components and Ammunitions supplementing the United Nations Convention against Transnational Organized Crime, supra* note 144.

155 *UN Convention against Illicit Traffic in Narcotic Drugs and Psychotropic Substances, supra* note 145 at preamble.

156 Ibid.

In adopting the *Inter-American Convention against Corruption*, State Parties noted that "corruption undermines the legitimacy of public institutions and strikes at society, moral order and justice, as well as the comprehensive development of peoples."[157] Further, the State Parties emphasized that the development of democracy in the region is threatened by corruption and the links between corruption and organized crime.[158] State Parties to the *African Union Convention on Preventing and Combating Corruption* stressed the inherent harms caused to society and the region by corruption and associated practices.[159] The objectives of the State Parties in creating the *Convention* included combatting corruption as well as strengthening development and democracy in the region and harmonizing national policies and laws relating to corruption and transparency.[160]

3.2.2 *Governance mechanisms*

The primary decision-making entity for the UNCAC is the CoP, which is tasked with reviewing reports and information on the implementation of the Convention, issuing recommendations, creating methods for sharing and mobilizing resources between States and cooperating with international organizations.[161] The UN Secretary General and UN system are collectively to serve the Secretariat role for the UNCAC and for the other UN associated treaty regimes discussed in this section.[162]

The *UN Convention against Transnational Organized Crime* establishes the CoP as the decision-making entity for governance purposes, including the ability to review information and make recommendations, facilitate exchanges and cooperation with international organizations, perform oversight and compliance reviews and render funding decisions.[163] The primary decision-making entity for the *Convention* is the Commission, which is also tasked with reviewing the status and implementation of the treaty regime as a whole.[164] Additionally, the Board is established as the highest level for oversight and guidance within the governance system for the *Convention*.[165]

Implementation of the *American Convention* through decision-making is conducted under the auspices of the Organization of American States

157 *Inter-American Convention against Corruption*, *supra* note 146 at preamble.

158 Ibid.

159 *African Union Convention on Preventing and Combating Corruption*, *supra* note 147 at preamble.

160 Ibid. at art 2.

161 *UN Convention against Corruption*, *supra* note 140 at art 63.

162 Ibid. at art 64; *UN Convention against Transnational Organized Crime*, *supra* note 141 at art 33.

163 *UN Convention against Transnational Organized Crime*, *supra* note 141 at art 32.

164 *UN Convention against Illicit Traffic in Narcotic Drugs and Psychotropic Substances*, *supra* note 145 at art 21.

165 Ibid. at art 22.

(OAS).[166] The *African Convention* establishes the Advisory Board on Corruption within the African Union as the primary oversight body for the treaty regime.[167] The Advisory Board promotes adoption of the *African Convention*, gathers, analyzes and shares data and information relating to the topics in the *Convention*, provides compliance advice to States, provides guidance and support for harmonized codes of conduct and creates alliances with non-governmental organizations and other entities.[168]

3.2.3 *Dispute settlement mechanisms*

Generally, disputes arising from the criminal treaty regimes in the UN context are to be settled by negotiation as a first effort and by arbitration as a second step. In the event that neither of these efforts is successful, or where arbitration fails to yield a result after six months, the matter may be referred to the International Court of Justice.[169] Similar measures in terms of negotiation and peaceful solutions are to be used in the *Inter-American* and *African Conventions.*

3.2.4 *Hard law elements in governance systems*

Under the UNCAC, State Parties have the obligation "to develop and implement or maintain effective, coordinated anti-corruption policies that promote the participation of society and reflect the principles of the rule of law, proper management of public affairs and public property, integrity, transparency and accountability."[170] This is accompanied by soft law encouragements to promote effective anti-corruption practices and evaluate national laws and rules.[171] To implement its purposes, the UNCAC contains a number of hard law obligations for State Parties. Importantly, it requires States to designate bodies to prevent corruption, including through policy creation and sharing of knowledge about corruption.[172] States are to "adopt, maintain and strengthen systems for the recruitment, hiring, retention, promotion and retirement of civil servants" and non-elected government officials by incorporating transparency, nuanced hiring in high-risk sectors for corruption, equality of pay, education and training in corruption.[173]

166 See *Inter-American Convention against Corruption, supra* note 146.
167 *African Union Convention on Preventing and Combating Corruption, supra* note 147 at art 22.
168 Ibid.
169 *UN Convention against Corruption, supra* note 140 at art 66; *UN Convention against Transnational Organized Crime, supra* note 141 at art 35; *UN Convention against Illicit Traffic in Narcotic Drugs and Psychotropic Substances, supra* note 164 at art 32.
170 *UN Convention against Corruption, supra* note 140 at art 5.
171 Ibid.
172 Ibid. at art 6.
173 Ibid. at art 7.

In the context of government procurement, State Parties to the UNCAC are required to "establish appropriate systems ... based on transparency, competition and objective criteria in decision-making that are effective ... in preventing corruption."[174] Money laundering is another area of concern under the UNCAC, and State Parties are required to create robust legal and regulatory systems, including those for monitoring and evaluation, to prevent and prosecute it.[175] Further areas constituting crimes at the national level in State Parties include bribery of national public officials, bribery of foreign public officials and officials of public international organizations, embezzlement, misappropriation or diversion of property by a public official, laundering the proceeds of a crime and obstruction of justice.[176]

To enforce and address the criminal aspects of the UNCAC's obligations, State Parties are required to enact laws, rules and policies that relate to freezing, seizure and confiscation of illegally obtained assets.[177] States are obligated to enact laws and rules relating to the protection of witnesses, experts and victims in association with corruption and associated crimes, and also to provide for compensation systems for damage caused by corruption.[178] Additional areas of anti-corruption focus for State Parties to the UNCAC include enhancing public reporting and transparency in public administration[179] and strengthening the independence and integrity of judges, prosecutors and the judicial system.[180] States are also obligated to prevent corruption in the domestic private sectors.[181] Further, State Parties to the UNCAC are required to ensure that members of society, especially civil society, are included in efforts to address corruption, including through public education campaigns.[182] At the international level, States are required to provide assistance to each other in corruption investigations and anti-corruption efforts.[183]

State Parties to the *UN Convention against Transnational Organized Crime* are obligated to enact laws and rules relating to a number of crimes and acts, notably the participation in an organized criminal group, laundering of proceeds of a crime, money laundering, transnational corruption and organized crimes networks, corruption of public officials and obstruction of justice.[184] Institutionally, State Parties are required to create systems for prosecution, adjudication and sanctions to enforce the terms of the

174 Ibid. at art 9.
175 Ibid. at art 14.
176 Ibid. at arts 15–17, 23, 25.
177 Ibid. at art 31.
178 Ibid. at arts 32, 35.
179 Ibid. at art 10.
180 Ibid. at art 11.
181 Ibid. at art 12.
182 Ibid. at art 13.
183 Ibid. at arts 37–39, 43, 46, 48, 60.
184 *UN Convention against Transnational Organized Crime*, *supra* note 141 at arts 5–9, 23.

Convention.[185] In terms of protections, States are required to make legal and regulatory provisions for witness protection, assistance to and protection of victims and ensure the involvement of the public in gathering information on organized crime.[186] There are numerous ways in which the State Parties are required to provide cooperation and assistance under the *Convention*, including mutual legal assistance for matters involving investigations, prosecutions and judicial procedures, law enforcement activities and training and technical assistance.[187]

Under the *UN Convention against Illicit Traffic in Narcotic Drugs and Psychotropic Substances*, State Parties are obligated to create laws and rules relating to a number of criminal offences relating to drugs and trafficking, as well as the profits and proceeds of these crimes.[188] In this context, State Parties are required to engage in confiscation activities related to the proceeds and profits of crimes established in the *Convention*.[189] Further, there is an obligation for States to take measures to eradicate illicit cultivation of narcotic plants and eliminate illicit demand for narcotic drugs and psychotropic substances at the national level.[190] State Parties also have obligations regarding cooperation and mutual assistance, including for information sharing, law enforcement activities and training.[191]

State Parties to the *Inter-American Convention against Corruption* are required to enact laws and rules entrenching standards of conduct for public officials, enforcing codes of conduct and training requirements for public servants, registering income, assets and investments for public officials, overseeing mechanisms for collecting tax data, protecting whistleblowers, creating oversight bodies and mechanisms, deterring bribery of foreign and national governmental officials and involving non-governmental organizations in efforts to combat bribery and corruption.[192] In terms of specific requirements, States must ensure that their definitions of corruption as a matter of law are in accord with the terms of the *Convention* and also adopt laws criminalizing transnational bribery and illicit enrichment.[193] At the international level, State Parties are required to provide assistance and cooperation in implementation of the *Convention* and are to designate central authorities at the national level to implement and oversee the *Convention*.[194]

185 Ibid. at art 11.
186 Ibid. at arts 24–25, 28.
187 Ibid. at arts 18, 26, 29.
188 *UN Convention against Illicit Traffic in Narcotic Drugs and Psychotropic Substances*, *supra* note 145 at art 3.
189 Ibid. at art 5.
190 Ibid. at art 14.
191 Ibid. at arts 7, 9, 10.
192 *Inter-American Convention against Corruption*, *supra* note 146 at art III.
193 Ibid. at arts VI–IX.
194 Ibid. at arts XIV, XVIII.

The *African Union Convention on Preventing and Combating Corruption* defines a number of activities and actions which are to qualify as crimes and illicit acts to which its prohibitions apply.[195] In conjunction with this, State Parties are obligated to enact laws and rules which fully incorporate these acts as part of the national criminal law system.[196] This includes operationalizing laws regarding confiscation and seizure of the proceeds and instrumentalities of corruption, designating national authorities for the purposes of cooperation and assistance, engaging in mutual legal assistance with other State Parties and generally cooperating with other States on corruption-related issues.[197]

3.2.5 *Soft law elements in governance systems*

State Parties to the UNCAC are encouraged to adopt codes of conduct and guidelines for public servants to assist in understanding acceptable and illicit conduct.[198] In terms of criminal law, State Parties to the UNCAC agree to consider establishing a number of crimes, including trading in influence, abuse of functions, illicit enrichment, bribery in the public sector, embezzlement of property in the private sector and concealment.[199] Additionally, State Parties are encouraged to enact whistleblower protections as a matter of law.[200]

As part of the *African Union Convention on Preventing and Combating Corruption*, State Parties commit to fight against corruption and related offences in the public services, as well as to make illicit enrichment an offense, to criminalize corruption in private sector activities and to involve civil society and the media in anti-corruption campaigns.[201]

3.3 Health and food regimes

Health and food regimes are cross-cutting however, given recent focus resulting from the COVID-19 pandemic and also interlinkages with human rights and the SDGs, are included in the social regime discussions. Essential to full enjoyment and realization of associated human rights regimes before, the pandemic has highlighted this and stressed the human rights aspects of these regimes and governance systems. The two treaty regimes discussed in

195 *African Union Convention on Preventing and Combating Corruption*, *supra* note 147 at art 4.
196 Ibid. at art 5.
197 Ibid. at arts 16, 18–20.
198 *UN Convention against Corruption*, *supra* note 140 at art 8.
199 Ibid. at arts 18–22, 24.
200 Ibid. at art 33.
201 *African Union Convention on Preventing and Combating Corruption*, *supra* note 147 at arts 7–8, 11–12.

this section are the *Constitution of the World Health Organization*[202] and the *Constitution of the Food and Agriculture Organization.*[203]

3.3.1 *Treaty regime purposes and objectives*

As a UN specialized entity, the *Constitution of the World Health Organization* (WHO) establishes that the organization is to work in tandem with the goals and purposes of the *Charter of the United Nations.*[204] State Parties recognize that "the enjoyment of the highest attainable standard of health is one of the fundamental rights of every human being without distinction of race, religion, political belief, economic or social condition," and that "the health of all peoples is fundamental to the attainment of peace and security and is dependent upon the fullest co-operation of individuals and States."[205] This informs the commitment of State Parties to the idea that "governments have a responsibility for the health of their peoples which can be fulfilled only by the provision of adequate health and social measures."[206]

The Food and Agriculture Organization (FAO) is also a UN specialized entity carrying a specific remit. The FAO is intended to address the need for increased nutritional and food access systems throughout State Parties, as well as the need to include rural populations in food access and food security issues, with the ultimate goal of "contributing towards an expanding world economy and ensuring humanity's freedom from hunger."[207] Organizationally, the FAO is empowered to generate and disseminate relevant information relating to food, nutritional concerns and agriculture, suggest policies and practices to assist in food and agricultural production, generate recommendations for relevant national and international policies regarding food and agriculture and assist State Party governments as requested.[208]

3.3.2 *Governance mechanisms*

Unlike many of the treaty regimes discussed in this book, the *WHO Constitution* – and the *FAO Constitution* below – establishes the parameters of an international organization as well as a treaty regime.[209] In this sense, the entirety of the *WHO Constitution* establishes a governance framework, although within this system there are still hard and soft law elements.[210]

202 *Constitution of the World Health Organization* (1948).
203 *Constitution of the Food and Agriculture Organization* (1945).
204 *Constitution of the World Health Organization, supra* note 202 at preamble.
205 Ibid.
206 Ibid.
207 *Constitution of the Food and Agriculture Organization, supra* note 203 at preamble.
208 Ibid. at art I.
209 See *Constitution of the World Health Organization, supra* note 202 at Ch I.
210 See ibid. at Ch II.

Indeed, the WHO as a whole is tasked with significant policy-generating, data gathering, coordinating and assisting of governments, regions and vulnerable communities functions in order to facilitate its purposes, generating suggestions for new conventions and agreements, creating guidelines for health policy and technical health response implementation and coordinating with specific international organizations to address cross-cutting goals, such as nutrition and food access.[211] To accomplish this, a significant portion of these functions are delegated to the Secretariat, which serves as the administrative entity for the WHO.[212] Given the specialized and highly technical nature of the WHO, the Secretariat serves as a liaison between and with State Parties and other international organizations for promotion of health goals.[213]

Overall, the WHO is comprised of three essential organs – the World Health Assembly, the Executive Board and the Secretariat.[214] The World Health Assembly is a general membership body for all State Parties to the *WHO Constitution* and is the primary policy-making entity in the WHO governance system.[215] It has the ability to create additional committees and subsidiary bodies within the WHO structure, receive and review reports and other information from State Parties and the Secretariat and adopt agreements or other treaty regimes.[216] Additionally, and of increasing importance since the advent of the *International Health Regulations* (IHRs), the World Health Assembly has the ability to create and adopt regulations and directives relating to health and associated topics.[217] This includes the ability to declare and issue regulations for quarantines and responsive measures.[218] The World Health Assembly meets at designated sessions throughout the year and can be convened as necessary in times of emergency.[219] Under the terms of the IHRs, an Emergency Committee and a Review Committee are established within the WHO governance system as well.[220]

The Executive Board is a smaller group of State Party representatives which acts as the executive entity in the WHO governance structure.[221] In this capacity, it is a source of advice to the World Health Assembly and the WHO as a whole and provides suggested policies for the Assembly to consider as well as retain the ability to take emergency actions where the situation warrants and the Assembly is unable to convene in time.[222] In addition,

211 Ibid. at Ch II, art 2.
212 Ibid. at Ch VII, art 30.
213 Ibid. at Ch VI.
214 Ibid. at Ch IV, art 9.
215 Ibid. at Ch V, art 18.
216 Ibid. at Ch V, arts 18, 19.
217 Ibid. at Ch V, art 21.
218 Ibid. at Ch V, art 21(a).
219 Ibid. at Ch V.
220 *International Health Regulations* (2006) at pt. IX.
221 *Constitution of the World Health Organization*, *supra* note 202 at Ch VI, art 28.
222 Ibid.

a series of regional committees are created for the purposes of addressing specific health concerns among differing regions and coordinating responses to these concerns in a context-appropriate manner.[223] The WHO may create joint committees with the International Labour Organization,[224] FAO,[225] UNESCO[226] and the United Nations Industrial Development Organization.[227]

The FAO is similarly an international organization within the UN system at the same time as a treaty regime with a significant governance system. The core decision-making body for the FAO is the Conference, which is the full representative body for all State Parties.[228] In this capacity, the Conference is responsible for the generating rules of the FAO, creating recommendations in general and for specific State Parties regarding food, agriculture and related issues, liaising with other international organizations and establishing Regional Conferences similar to those used by the WHO.[229]

The Council of the FAO is a smaller body comprised of rotating representatives of State Parties and working through a series of committees including the Programme Committee, Finance Committee, Committee on Constitutional and Legal Matters, Committee on Commodity Problems, Committee on Fisheries, Committee on Forestry and Committee on Agriculture.[230] Generally, the Council is empowered to address issues and provide recommendations at the request of the Conference.[231] At present, a number of subsidiary committees and groups exist as part of this structure, clustered under the headings of agriculture, animal production and health, commodities and trade, fisheries, food policy and nutrition, forestry, genetic resources for food and agriculture, land and water development, plant production and protection and statistics.[232]

The Secretariat serves as the administrative entity for the FAO under the authority of the Director-General.[233] The Conference, Council and Director-General have the ability to create additional committees, commissions,

223 Ibid. at Ch XI.

224 See *Agreement between the International Labour Organization and the World Health Organization* at art III.

225 See *Agreement between the Food and Agriculture Organization of the United Nations and the World Health Organization* at art III.

226 See *Agreement between the United Nations Educational, Scientific and Cultural Organization and the World Health Organization* at art IV.

227 See *Agreement between the United Nations Industrial Development Organization and the World Health Organization* at art 6.

228 *Constitution of the Food and Agriculture Organization*, *supra* note 203 at art III.

229 Ibid. at art IV.

230 Ibid. at art V.

231 Ibid.

232 FAO, Statutory Bodies by subject matter, available at http://www.fao.org/unfao/govbodies/gsb-subject-matter/subject-matter/en/.

233 *Constitution of the Food and Agriculture Organization*, *supra* note 203 at arts VII, VIII.

topic-specific conferences and working groups as deemed necessary.[234] Additionally, the FAO has established a framework for evaluating and, where appropriate, allowing non-State actors to participate in and contribute to certain aspects of its functioning.[235]

3.3.3 *Dispute settlement mechanisms*

Disputes relating to the WHO's activities or between State Parties arising out of WHO commitments are first to be addressed by negotiation.[236] If this does not prove successful, the World Health Assembly may attempt to resolve the issue and, ultimately, may refer the matter to the ICJ for resolution where necessary.[237] Provided the United Nations agrees to such a request, the WHO may also seek an advisory opinion from the ICJ.[238] In terms of disputes specifically arising in connection with the IHRs, State Parties are to first attempt the use of negotiation, then refer the matter to the WHO Director-General and, finally, may pursue an arbitral solution.[239]

Under the FAO system, disputes between State Parties are to be first addressed through negotiations or other peaceful means and, should these fail, may be referred to the ICJ for a final decision or to a designated arbitral body agreed on by the Parties.[240] Further, it is possible for the FAO to request an advisory opinion on matters within its jurisdiction from the ICJ.[241]

3.3.4 *Hard law elements in governance systems*

Perhaps the most significant aspect of hard law generated through the WHO structure is the IHRs. As an outgrowth of the regulatory powers granted to the World Health Assembly in the *Constitution*, the IHRs were first issued in 1969 and have been updated on a regular basis ever since.[242] Tellingly, the IHRs began as an effort to define and regulate the handling of significant diseases which required quarantines or other restrictive measures at the national level as well as concomitant international attention and prioritization.[243] At present, the purposes of the IHRs are "to prevent, protect against, control and provide a public health response to the international spread of

234 Ibid. at art VI.

235 See Food and Agriculture Organization Policy Governing Relations with International Non-Governmental Organizations (2020).

236 *Constitution of the World Health Organization*, *supra* note 202 at Ch XXVIII, art 75.

237 Ibid.

238 Ibid. at Ch XXVIII, art 76.

239 *International Health Regulations*, *supra* note 220 at art 56.

240 *Constitution of the Food and Agriculture Organization*, *supra* note 203 at art XVII.

241 Ibid. at art XVII.

242 *International Health Regulations*, *supra* note 220 at foreword.

243 Ibid.

disease in ways that are commensurate with and restricted to public health risks, and which avoid unnecessary interference with international traffic and trade."[244] Each State Party is required to designate a national focal point for coordination purposes as well as indicate the domestic authorities that will be directly responsible for implementing the IHRs.[245]

The current iteration of the IHRs, which became operational in 2007, contain significant legal and regulatory elements at the national and international levels, notably that State Parties are to "develop, strengthen and maintain, as soon as possible but no later than five years from the entry into force of these Regulations for that State Party, the capacity to detect, assess, notify and report events in accordance with these Regulations."[246] Pursuant to the IHRs, State Parties are obligated to report "all events which may constitute a public health emergency of international concern within [their] territory in accordance with the decision instrument, as well as any health measure implemented in response to those events" within 24 hours of determining that this situation exists.[247] Once this communication has been made, the State Party is under a continuing requirement to inform the WHO of progress and medical information which becomes available in regard to the issue.[248] Further, where there is a suspicion of a public health event, State Parties also have an obligation to share this information with the WHO.[249] Additionally, the WHO Secretariat is allowed to receive and consider information from non-State actors regarding potential public health events occurring in a State Party.[250] Where follow-up is deemed appropriate, the State Party must then cooperate with the WHO in assessing the validity of the situation and necessary steps.[251] Should these measures regarding public health events be triggered, the WHO itself is under a duty to share the information with other State Parties and with relevant non-State actors.[252]

Ultimately, the determination as to whether there is a public health event under the IHRs is to be made by the WHO Director-General as the head of the Secretariat.[253] In making this determination, the Director-General has the ability to issue both temporary and standing recommendations for State response to the public health threat.[254] These recommendations can extend beyond the treatment of people and to the handling of animals and wildlife,

244 Ibid. at art 2.
245 Ibid. at art 4.
246 Ibid. at art 5.
247 Ibid. at art 6.
248 Ibid.
249 Ibid. at art 7.
250 Ibid. at art 9(1).
251 Ibid. at art 10.
252 Ibid. at art 11.
253 Ibid. at art 12.
254 Ibid. at arts 15–16.

goods in transit, methods of travel and packages.[255] The recommendations are to be made after discussions with the State Parties, the World Health Assembly, Executive Board and committees, scientific and health experts and others as necessary.[256]

As a planning matter, State Parties are required by the IHRs to create and update response strategies for public health events in their territory and originating in other States but with the possibility of spreading.[257] In situations where States are called on to put such plans into effect, the WHO has the ability to provide them with assistance as requested and deemed appropriate.[258] This requirement includes the designation of airports and other ports of entry that have the capacity to address the issue and directives at the domestic level as they relate to regulation of travel and movement in response to the public health threat.[259] Additionally, there is an effort to ensure that the IHRs are communicated to and utilized by other relevant international organizations including the International Civil Aviation Organisation.[260]

The *Codex Alimentarius* International Food Standards exists as a joint effort between the FAO and WHO for the promotion of safe and nutritious food access as well as for food quality and food security for current and future generations.[261] Additionally, the *Codex Alimentarius* seeks to ensure that trade in food and agriculture-related products is facilitated and that trade barriers are reduced provided this is done in a safe manner.[262] While the standards adopted under the *Codex Alimentarius* system are not automatically binding at the domestic level without additional national legislation, they serve as the internationally accepted requirements.[263]

3.3.5 *Soft law elements in governance systems*

As part of the IHRs, State Parties have the ability to report lower-level events and medical issues to the WHO and other State Parties as they believe appropriate and to seek consultations on these issues.[264] Additionally, when there is a public health event that has been recognized as such by the WHO Director-General, the principle of sovereignty requires that State Parties

255 Ibid. at art 16.
256 Ibid. at art 17.
257 Ibid. at art 13.
258 Ibid.
259 Ibid. at pt. IV.
260 WHO-IHR, Revision of the International Health Regulations (2015) sect 6.
261 See Food and Agriculture Organization, Codex Alimentarius, available at http://www.fao.org/fao-who-codexalimentarius/about-codex/en/.
262 Ibid.
263 Ibid.
264 *International Health Regulations*, *supra* note 220 at art 8.

are subject to soft law provisions for determining the appropriate public health measures to put in place at the domestic level.[265] An exception to this exists to prohibit as a matter of hard law invasive medical examinations or measures for travelers arriving in a State Party's jurisdiction except for testing and certain vaccination requirements.[266]

In the FAO context, the *Codex Alimentarius* is supplemented by soft law guidelines and codes of practice.[267] The guidelines and codes of practice are based on technical skills and expertise, allowing States and industry representatives to find the most analogous standards to implement within their own legal and regulatory systems.[268] At the same time, the FAO is able to exercise an oversight function for these soft law instruments and update them quickly as the situation warrants.[269]

3.4 Weapons and hazardous substance regimes

Weapons and hazardous substances pose an existential threat to humanity in a cross-cutting manner. At their heart, weapons and hazardous substances endanger individuals and communities, invoking concerns over the fundamental right to life that is a core element of human rights treaties. They also link to issues of health and food access, potentially exposing victims to incalculable immediate and generational harms that also impact on environmental rights and concerns. Further, weapons and hazardous substances have the ability to undermine the rule of law through their status as an illicit commodity. For these reasons, they are included in this chapter although there are also strong links to environmental and economic issues and governance systems.

In this context, the following treaty regimes are grouped together for analysis: the *Treaty on the Prohibition of Nuclear Weapons*,[270] the *Convention on Cluster Munitions*,[271] the *Convention on the Prohibition of the Development, Production, Stockpiling and Use of Chemical Weapons and on Their Destruction*,[272] the *Arms Trade Treaty*,[273] the *African Nuclear*

265 Ibid. at pt. V.
266 Ibid. at art 31.
267 Food and Agriculture Organization, Codex Alimentarius: Guidelines, available at http://www.fao.org/fao-who-codexalimentarius/codex-texts/guidelines/en/; Food and Agriculture Organization, Codex Alimentarius: Codes of Practice, available at http://www.fao.org/fao-who-codexalimentarius/codex-texts/codes-of-practice/en/.
268 Ibid.
269 Ibid.
270 *Treaty on the Prohibition of Nuclear Weapons* (2017) (to enter into force on 22 January 2021).
271 *Convention on Cluster Munitions* (2010).
272 *Convention on the Prohibition of the Development, Production, Stockpiling and Use of Chemical Weapons and on Their Destruction* (1992).
273 *Arms Trade Treaty* (2014).

Weapon-Free-Zone Treaty[274] and the *Bamako Convention on the Ban of the Import into Africa and the Control of Transboundary Movement and Management of Hazardous Wastes within Africa*.[275]

3.4.1 *Treaty regime purposes and objectives*

The *Treaty on the Prohibition of Nuclear Weapons* was created by State Parties based on the understanding of the threats posed by nuclear weapons to current and future generations in the transboundary context, as well as the national context, and especially for vulnerable and marginalized groups such as women and children.[276] The *Convention on Cluster Munitions* stresses that the use of cluster munitions poses not only a short-term threat but also exists as a generational threat to civilians long after the fighting has concluded and the conflict has been settled.[277]

In the *Arms Trade Treaty*, there is an attempt to balance the sovereign right to self-defense with the rights of civilians, particularly vulnerable populations, and the interests of the international community in promoting peace and non-violence.[278] With this interest in balancing in mind, the objectives of the *Treaty* include to "establish the highest possible common international standards for regulating or improving the regulation of the international trade in conventional arms; and prevent and eradicate the illicit trade in conventional arms and prevent their diversion."[279]

In crafting the *African Nuclear Weapon-Free-Zone Treaty*, the State Parties recognized and stressed the potential for the treaty regime to assist generating peace and stability in the region and ensuring the achievement of the intended environmental policy goals for the region as well.[280]

3.4.2 *Governance mechanisms*

For the purposes of *Treaty on the Prohibition of Nuclear Weapons* decision-making and oversight, the Meeting of the Parties is established as the key review and verification entity.[281] Similarly, the primary governance mechanism of the *Convention on Cluster Munitions* is the Meeting of the Parties, which is tasked with reviewing the status of the *Convention* and its implementation, reports and other materials, cooperation and other means of

274 *African Nuclear Weapon-Free-Zone Treaty* (2009).
275 *Bamako Convention on the Ban of the Import into Africa and the Control of Transboundary Movement and Management of Hazardous Wastes within Africa* (1998).
276 *Treaty on the Prohibition of Nuclear Weapons*, *supra* note 270 at preamble.
277 *Convention on Cluster Munitions*, *supra* note 271 at preamble.
278 *Arms Trade Treaty*, *supra* note 273 at preamble.
279 Ibid. at art 1.
280 *African Nuclear Weapon-Free-Zone Treaty*, *supra* note 274 at preamble.
281 *Treaty on the Prohibition of Nuclear Weapons*, *supra* note 270 at art 8.

international assistance, technological development and submissions from State Parties regarding the *Convention*.[282] Additionally, every five years there is a requirement for the States to convene a Review Conference under the auspices of the UN Secretary General.[283]

The *Convention on the Prohibition of the Development, Production, Stockpiling and Use of Chemical Weapons and on Their Destruction* establishes the Organization as the overarching governance system, comprised of the Conference of the State Parties, the Executive Council and the Technical Secretariat.[284] The CoP has standard functions of oversight and policy-generation, and has the ability to call special sessions when deemed necessary.[285] The Executive Council consists of 41 rotating State Party members and is the equivalent of the UN Security Council in terms of decision-making authority.[286] The Technical Secretariat is tasked with carrying out standard administrative functions and providing technical expertise as necessary.[287]

The primary governance entity under the *Arms Trade Treaty* is the CoP, which has oversight and recommendation authority over State Parties and the development of the *Treaty* apparatus.[288] There is a standing Secretariat charged with administrative and communications functions.[289] The CoP exists as the primary decision-making entity under the *African Nuclear Weapon-Free-Zone Treaty*'s terms and is vested with oversight requirements, reporting reviews and generation of recommendations, amendments and other *Treaty* revisions.[290] Ensuring that State Parties meet their obligations is a matter assigned to the African Commission on Nuclear Energy, which is the *Treaty*'s compliance mechanism.[291] Compliance matters are intertwined with the annual reporting requirements for all State Parties.[292]

Under the *Bamako Convention on the Ban of the Import into Africa and the Control of Transboundary Movement and Management of Hazardous Wastes within Africa*, the CoP exists as the senior decision-making body, tasked with harmonizing policies and laws, creating amendments and proposed protocols, reviewing and providing guidance on reports, creating subsidiary bodies and assisting in peaceful settlement of disputes.[293] While the Secretariat carries out basic administrative functions, it is also tasked with

282 *Convention on Cluster Munitions*, *supra* note 271 at art 11.
283 Ibid. at art 12.
284 *Convention on the Prohibition of the Development, Production, Stockpiling and Use of Chemical Weapons and on Their Destruction*, *supra* note 272 at art VIII.
285 Ibid. at art VIII (B).
286 Ibid. at art VIII (C).
287 Ibid. at art VIII (D).
288 *Arms Trade Treaty*, *supra* note 273 at art 17.
289 Ibid. at art 18.
290 *African Nuclear Weapon-Free-Zone Treaty*, *supra* note 274 at art 14.
291 Ibid. at art 12.
292 Ibid. at art 13.
293 *Bamako Convention*, *supra* note 275 at art 15.

facilitating the exchange of technical information needed to fully implement the *Convention* at all levels.[294]

3.4.3 *Dispute settlement mechanisms*

Negotiation and other peaceful means of settling disputes between the State Parties is at the foundation of *Treaty on the Prohibition of Nuclear Weapons*' mechanisms for addressing disputes.[295] If this proves unsuccessful in addressing the issues raised, the dispute may then be brought to the next MoP for a decision.[296] Under the *Arms Trade Treaty*'s terms, disputes are to be settled by peaceful means where possible and then can be brought before the CoP for a decision.[297] Should this step prove unable to address the concerns raised in the dispute it is possible for the matter to be referred to the ICJ.[298]

In the event of disputes between the State Parties or between a State Party and the *Convention on Cluster Munitions*, there is a requirement to consult together for a speedy settlement of the issues.[299] The next option is to bring the matter to the MoP, which can address the issues contained or refer the dispute to the ICJ.[300] Dispute settlement under the *Convention on the Prohibition of the Development, Production, Stockpiling and Use of Chemical Weapons and on Their Destruction* is first to go to the CoP for attempts at peaceful settlement or negotiation and then to the ICJ if this proves difficult.[301] The Executive Council is also able to assist and provide guidance during dispute settlement efforts.[302]

Issues of *African Nuclear Weapon-Free-Zone Treaty* interpretation are to be handled through either recourse to the ICJ or through an arbitral tribunal established under the *Treaty*'s auspices.[303] Similarly, complaints and disputes arising from the *Treaty* are to be settled through a three-step process if necessary.[304] In this context, the first step is an attempt at peaceful settlement; the second step is recourse to the Commission for a determination; and finally, the third steps is reference of the matter to the International Atomic Energy Agency in the event of an allegation involving a significant breach of the *Treaty*'s terms.[305]

294 Ibid. at art 16.
295 *Treaty on the Prohibition of Nuclear Weapons*, *supra* note 270 at art 11.
296 Ibid.
297 *Arms Trade Treaty*, *supra* note 273 at art 19.
298 Ibid.
299 *Convention on Cluster Munitions*, *supra* note 271 at art 10.
300 Ibid.
301 *Convention on the Prohibition of the Development, Production, Stockpiling and Use of Chemical Weapons and on Their Destruction*, *supra* note 272 at art XIV.
302 Ibid.
303 *African Nuclear Weapon-Free-Zone Treaty*, *supra* note 274 at art 15.
304 Ibid. at Annex VI.
305 Ibid.

Dispute settlement under the *Bamako Convention on the Ban of the Import into Africa and the Control of Transboundary Movement and Management of Hazardous Wastes within Africa* begins with negotiations and other attempts at peaceful settlement between the States involved.[306] Following this, a dispute would be sent to the ICJ or a dedicated ad hoc arbitral body established pursuant to the terms of the *Convention*.[307]

3.4.4 *Hard law elements in governance systems*

Pursuant to the terms of the *Treaty on the Prohibition of Nuclear Weapons*, State Parties have the obligation to refrain from developing and testing nuclear weapons and delivery systems, transferring nuclear weapons and delivery systems, receiving control of nuclear weapons and delivery systems, threatening the use of nuclear weapons and delivery systems, bypassing the prohibitions in the *Treaty* and allowing nuclear weapons to be in the State's territory.[308] With these obligations in mind, States are required to take legal and regulatory measures at the national level.[309] In instances where States have used nuclear weapons in their territories, including during previous conflicts, there is a requirement to provide assistance to victims and environmental remediation.[310] For this, and for the general implementation of the *Treaty*'s obligations, there is a requirement that States cooperate with each other and render assistance where available.[311]

As a fundamental premise, all State Parties to the *Convention on Cluster Munitions* are obligated to refrain from using cluster munitions and developing, creating, stocking, transferring or taking other actions which would assist in cluster munitions trafficking.[312] Connected to these obligations, States are required to separate any cluster munitions in their arsenals and either destroying them or providing information on their quantity, as well as requirements regarding the clearance and destruction of cluster munitions remnants and education on risk reduction for those who are potentially exposed to them.[313] There is also an obligation for States to provide victim assistance to those who have suffered harm within their jurisdiction.[314] At the international level, there are hard law obligations for States to report on the transparency mechanisms used as part of the implementation system for *Convention* requirements and to share information on how legal

306 *Bamako Convention*, *supra* note 275 at art 20.
307 Ibid.
308 *Treaty on the Prohibition of Nuclear Weapons*, *supra* note 270 at art I.
309 Ibid. at art 5.
310 Ibid. at art 6.
311 Ibid. at art 7.
312 *Convention on Cluster Munitions*, *supra* note 271 at art 1.
313 Ibid. at arts 3–4.
314 Ibid. at art 5.

and regulatory systems at the national level have been changed to reflect *Convention* terms.[315]

Due to the nature of chemical weapons and their harms, State Parties to the *Convention on the Prohibition of the Development, Production, Stockpiling and Use of Chemical Weapons and on Their Destruction* have obligations to refrain from developing, creating, keeping or otherwise deploying chemical weapons, engaging in any form of sale or transfer of chemical weapons and using chemical weapons.[316] Additionally, there are requirements for States to destroy their stocks of chemical weapons and to refrain from using chemical weapons in the control or prevention of riots.[317] To ensure the entrenchment of these requirements as a matter of law, the *Convention* contains obligations for the implementation of national legal and regulatory measures.[318]

The *Arms Trade Treaty* contains a number of hard law requirements regarding the implementation of the terms at the national level, the designation of national contact points and authorities, the prevention of prohibited transfers, record-keeping regarding arms production and transfers, reporting and enforcement measures.[319] Further, States are required to place limits on exports and impose export assessments to determine whether arms should be transferred to regimes based on their human rights, humanitarian law and general legal compliance.[320] Similar requirements exist for import restrictions, transportation and transshipment of arms, arms brokering and diversion of arms shipments.[321]

Under the *African Nuclear Weapon-Free-Zone Treaty*, State Parties are obligated to legally renounce the use of nuclear explosive devices, including not to conduct research or seek to assist others in these activities[322] and to ensure that nuclear explosive devices are not present in the State.[323] Additionally, States are obligated to declare, dismantle and destroy or convert nuclear devices in their jurisdictions and to prohibit dumping of radioactive wastes.[324]

The *Bamako Convention* contains binding requirements for State Parties to create and share a national definition of hazardous waste.[325] Following on from this, States are obliged to undertake hazardous waste importation bans

315 Ibid. at arts 7–9.
316 *Convention on the Prohibition of the Development, Production, Stockpiling and Use of Chemical Weapons and on Their Destruction*, *supra* note 272 at art 1.
317 Ibid. at arts I, III.
318 Ibid. at art IV.
319 *Arms Trade Treaty*, *supra* note 273 at arts 5–6, 12–14.
320 Ibid. at art 7.
321 Ibid. at arts 8–11.
322 *African Nuclear Weapon-Free-Zone Treaty*, *supra* note 274 at art 3.
323 Ibid. at art 4.
324 Ibid. at arts 6–7.
325 *Bamako Convention on the Ban of the Import into Africa and the Control of Transboundary Movement and Management of Hazardous Wastes within Africa*, *supra* note 275 at art 3.

and share information on violations with the Secretariat,[326] and to impose a ban on dumping of hazardous wastes at sea and in internal waters.[327] In addition, States are required to create transboundary movement and notification procedures, including elements requiring consent prior to the commencement of the shipment activity,[328] and to adopt the duty to re-import where there are issues with the full exportation of the covered substances.[329] To comply with these requirements and facilitate the exchange of information, States are obligated to designate competent authorities, a national focal point and create additional oversight mechanisms.[330] States undertake a duty to prevent and report illegal trafficking in hazardous wastes, including the obligation for transmission of information regarding accidents and hazardous waste movements.[331]

3.5 Pandemic responses

Among the treaty regimes discussed in this Chapter, it is perhaps unsurprising that the most robust response to the COVID-19 pandemic has come from the WHO. Indeed, the WHO was the first global governance system to be faced with COVID-19 when the People's Republic of China officially informed the Director-General of the existence of a novel virus on December 31, 2019.[332] This triggered a response from the WHO in the form of sending an investigatory team to review the situation, which rapidly began involving additional offices and areas of expertise concentrated under the WHO Secretariat structure.[333] As a result, the international notification requirements for the WHO Director-General under the IHRs were invoked on January 5, 2020.[334]

Since that time, the WHO has been at the governance center of the pandemic at the international level. The criticism brought against the WHO by various State Parties is without the scope of this book except to highlight the inherent tensions which can emerge in a globally focused governance system when States act first as nationalistically focused actors rather than as members of an active and collaborative system.

From a governance perspective, the WHO is the entity responsible for declaring a global pandemic, which it did on March 10, 2020, and for

326 Ibid. at art 4(1).
327 Ibid. at art 4(2).
328 Ibid. at art 6.
329 Ibid. at art 8.
330 Ibid. at art 5.
331 Ibid. at arts 9, 13.
332 WHO, Timeline: WHO's COVID-19 response, available at https://www.who.int/emergencies/diseases/novel-coronavirus-2019/interactive-timeline#!.
333 Ibid.
334 Ibid.

monitoring and oversight of the pandemic's progress as well as the progress of legal, policy and scientific progress in addressing it.[335] Against this backdrop, the WHO has issued a series of guidelines and suggestions for State governments as well as private industry and individuals on how to address the spread of the virus.[336] The Executive Committee has served as a critical oversight body throughout the duration of the pandemic and in the weeks beforehand.[337]

Food safety and transportation have become critical issues during the pandemic, and the FAO has responded to this through the *Codex Alimentarius* Commission, which has taken an active role in coordinating with State Parties and other constituencies to ensure that factual information has reached them and informs their rules and practices.[338] As an organization, the FAO has operationalized the expertise of its committees and other working groups as well as the knowledge of those working within the Secretariat to generate policy guides and other research reports that are intended to assist State Parties in crafting short- and long-term responses to the pandemic that protect agriculture, food access and food security.[339]

As in other contexts, the treaty regimes discussed in this Chapter have seen changes to their scheduled meeting and decision-making processes.[340] A number of the core human rights governance systems have responded to the pandemic by issuing policy statements and other documents that highlight the vulnerabilities of human rights in the face of State Party responses

335 Ibid.

336 See Public health surveillance for COVID-19: interim guidance, WHO/2019-nCoV/SurveillanceGuidance/2020.7 (7 August 2020); Global surveillance of COVID-19: WHO process for reporting aggregated data, WHO/2019-nCoV/surveillance_aggr_CRF/2020.3 (7 August 2020); Considerations for the provision of essential oral health services in the context of COVID-19, WHO/2019-nCoV/Oral_health/2020.1 (3 August 2020); Considerations for implementing mass treatment, active case-finding and population-based surveys for neglected tropical diseases in the context of the COVID-19 pandemic, WHO/2019-nCoV/neglected_tropical_diseases/2020.1 (27 July 2020); Preventing and managing COVID-19 across long-term care services: Policy brief, WHO/2019-nCoV/Policy_Brief/Long-term_Care/2020.1 (24 July 2020); Biomedical equipment for COVID-19 case management - inventory tool: Interim guidance, WHO/2019-nCov/biomedical_equipment_inventory/2020.1 (26 June 2020).

337 WHO, Statement on the fourth meeting of the International Health Regulations (2005) Emergency Committee regarding the outbreak of coronavirus disease (COVID-19), available at https://www.who.int/news-room/detail/01-08-2020-statement-on-the-fourth-meeting-of-the-international-health-regulations-(2005)-emergency-committee-regarding-the-outbreak-of-coronavirus-disease-(covid-19).

338 Codex Alimentarius, COVID-19, available at http://www.fao.org/fao-who-codexalimentarius/thematic-areas/covid-19/en/.

339 FAO, Policy support and governance gateway, available at http://www.fao.org/policy-support/coronavirus-pandemic/en/.

340 See CRC, *supra* note 2; FAO *Constitution*, *supra* note 203; CERD, *supra* note 5; CEDAW, *supra* note 6; CAT, *supra* note 7; ICCPR, *supra* note 1; ICESCR, *supra* note 2.

to COVID-19.[341] For instance, the Committee on the Rights of the Child has emphasized the inherent threats that closing or altering education poses to children,[342] and the Committee on the Protection of the Rights of All Migrant Workers and Members of their Families highlighted the health and security issues faced by migrant workers unable to return home and without social protections in the States where they have been working.[343] In the regional context, the Inter-American Commission on Human Rights has issued a formal resolution on the human rights of people with COVID-19[344] and the African Commission on Human and Peoples' Rights has issued a statement on the need to protect and preserve electoral rights during the pandemic.[345]

While many of the UN-associated criminal regimes discussed in this Chapter have had their official meetings postponed during the pandemic, it should be highlighted that they have continued work on policy documents and recommendations. This has been emphasized as a significant aspect of ensuring that corruption does not hinder the delivery of pandemic-related relief and of protecting an increasingly online international community from threats posed by cybercrimes.[346]

3.6 Trends and summaries

This Chapter has surveyed treaty regimes and concomitant governance mechanisms across a range of topics relating to human rights, criminal conduct, health and agricultural and weapons and hazardous substances. It

341 CRC, The Committee on the Rights of the Child warns of the grave physical, emotional and psychological effect of the COVID-19 pandemic on children and calls on States to protect the rights of children (2020); UN Committee on the Protection of the Rights of All Migrant Workers and Members of Their Families and UN Special Rapporteur on the human rights of migrants, Joint Guidance Note on the Impacts of the COVID-19 Pandemic on the Human Rights of Migrants 1 (26 May 2020); Committee on the Elimination of Discrimination against Women, Guidance Note on CEDAW and COVID-19 (2020); Committee on Economic, Social and Cultural Rights, Statement on the coronavirus disease (COVID-19) pandemic and economic, social and cultural rights, E/C.12/2020/1 (17 April 2020).

342 CRC, The Committee on the Rights of the Child warns of the grave physical, emotional and psychological effect of the COVID-19 pandemic on children and calls on States to protect the rights of children (2020).

343 UN Committee on the Protection of the Rights of All Migrant Workers and Members of Their Families and UN Special Rapporteur on the human rights of migrants, Joint Guidance Note on the Impacts of the COVID-19 Pandemic on the Human Rights of Migrants 1 (26 May 2020).

344 IACHR, Human Rights of Persons with COVID-19, Resolution No. 4/2020 (27 July 2020).

345 African Commission on Human and Peoples' Rights, Statement of the African Commission on Human and Peoples' Rights on Elections in Africa during the COVID-19 Pandemic, available at https://www.achpr.org/pressrelease/detail?id=522.

346 United Nations Office of Drugs and Crime, Coronavirus disease (COVID-19) – UNODC updates, available at https://www.unodc.org/unodc/en/covid-19.html.

found that there are significant trends within and across regime classifications that relate to global governance issues and correlate to the SDGs as a whole as well as to particular elements of the SDGs, especially SDGs 2, 3, 5, 8, 10 and 16. Among these, the strongest correlation between the treaty regimes and governance systems discussed occurs in terms of SDG 16 given the breadth of its remit, embracing everything from violence reduction to transparency and social inclusion to public participation to reductions in threats from weapons.

A critical trend in the treaty regimes discussed is their focus on various human rights concerns – be they regarding acts of torture, rights of children, societal ability to progress beyond corruption, the right to health, the right to live without generational threats from weapons or beyond – and the translation of these concerns into governance structures that are tailored to meet the needs of the populations affected.

By allowing private individuals and communities to bring claims regarding human rights violations to regional and international bodies, the core human rights treaties pierced the well-worn veil of international law as the realm of States. Indeed, this has created a unique governance structure which attempts to balance sovereignty and the supremacy of the State in international law with the realization that the rights created belong to private actors and that there must be a place for claims regarding infringements on these rights to occur. At the same time, while the other sectors discussed in this Chapter have adopted a more traditional international law perspective on governance systems, especially the WHO and FAO which act as formalized international organizations, they too recognize the importance of non-State voices in creating highlight technical and specialized policy that is often dependent on knowledge outside that possessed by international policy makers. These differing responses to related issues demonstrate the importance of open and innovative governance systems for social sector regimes as well as for regimes which are highly technical and continue to evolve.

Relatedly, the treaty regimes discussed in this Chapter require that domestic actors be either designated or created by State Party governments in order to enforce the terms of the international law instrument at issue. This entrenches the State's commitments under the treaty regime as part of the national governance system while also linking the national governance sector to the global governance system established in the regime. This duality of governance is both mutually reinforcing and allows States to be held to account when there are failures of governance as a national matter since the failure is in regard to an international commitment.

Each of the treaty regimes discussed emphasized the need to incorporate and act to protect vulnerable and marginalized populations in different contexts and with different needs. However, whether the rights to be protected are of children today or their grandchildren, the governance systems put in place by these regimes require States to actively report on – and thus, at least in theory, act on – their progress toward achieving their hard law obligations. These governance systems also allow for the evolution of their terms as science and technology becomes further advanced while seeking to include the voice of marginalized peoples in their decision-making.

Finally, the governance systems created by treaty regimes discussed in this Chapter must be framed against the larger intention of human rights and social treaties to entrench the laws and rules they contain as elements in a durable and evolving human rights system. This system functions as a duality of national and international, which from a governance perspective can seem uneven and yet allows the system to be reinforcing of the overarching global needs and commitments while giving space for national variations and needs provided they do not conflict. This is as true for the core human rights treaties as it is for the WHO and IHRs, both of which represent governance systems that are designed to function through this duality and, if they are to be criticized, should be criticized at the level of human fallibility in implementation rather than governance system design.

4 Economic treaty regimes

Economic treaty regimes include a wide range of activities, interests and opportunities to craft governance systems. In this setting, it could be expected that various regimes and sectors would share little in common in terms of governance systems and goals, however, the opposite is true. Regardless the differences in industry, function and form of governance system, there are core interconnections between the economic aspects of these entities and environmental and social aspects which make the regimes relatable to each other and to regimes set out in Chapters 2 and 3. Additionally, these interconnections demonstrate the ways in which these regimes can be directly connected to and entrench the Sustainable Development Goals (SDGs).

4.1 Trade regimes

Trading regimes have historically given rise to a significant body of international law and defined the ways States interacted in everything from diplomacy to warfare. In the modern international law context, the primary governance system for trade in the World Trade Organization (WTO), which is comprised of an international organization based on a set of trade-focused treaty regimes that State Parties must adopt as national law prior to becoming members.

Given the depth of WTO influence on trade regimes, it will be the primary focus of this section however the role of free trade agreements as trade regimes that create governance mechanisms must be noted here as well. While the volume of free trade agreements and their specialized nature precludes a discussion in this book, their contributions to governance systems should not be overlooked. Indeed, free trade agreements increasingly incorporate specialized joint review committees, dispute settlement systems and, in some instances, provisions establishing separate oversight and review organizations for issues such as environmental and labor law enforcement at the national levels in the State Parties.

4.1.1 *Treaty regime purposes and objectives*

The origins of the WTO can be traced to the 1947 *General Agreement on Tariffs and Trade* (GATT), which survived as the guiding treaty regime for the international community until 1995. The *GATT* stressed that trade and economic advancement "should be conducted with a view to raising standards of living, ensuring full employment and a large and steadily growing volume of real income."[1] When the international community created the WTO as an independent international organization in 1995 it did so under the auspices of the *Agreement Establishing the World Trade Agreement* (*Marrakech Agreement*), which included the GATT's terms.[2] In the *General Agreement on Trade in Services* (GATS), WTO State Parties stressed the importance of liberalizing the system of trade in services to be reflective of current economic trends and regimes.[3] The *Agreement on Agriculture* notes the significant connections between environmental concerns and agricultural trade and that the *Agreement* is a regime meant to assist in this interrelationship.[4] The *Revised Agreement on Government Procurement* focuses on the need to balance between sovereign undertakings and security interests on the one hand and the concern that these grounds not be used as an excuse for unfairly and illegally assisting domestic businesses on the other.[5]

4.1.2 *Governance mechanisms*

The essential framework for a Conference of the Parties (CoP) system of governance in the trade regime context was established in the 1947 *GATT*.[6] This GATT-based regime was, however, without a governance structure.[7] The 1995 *Marrakech Agreement* remedied this by establishing the WTO as an international organization with concomitant governance systems and organs.[8] In this context, the most senior organ is the Ministerial Council, which meets biennially and addresses significant issues of law and policy for international trade.[9] Additionally, the General Council serves as the secondary decision-making entity within the WTO governance system, with the ability to make policy decisions between meetings of the Ministerial

1 *General Agreement on Tariffs and Trade* (1947).
2 *Agreement Establishing the World Trade Organization* (1995).
3 *General Agreement on Trade in Services* (1995).
4 *Agreement on Agriculture* (1995).
5 *Revised Agreement on Government Procurement* (1995).
6 GATT, *supra* note 1 at XXV.
7 Ibid.
8 *Marrakech Agreement*, *supra* note 2.
9 Ibid. at art IV.

Council and oversight authority for the Trade Policy Reviews that States are obligated to file as an aspect of their reporting requirements.[10]

GATS established the Council for Trade in Services, which is authorized to address measures needed to implement its terms and to hear initial complaints if the State Parties involved agree.[11] The *Marrakech Agreement* also established the Council for Trade-Related Aspects of Intellectual Property and the Council for Trade in Goods, and these Councils operate under the jurisdiction of the General Council.[12] Pursuant to the *Marrakech Agreement*, the Ministerial Council is vested with jurisdiction over the Committee on Trade and Development, Committee on Balance-of-Payments Restrictions and Committee on Budget, Finance and Administration.[13] Similar provisions exist for the creation of the Committee on Agriculture,[14] Committee on Customs Valuation,[15] Committee on Import Licensing,[16] Committee on Government Procurement,[17] Committee on Safeguards,[18] Committee on Sanitary and Phytosanitary Measures,[19] Committee on Subsidies and Countervailing Measures and Subsidiary Bodies,[20] Committee on Technical Barriers to Trade,[21] and Committee on Trade-Related Investment Measures under their respective treaty regimes.[22] The WTO Secretariat, under the leadership of the Director-General, is tasked with administrative and bureaucratic functions.[23]

4.1.3 *Dispute settlement mechanisms*

The trade regimes established under the WTO system are highly nuanced and disputes stemming from them require significant expertise to resolve. At the same time, the rights and obligations created in these treaties are binding on the State Parties in their capacities as sovereign representatives and, as such, disputes must be brought at the State-to-State level rather than involving individuals, businesses or investors who might suffer harms as a result of State laws and rules contravening WTO treaty terms. In this context,

10 Ibid.
11 GATS, *supra* note 3 at arts XXII, XXIV.
12 *Marrakech Agreement, supra* note 2 at art IV.
13 Ibid.
14 *Agreement on Agriculture, supra* note 4 at 17–18.
15 *Agreement on Implementation of Article VII of the GATT* (1994) at art 18.
16 *Agreement on Import Licensing Procedures* (1995) at art 4.
17 *Revised Agreement on Government Procurement, supra* note 5 at art XXI.
18 *Agreement on Safeguards* (1995) at art 13.
19 *Agreement on the Application of Sanitary and Phytosanitary Measures* (1995) at art 12.
20 *Agreement on Subsidies and Countervailing Measures* (1995) at art 24.
21 *Agreement on Technical Barriers to Trade* (1995) at art 13.
22 *Agreement on Trade-Related Investment Measures* (1995) at art 7.
23 *Marrakech Agreement, supra* note 2 at art VI.

the WTO Dispute Settlement Body (DSB) serves as the entity authorized to receive and oversee the settling of disputes between State Parties.[24]

Where a State believes a contravention of one or more WTO treaties exists, there is typically an attempt at informal dialogue between the States involved in order to settle the matter quickly and with minimal cost.[25] Should this fail, the complaining State then has the ability to file an initial notice with the DSB, which triggers a mandatory period during which efforts at conciliation and settlement are to be undertaken.[26] If these efforts are successful, the matter is officially closed.[27] If, however, these efforts are unsuccessful the complaining State will file the official complaint, after which the respondent State will have the opportunity to respond and a panel of experts will be convened to hear the complaint.[28]

When the Panel has received the responsive pleadings and any additional comments from third-party States with interests in the matters at issue, it will then issue its report and findings.[29] At this point, the States may accept the report and enter into discussions as to how to implement it or either one or both of the States may appeal the report to the Appellate Body.[30] The Appellate Body, comprised of a separate panel of experts, has the ability to review the matters on appeal and issue a report that then becomes binding on the States, which are to agree on the manner and timing of its implementation.[31] However, in instances where a State fails to implement the Appellate Report, and after attempts to ensure compliance have failed, the injured State may receive organizational approval to impose reciprocal sanctions until the Appellate Report is implemented or the contested measure is removed.[32]

4.1.4 *Hard law elements in governance systems*

The GATT entrenched significant economic and trade practices as a matter of international law to be implemented within national legal systems of State Parties, including most favored nation status and concomitant rights,[33] national treatment of other GATT State Parties for the purposes of internal taxation and regulation,[34] freedom of transit for goods in commerce,[35]

24 Ibid. at Annex 2 on DSB.
25 Ibid.
26 Ibid.
27 Ibid.
28 Ibid.
29 Ibid.
30 Ibid.
31 Ibid.
32 Ibid.
33 GATT, *supra* note 1 at art I.
34 Ibid. at III.
35 Ibid. at IV.

anti-dumping protections,[36] customs valuation uniformity,[37] marks of origin of goods requirements,[38] publication of trade regulations to allow for transparency,[39] quarantine restrictions,[40] safeguards,[41] subsidies restrictions,[42] restrictions on government assistance for economic development,[43] accepted general and security-related exceptions,[44] and nullification and impairment responses.[45] Many of these initial terms have been further amplified through subsequent WTO promulgated treaty regimes.[46]

The GATS terms include most favored nation status for services,[47] transparency in rules and requirements relating to services,[48] obligations for developed States to increase the potential of developing States to participate in the global service economy,[49] restrictions on monopolies and exclusive service suppliers in the domestic context,[50] business practices in the services context,[51] negotiation abilities for emergency safeguard measures,[52] reduction and elimination of subsidies,[53] market access and services allowances at the domestic level,[54] and progressive liberalization of systems and trade laws on services.[55]

The *Agreement on Agriculture* addresses a number of agricultural trade elements as well as practices associated with agricultural trade which can be used to help or hinder it as part of the international trading system. These include issues such as market access,[56] special safeguard provisions and agricultural laws and rules stemming from them,[57] commitments regarding levels of domestic support to the agriculture sector,[58] export competition and export commitments,[59] and, in limited circumstances, allowances for

36 Ibid. at VI.
37 Ibid. at VII.
38 Ibid. at IX.
39 Ibid. at X.
40 Ibid. at XI.
41 Ibid. at XII.
42 Ibid. at XVI.
43 Ibid. at XVIII.
44 Ibid. at XX, XXI.
45 Ibid. at XXIII.
46 *Agreement of Implementation of Article VI of the General Agreement on Tariffs and Trade, supra* note 15.
47 GATS, *supra* note 3 at II.
48 Ibid. at III.
49 Ibid. at IV.
50 Ibid. at VIII.
51 Ibid. at IX.
52 Ibid. at X.
53 Ibid. at XV.
54 Ibid. at XVI.
55 Ibid. at XV.
56 *Agreement on Agriculture, supra* note 4 at 4.
57 Ibid. at 5.
58 Ibid. at 6–7.
59 Ibid. at 8–9.

divergence for least-developed States and net food-importing developing States.[60]

Under the *Agreement on Trade in Civil Aircraft*, WTO State Parties adopted significant trade-related obligations, including those relating to customs duties,[61] the application of technical barrier to trade in the civil aircraft context,[62] the non-application of certain trade restrictions,[63] and to ensure that the regional and local governments in their jurisdictions also apply these undertakings.[64] The *Revised Agreement on Government Procurement* establishes the scope and coverage of acts to be classified as within the realm of government procurement,[65] provides allowances for security and general exceptions for procurement contexts,[66] establishes general principles for reconciling government procurement with international trade,[67] generates requirements that State Parties share information on national procurement systems, laws and policies in order to foster transparency,[68] and stipulates technical requirements for the procurement system in all State Parties.[69]

Specific regulatory requirements across all sectors of the economy exist under the *Agreement on Implementation of Article VII of the GATT*, relating to customs valuations provisions,[70] *Agreement on Import Licensing Procedures*,[71] the *Agreement on Pre-Shipment Inspection*,[72] the *Agreement on Safeguards*,[73] the *Agreement on the Application of Sanitary and Phytosanitary Measures*,[74] the *Agreement on Subsidies and Countervailing Measures*,[75] the *Agreement on Technical Barriers to Trade*,[76] *Agreement on Trade-Related Investment Measures* (TRIMs)[77] and the *Agreement on Trade-Related Aspects of Intellectual Property Rights* (TRIPs).[78]

60 Ibid. at 16.
61 *Agreement on Civil Aircraft* (1995) at 2.
62 Ibid. at 3.
63 Ibid. at 5.
64 Ibid. at 7.
65 *Revised Agreement on Government Procurement*, *supra* note 5 at II.
66 Ibid. at III.
67 Ibid. at IV.
68 Ibid. at VI.
69 Ibid. at VII–XVIII.
70 *Agreement on Implementation of Article VII of the GATT*, *supra* note 15.
71 *Agreement on Import Licensing Procedures*, *supra* note 16.
72 *Agreement on Pre-Shipment Inspection* (1995).
73 *Agreement on Safeguards*, *supra* note 18.
74 *Agreement on the Application of Sanitary and Phytosanitary Measures*, *supra* note 19.
75 *Agreement on Subsidies and Countervailing Measures*, *supra* note 20.
76 *Agreement on Technical Barriers to Trade*, *supra* note 21.
77 TRIMs, *supra* note 22.
78 *Agreement on Trade-Related Aspects of Intellectual Property Rights* (1995).

4.1.5 *Soft law elements in governance systems*

GATT established the ability of State Parties to assist developing States in trade policy and related activities,[79] which was the precursor to the current Aid-for-Trade programme implemented through the WTO system.[80] Under GATS, there are similar provisions regarding technological cooperation and transfer for the services sector.[81]

4.2 Economic policy regimes

The regimes discussed in this section might at first seem at opposite ends of a spectrum between attempts to regulate corporate actor conduct overseas and attempts to regulate the exploration and exploitation of space. And yet, at their core these regimes are both economic in nature and cross-cutting in impact, seeking to regulate conduct that is inherently driven by profit and economic power while having the ability to cause damage and destruction to communities and humanity alike. Indeed, the efforts at balancing profit with protection can be seen as a fundamental bridge that brings these otherwise separate fields together. In this context, the following treaty regimes are grouped together for analysis: the *OECD Guidelines for Multinational Enterprises*[82] and the *OECD Convention on Combatting Bribery of Foreign Public Officials in International Business Transactions*.[83]

Since the inception of the *Moon Treaty*, the international community has established a system that seeks to create laws, regulatory systems and governance mechanisms that are standard to international practice and transfer them to a constantly emerging field of science, technology and capacity. In many ways, this perhaps offers the closest analogy to the SDGs given the depth of issues involved, the proliferation of soft law standards, and the use of evolving knowledge and understanding as benchmarks for the achievement of goals and targets. While the SDGs are time-sensitive and international space law is decidedly not fixed to a date requirement, the fast-moving pace of science and technology surrounding outer space is such that there is an implicit time sensitivity to decisions taken.

International space law lacks a centralized treaty regime, instead relying on five treaties for form the core of its functions[84]: the *Treaty on Principles Governing the Activities of States in the Exploration and Use of Outer Space,*

79 GATT, *supra* note 1 at XXXVII.

80 WTO, Aid for Trade, available at https://www.wto.org/english/tratop_e/devel_e/a4t_e/aid4trade_e.htm.

81 GATS, *supra* note 3 at XXV.

82 *OECD Guidelines for Multinational Enterprises* (2011).

83 *OECD Convention on Combatting Bribery of Foreign Public Officials in International Business Transactions* (1999).

84 United Nations Office for Outer Space Affairs, *International Space Law: United Nations Instruments* (Vienna, 2017) iii–iv.

Including the Moon and Other Celestial Bodies,[85] the *Agreement on the Rescue of Astronauts, the Return of Astronauts and Return of Objects Launched into Outer Space,*[86] the *Convention on International Liability for Damage Caused by Space Objects,*[87] *the Agreement Governing the Activities of States on the Moon and Other Celestial Bodies,*[88] and the *Convention on Registration of Objects Launched into Outer Space.*[89]

4.2.1 *Treaty regime purposes and objectives*

From the outset, the *OECD Convention on Combatting Bribery of Foreign Public Officials in International Business Transactions* can be viewed as a combination of hard law and soft law mechanisms seeking to address what is both a national and transnational issue.[90] This reflects the multifaceted nature of the industries, entities and conduct to be regulated as well as the difficulty in ensuring that this conduct is evenly regulated on a global scale.

The *Treaty on Principles Governing the Activities of States in the Exploration and Use of Outer Space, Including the Moon and Other Celestial Bodies* vested oversight and reporting jurisdiction for its terms and requirements in the United Nations Secretary General (UNSG).[91] This includes State Party requirements to register the objects launched into Outer Space under their jurisdiction and to provide information on scientific discoveries made.[92] While the Treaty leaves open the option to have other governance issues handled by unspecified international organizations, in practice these issues have all been addressed to the UNSG system.[93] These registration requirements are amplified in the *Convention on Registration of Objects Launched into Outer Space*[94] and the *Moon Treaty.*[95] Under the terms of the

85 *Treaty on Principles Governing the Activities of States in the Exploration and Use of Outer Space, Including the Moon and Other Celestial Bodies,* United Nations, Treaty Series, vol. 610, No. 8843 (1967).

86 *Agreement on the Rescue of Astronauts, the Return of Astronauts and Return of Objects Launched into Outer Space,* United Nations, Treaty Series, vol. 672, No. 9574 (1967).

87 *Convention on International Liability for Damage Caused by Space Objects,* United Nations, Treaty Series, vol. 961, No. 13810 (1972).

88 *Agreement Governing the Activities of States on the Moon and Other Celestial Bodies,* United Nations, Treaty Series, vol. 1363, No. 23002 (1984).

89 *Convention on Registration of Objects Launched into Outer Space,* United Nations, Treaty Series, vol. 1023, No. 15020 (1974).

90 *OECD Convention on Combatting Bribery of Foreign Public Officials, supra* note 83 at preamble.

91 *Treaty on Principles Governing the Activities of States in the Exploration and Use of Outer Space, Including the Moon and Other Celestial Bodies, supra* note 85 at art XIII.

92 Ibid.

93 Ibid.

94 *Convention on Registration of Objects Launched into Outer Space, supra* note 89 at arts II, IV.

95 *Agreement Governing the Activities of States on the Moon and Other Celestial Bodies, supra* note 88 at art 5.

Moon Treaty, State Parties are obligated to inform the public and the UNSG of exploration and use activities involving the Moon, as well as informing States working in the same area of the Moon of their exploration and use intent and notifying the UNSG, other States and the public of significant scientific findings from Moon and space exploration, including those potentially having a harmful impact on Earth or human life.[96] Further, under the *Moon Treaty* there are obligations that State Parties adopt laws and rules for environmental protection on Earth from potential impacts of space activities and protection of the Outer Space environment.[97]

4.2.2 *Governance mechanisms*

United Nations General Assembly (UNGA) decisions regarding the implementation and governance structure of the UN elements for space policy centered on the creation of the United Nations Office for Outer Space Activities (UNOOSA) and the Committee in the Peaceful Uses of Outer Space. The Committee is charged with carrying out the functions delegated to the UNSG under the space law treaties, including handling registration issues, with a focus on enabling the participation of developing States in the space exploration process.[98] While the Committee and associated specialized entities under its jurisdiction, such as the United Nations Platform for Space-based Information for Disaster Management and Emergency Response, address policy issues and take decisions according to the mandates established in core space treaties, the UNOOSA engages in more administrative functions as well as conducting educational activities and meetings of various constituencies.[99] The Committee and associated organs meet several times a year as a standard practice and take decisions during these meetings.[100] However, there is no organized CoP system as such, and the ability of civil society and non-governmental actors to participate in these meetings is strictly limited.[101]

4.2.3 *Dispute settlement mechanisms*

Similar to the SDGs, the multifaceted nature and reliance on a significant body of soft law makes space law difficult to establish a fulsome dispute resolution system over. Generally, the core treaties and UNGA principles

96 Ibid.
97 Ibid. at art 7.
98 See *Declaration on International Cooperation in Exploration and Use of Outer Space for the Benefit and in the Interest of All States, Taking into Particular Account the Needs of Developing Countries*, resolution 51/122 of 13 December 1996.
99 United Nations Office for Outer Space Affairs, About Us, available at https://www.unoosa.org/oosa/en/aboutus/index.html.
100 Ibid.
101 Ibid.

relating to them require State Parties to adopt domestic legislation regarding environmental protection on Earth and in Outer Space, as well as liability for the actions of their space programs and nationals in space. Further, the treaties extend international responsibility for States regarding the activities on their nationals in Outer Space.[102]

The *Convention on International Liability for Damage Caused by Space Objects* establishes that claims regarding damage should first be commenced in national courts and heard under national law to the extent possible.[103] To assist in this, the *Convention* establishes a filing procedure to be used in the event of a claim.[104] Should these claims prove unable to be addressed through the appropriate domestic court systems, the *Convention* requires that the issues be submitted for diplomatic proceedings and attempts at crafting a solution.[105] In the event that diplomatic means cannot settle the dispute, the *Convention* allows for the creation of a dedicated Claims Commission to hear the issues complained of and render a decision. The Commission is to be comprised of one member appointed by each State Party involved in the complaint as well as an independent representative upon whom the Parties must agree.[106] Once the Commission has made its determination there is no further appellate body or process.[107]

Under the *Agreement Governing the Activities of States on the Moon and Other Celestial Bodies*, a number of protections for lunar resources and Outer Space resources are created, including prohibitions on the assertion of private ownership of natural resources and the concomitant requirement that States act to stop such assertions from being made by those under their jurisdiction.[108] Should there be a dispute between State Parties over the implementation of these terms, the *Agreement* sets out a dispute resolution system which starts with formal consultations over the alleged violation.[109] If the consultations are unsuccessful, the matter is then referred to the UNSG for further mediation.[110]

Additionally, the soft law instruments that provide amplification of and support for the core space law treaties create new avenues for the use of peaceful settlement of disputes between State Parties. The UNGA's *Principles Relating to Remote Sensing of the Earth from Outer Space* provide

102 *Treaty on Principles Governing the Activities of States in the Exploration and Use of Outer Space, Including the Moon and Other Celestial Bodies*, *supra* note 85 at art VI.

103 *Convention on International Liability for Damage Caused by Space Objects*, *supra* note 87.

104 Ibid. at art VIII.

105 Ibid. at art IX.

106 Ibid. at arts XIV–XX.

107 Ibid.

108 *Agreement Governing the Activities of States on the Moon and Other Celestial Bodies*, *supra* note 88 at arts 11, 14.

109 Ibid. at art 14.

110 Ibid.

that disputes are to be handled through good offices,[111] while the *Principles Relevant to the Use of Nuclear Power Sources in Outer Space* establish grounds for state responsibility, liability and compensation and peaceful settlement of disputes as called for in the UN Charter.[112]

4.2.4 *Hard law elements in governance systems*

The *OECD Convention on Combatting Bribery of Foreign Public Officials in International Business Transactions* makes extensive provisions under which States are required to create domestic laws criminalizing activities and sanctions related to bribery and associated offenses. This is the case for the creation of the offense of bribery of foreign public officials,[113] as well as associated penalties and sanctions,[114] domestic jurisdiction for enforcement of these laws and penalties,[115] the application of rules and laws of States to the prosecution for related offenses,[116] and the designation of money laundering crimes.[117]

Although the *Treaty on Principles Governing the Activities of States in the Exploration and Use of Outer Space, Including the Moon and Other Celestial Bodies* might seem to emphasize soft law principles over binding hard law on the surface, in fact there are significant hard law elements in its terms.[118] The two key examples of this are the implementation of bans on military and related activities in Outer Space and the requirement of universal protections for astronauts in Outer Space and upon their re-entry.[119] Concerns over military use of Outer Space, particularly involving nuclear materials, are discussed as hard law prohibitions in the *Agreement Governing the Activities of States on the Moon and Other Celestial Bodies*.[120] As noted above, the *Agreement* strictly prohibits private or State ownership claims over the territory and natural resources found on the Moon and instead designates the Moon as an internationalized territory for the purposes of ownership and control.[121] The *Convention on International Liability for Damage Caused by Space Objects* is primarily a hard law treaty in the sense that it articulates and seeks to entrench the concept of international legal liability for acts

111 *Principles Relating to Remote Sensing of the Earth from Outer Space*, *supra* note 84.
112 Ibid. at principles 8–10.
113 *OECD Convention on Combatting Bribery of Foreign Public Officials*, *supra* note 83 at art 1.
114 Ibid. at art 3.
115 Ibid. at art 4.
116 Ibid. at art 5.
117 Ibid. at art 7.
118 *Treaty on Principles Governing the Activities of States in the Exploration and Use of Outer Space, Including the Moon and Other Celestial Bodies*, *supra* note 85.
119 Ibid.
120 *Agreement Governing the Activities of States on the Moon and Other Celestial Bodies*, *supra* note 88 at art 3.
121 Ibid. at art 11.

of States and their citizens committed in and in relation to Outer Space in domestic legal systems as well as at the international level.[122]

4.2.5 *Soft law elements in governance systems*

It is perhaps obvious that the *OECD Guidelines for Multinational Enterprises* are voluntary and thus the source of soft law in terms of their relationship with States and in terms of the types of legal and regulatory systems suggested at the domestic level. The intention behind the *Guidelines* is fostering harmony between corporate practices and national laws and policies, as well as making States more attractive to foreign investment because of the transparency of their regulatory systems and the promotion of sustainable development through the activities of multinational enterprises.[123] Additionally, taking note of the ways in which multinational enterprises operate, the *Guidelines* highlight the need for cooperation and coordinate between States where they have a presence.[124]

While the majority of the *OECD Convention on Combatting Bribery of Foreign Public Officials in International Business Transactions*' requirements relate to the creation and implementation of hard law, soft law plays an important element in the provisions relating to mutual legal assistance between States.[125] Soft law is predominant in the *OECD Guidelines for Multinational Enterprises*. In this context, State Parties are to encourage their multinational enterprises to "develop and apply effective self-regulatory practices and management systems that foster a relationship of confidence and mutual trust between enterprises and the societies in which they operate."[126] States are also to provide encouragement and support to their multinationals in terms of extending the terms of the *Guidelines* and associated concerns to sub-contracts, sub-agents and others used throughout the business chain of operations.[127]

The *Guidelines* are firm in their provisions that multinationals should adhere to international and national environmental rules, policies and practices, especially those seeking to promote environmental concerns, public health and public safety.[128] Where appropriate, the *Guidelines* stress the need to prepare and cooperate with requests for the preparation of an environmental impact assessment for proposed actions and activities attributable to the multinational and its subsidiaries.[129] Further provisions of the

122 *Convention on International Liability for Damage Caused by Space Objects*, *supra* note 87.
123 *OECD Guidelines for Multinational Enterprises*, *supra* note 82 at preface.
124 Ibid. at pt. I.
125 *OECD Convention on Combatting Bribery of Foreign Public Officials*, *supra* note 83 at art 9.
126 *OECD Guidelines for Multinational Enterprises*, *supra* note 82 at pt. II, para 7.
127 Ibid. at pt. II, para 10.
128 Ibid. at pt. V.
129 Ibid. at pt. V, para 3.

Guidelines relate to technology transfer as part of multinational operations[130] and the necessity of taking actions to combat bribery and corruption in the public and private spheres.[131]

Many aspects of space law have historically been soft law-based and this continues to be the trend in current international law and governance practice. In seeking to "prevent the Moon from becoming an area of international conflict,"[132] the *Agreement Governing the Activities of States on the Moon and Other Celestial Bodies* states that all activities in this sphere are to be governed by the *UN Charter* and international law as well as soft law instruments adopted by the international community.[133] The *Agreement* promotes scientific freedom of investigation on the Moon for all State Parties at the same time that it seeks to ensure State Parties are barred from exerting sovereign claims over territory or natural resources in Outer space.[134] In light of this, the *Agreement* establishes a general framework for how manned and unmanned stations on the Moon may be created.[135]

Soft law plays a significant role in complementing and amplifying the terms of the core space law treaties, especially as the UNGA as adopted a series of resolutions enshrining essential soft law understandings for the implementation of a flexible international space law regime. A critical component of this comes from the *Declaration of Legal Principles Governing the Activities of States in the Exploration and Use of Outer Space*, providing States are to carry out their space related activities in accordance with the principles of "coordination and mutual assistance and shall conduct all their activities in Outer Space with due regard for the corresponding interests of other States."[136]

Further, the generation and use of guidelines and criteria in space operations, although not binding as a matter of law, form an essential component of the emerging nature of space regulation at the national and international levels. This can be seen in the generation of governance systems in new technology areas such as television satellites and remote sensing of the Earth.[137] To advance the technological capacity of all States seeking to become active in Outer Space, the *Declaration on International Cooperation in Exploration and Use of Outer Space for the Benefit and in the Interest of All States, Taking into*

130 Ibid. at pt. VI.
131 Ibid. at pt. VIII.
132 *Agreement Governing the Activities of States on the Moon and Other Celestial Bodies*, *supra* note 88 at preamble.
133 Ibid. at art 2.
134 Ibid. at art 6.
135 Ibid. at art 9.
136 *Declaration of Legal Principles Governing the Activities of States in the Exploration and Use of Outer Space*, *supra* note 88.
137 See *Principles on TV Satellites; Principles Relating to Remote Sensing of the Earth from Outer Space*, *supra* note 84.

Particular Account Developing Countries provides for inter-governmental and technical support between States, as well as technology transfer assistance.[138] The *Principles Relevant to the Use of Nuclear Power Sources in Outer Space* provide for the creation of national guidelines and criteria for safe use of nuclear power in this context, including a safety assessment criteria.[139] Similarly, the *Space Debris Mitigation Guidelines of the Committee on the Peaceful Uses of Outer Space* emphasize the current and future dangers to Earth and Outer Space posed by space debris and provide for the generation of national mitigation plans that are to be overseen at the international level.[140]

4.3 Banking and finance regimes

Banking and finance related treaty regimes represent a different form of governance system and philosophy than many of the regimes discussed in this Chapter and this book in that they are more tightly tied to business operations. What these regimes demonstrate, however, is another aspect of the flexibility of global governance constructs and the inherent ability of these constructs to generate systems which are responsive to the needs of a particular constituency or sector while at the same time preserving core values of the international community.

In this context, the two primary treaty regime-based systems discussed are the World Bank Group and the International Monetary Fund (IMF). It should be noted that a variety of regional banking entities, such as the Inter-American Development Bank, the European Bank for Reconstruction and Development, the African Development Bank and the Asian Development Bank, perform vital functions in the realm of financing for activities which support and further the SDGs through governance systems which parallel those used at the purely global banking sector. A full profile of the work of banking regimes as agents of SDG implementation and entrenchment is unfortunately outside the scope of this book but would be a fascinating study for the future.

4.3.1 *Treaty regime purposes and objectives*

Despite the organizational terminology, the World Bank is indeed an umbrella entity for separate entities which together address a variety of banking and finance regimes operating at the international level for the benefit of

138 *Declaration on International Cooperation in Exploration and Use of Outer Space for the Benefit and in the Interest of All States, Taking into Particular Account Developing Countries*, *supra* note 84.

139 *Principles Relevant to the Use of Nuclear Power Sources in Outer Space*, *supra* note 84 at principles 3, 4.

140 *Space Debris Mitigation Guidelines of the Committee on the Peaceful Uses of Outer Space*, *supra* note 84.

States and, in some instances, actors within those States. The first of these entities is the International Bank for Reconstruction and Development (IBRD), which was created to provide direct assistance to States seeking to engage in reconstruction and development projects "including the restoration of economies destroyed or disrupted by war, the reconversion of productive facilities to peacetime needs and the encouragement of the development of productive facilities and resources in less developed countries."[141] It also serves to promote long-term and foreign investments in areas recovering from conflicts and other challenges and to ensure that there are pathways for the involvement of the private sector in development planning.[142]

The International Finance Corporation (IFC) exists "to further economic development by encouraging the growth of productive private enterprise in member countries, particularly in the less developed areas, thus supplementing the activities of the International Bank for Reconstruction and Development."[143] In this way, the IFC is empowered to assist with the types of private financing and involvement with which the IBRD cannot while furthering the same aims. The International Development Association (IDA) was created "to promote economic development, increase productivity and thus raise standards of living in the less-developed areas of the world included within the Association's membership, in particular by providing finance to meet their important developmental requirements on terms which are more flexible and bear less heavily on the balance of payments than those of conventional loans, thereby furthering the developmental objectives of the International Bank for Reconstruction and Development."[144] Further, the Multilateral Investment Guarantee Agency (MIGA) serves to supplement the activities of international banking institutions by "encourag[ing] the flow of investments for productive purposes among member countries, and in particular to developing member countries."[145]

Additionally, the IMF exists as a source of financing at the international level and, beyond this, is tasked with "facilitat[ing] the expansion and balanced growth of international trade, and [] contribut[ing] thereby to the promotion and maintenance of high levels of employment and real income and [] develop[ing] of the productive resources of all members as primary objectives of economic policy,"[146] as well as assisting in currency stability and confidence building for State Parties seeking funding from public and private sources.[147]

141 *IBRD Articles of Agreement* (2012) at art I (i).
142 Ibid. at art I.
143 *IFC Articles of Agreement* (2020) at art I.
144 *IDA Articles of Agreement* (1960) at art I.
145 *Convention Establishing the MIGA* (1988) at art 2.
146 *IMF Articles of Agreement* (1944) at art I.
147 Ibid.

4.3.2 *Governance mechanisms*

The IBRD governance system is comprised of the Board of Governors, Executive Board and President.[148] The Board of Governors is the primary decision-making entity for the IBRD and is a representative body for all State Parties,[149] having many responsibilities that relate to the function of the IBRD as an entity in a fashion similar to a corporate board of directors.[150] The Executive Board is a smaller entity charged with conducting the operations of the IBRD and is comprised of rotating members as well as members who represent the largest shareholders at given points in time.[151] The President serves as the head of the Secretariat equivalent within the IBRD structure.[152] Similar roles and responsibilities are established in the IFC,[153] IDA,[154] and MIGA.[155] Additionally, there is an Advisory Council comprised of private sector representatives of business and industry that is meant to serve as a source of expertise to the IBRD.[156] Although it is a separate organization, the IMF also uses this more corporate-based governance system and is under the leadership of the Director-General.[157]

4.3.3 *Hard law elements in governance systems*

Generally, the legal aspects of the governance systems established in the World Bank Group focus on the obligations of State Parties to provide financing in for the various entities. However, where States receive loans or other financing from any of the World Bank entities they are required to ensure that the terms of the contracts are implemented as a matter of national law. This is of particular importance in an increasing number of social and environmental contexts, as the World Bank entities have developed policies for including environmental protection, women, Indigenous communities and other often marginalized actors in all phases of carrying out internationally financed projects. These standards and policies are also used by the IMF and are essential to the lending and financial assistance process it has established.[158]

148 *IBRD Articles of Agreement*, *supra* note 141 at art V(1).
149 Ibid. at art V(2).
150 Ibid.
151 Ibid. at art V(4).
152 Ibid. at art V(5).
153 *IFC Articles of Agreement*, *supra* note 143 at art IV.
154 *IDA Articles of Agreement*, *supra* note 144 at art VI.
155 *Convention Establishing the MIGA*, *supra* note 145 at Ch V.
156 *IBRD Articles of Agreement*, *supra* note 141 at art V(6).
157 *IMF Articles of Agreement*, *supra* note 146 at art XII.
158 IMF, Factsheets, available at https://www.imf.org/en/About/Factsheets/IMF-Surveillance.

4.4 Industry focused regimes

Treaty regime-based global governance systems span a number of industries. While these governance systems and the treaty regimes which underlie them are often attenuated to the specific needs of an industry, they share significant forms of commonality in structure and in incorporating concerns such as environmental protection and sustainable development. The industries selected for this section range from fishing to energy to timber to tourism to waste disposal in a purposeful effort to demonstrate the diversity of treaty regime-based global governance systems relating to industries that have had often contentious relationships with sustainability yet have increasingly come to embrace it.

In this context, the following treaty regimes for fishing are discussed: the *Convention on the Determination of the Minimum Conditions for Access and Exploitation of Marine Resources within the Maritime Zones under Jurisdiction of the Member States of the Sub-Regional Fisheries Commission* (*Sub-Regional Fisheries Commission*),[159] the *Convention for the Establishment of an Inter-American Tropical Tuna Commission* (*IATTC Commission*),[160] the *Convention for the Conservation of Salmon in the North Atlantic Ocean*,[161] the *Convention on Future Multilateral Cooperation in North-East Atlantic Fisheries*,[162] the *Convention for the Conservation of Anadromous Stocks in the North Pacific Ocean*,[163] the *Northwest Atlantic Fisheries Convention*,[164] the *Convention on the Conservation and Management of Pollock Resources in the Central Bering Sea*,[165] the *Convention on the Conservation and Management of Fishery Resources in the South East Atlantic Ocean*,[166] the *Convention for the Conservation of Southern Bluefin Tuna*,[167] and the *Convention on the Conservation and Management of Highly Migratory Fish Stocks in the Western and Central Pacific Ocean*.[168]

In this context, the following treaty regimes for energy are discussed: the *International Renewable Energy Agency* (IRENA),[169] the *Energy Charter*

159 *Convention on the Determination of the Minimum Conditions for Access and Exploitation of Marine Resources within the Maritime Zones under Jurisdiction of the Member States of the Sub-Regional Fisheries Commission* (2012).
160 *Convention for the Establishment of an Inter-American Tropical Tuna Commission* (1949).
161 *Convention for the Conservation of Salmon in the North Atlantic Ocean* (1983).
162 *Convention on Future Multilateral Cooperation in North-East Atlantic Fisheries* (1982).
163 *Convention for the Conservation of Anadromous Stocks in the North Pacific Ocean* (1993).
164 *Northwest Atlantic Fisheries Convention* (1949).
165 *Convention on the Conservation and Management of Pollock Resources in the Central Bering Sea* (1995).
166 *Convention on the Conservation and Management of Fishery Resources in the South East Atlantic Ocean* (2001).
167 *Convention for the Conservation of Southern Bluefin Tuna* (1994).
168 *Convention on the Conservation and Management of Highly Migratory Fish Stocks in the Western and Central Pacific Ocean* (1995).
169 *International Renewable Energy Agency* (*IRENA*) (2008).

Treaty,[170] the *Convention of the African Energy Commission*,[171] and the *Protocol on Energy in the SADC Region*.[172]

In this context, the following treaty regimes for waste handling are discussed: the *Convention to Ban the Importation into Island Countries of Hazardous and Radioactive Wastes and to Control the Transboundary Movement and Management of Hazardous Wastes within the South Pacific Region* (*Waigani Convention*),[173] the *Basel Convention on the Control of Transboundary Movements of Hazardous Wastes and Their Disposal*,[174] and the *Rotterdam Convention on Prior Informed Consent Procedure for Certain Hazardous Chemicals and Pesticides in International Trade*.[175]

Additionally, the *International Tropical Timber Agreement*[176] is discussed as an example of an evolving treaty regime and associated governance system that balances a unique and diverse set of constituencies. Finally, the *Convention Establishing the Sustainable Tourism Zone of the Caribbean* is discussed as a treaty regime creating a governance system for a regional area that is used by tourists from around the globe and reflects the tenets of SDG 8 on sustainable tourism in a way that few other treaty regimes do.

4.4.1 *Treaty regime purposes and objectives*

4.4.1.1 *Fishing*

The *Convention on the Determination of the Minimum Conditions for Access and Exploitation of Marine Resources within the Maritime Zones* under jurisdiction of the Member States of the Sub-Regional Fisheries Commission represents a regional undertaking between Cabo Verde, Guinea, Guinea Bissau, Mauritania, Senegal and Sierra Leone.[177] By creating the *Convention*, the State Parties established that the terms are part of a concerted effort to bring national laws and rules into accord with existing international law obligations "for the benefit of current and future generations."[178] Additionally,

170 *Energy Charter Treaty* (1991).

171 *Convention of the African Energy Commission* (2001).

172 *Protocol on Energy in the SADC Region* (1996).

173 *Convention to Ban the Importation into Island Countries of Hazardous and Radioactive Wastes and to Control the Transboundary Movement and Management of Hazardous Wastes within the South Pacific Region* (2001).

174 *Basel Convention on the Control of Transboundary Movements of Hazardous Wastes and Their Disposal* (1992).

175 *Rotterdam Convention on Prior Informed Consent Procedure for Certain Hazardous Chemicals and Pesticides in International Trade* (2004).

176 *International Tropical Timber Agreement* (2006).

177 *Convention on the Determination of the Minimum Conditions for Access and Exploitation of Marine Resources within the Maritime Zones under Jurisdiction of the Member States of the Sub-Regional Fisheries Commission*, *supra* note 159.

178 Ibid. at preamble.

the *Convention* highlights the importance of regional and sub-regional cooperation for accomplishing the goals of maritime protection and fishing sustainability.[179]

In 1949, the *Convention for the Establishment of an Inter-American Tropical Tuna Commission* (*IATTC Convention*) was adopted with the goal of operationalizing a regional organization to address the shared issues surrounding tuna fishing.[180] This was updated in 2003 with the enactment of the *Antigua Convention*, which also reflects the adoption of the UNCLOS and associated governance regimes by the international community, as well as environmental and sustainable development laws which were not in existence at the time of the *IATTC Convention*'s signing.[181] As the *Antigua Convention* provides, "the objective … is to ensure the long-term conservation and sustainable use of the fish stocks covered by this Convention, in accordance with the relevant rules of international law."[182] In addition to the legal and contextual updates, the *Antigua Convention* reflects the reality that the Commission's membership has now grown to include 21 States throughout the Western Hemisphere as well as Asia and the South Pacific.[183]

The overall objective of the *Convention on Future Multilateral Cooperation in North-East Atlantic Fisheries* is "to ensure the long-term conservation and optimum utilization of the fishery resources in the Conservation Area, providing sustainable economic, environmental and social benefits."[184] The *Northwest Atlantic Fisheries Convention* was enacted with the goal "to conclude a convention for the investigation, protection and conservation of the fisheries of the Northwest Atlantic Ocean, in order to make possible the maintenance of a maximum sustained catch from those fisheries."[185]

As with many of the specialized fisheries regimes, the *Convention on the Conservation and Management of Pollock Resources in the Central Bering Sea* was established as an international regime allowing for conservation and management coordination and planning for a vital fish stock.[186] This includes efforts to restore the pollock stock and to maintain a sustainable stock for the future.[187] The *Convention for the Conservation of Southern Bluefin Tuna*'s

179 Ibid.

180 *Convention for the Establishment of an Inter-American Tropical Tuna Commission*, *supra* note 160.

181 *Convention for the Strengthening of the Inter-American Tropical Tuna Commission* (*Antigua Convention*) (2003).

182 Ibid. at art II.

183 Inter-American Tropical Tuna Commission, Main Page, available at https://www.iattc.org/HomeENG.htm.

184 *Convention on Future Multilateral Cooperation in North-East Atlantic Fisheries*, *supra* note 162 at art 2.

185 *Northwest Atlantic Fisheries Convention*, *supra* note 164 at preamble.

186 *Convention on the Conservation and Management of Pollock Resources in the Central Bering Sea*, *supra* note 165 at art 1.

187 Ibid.

general objective is "to ensure, through appropriate management, the conservation and optimum utilization of southern bluefin tuna."[188]

The *Convention on the Conservation and Management of Fishery Resources in the South East Atlantic Ocean* and the governance structure created by it is intended to adopt conservation and sustainable use measures for fishing activities and for measures relating to ecosystems sustaining fisheries, encourage State Parties to adopt and incorporate the precautionary approach into their legal regimes for fishery activities, and oversee fisheries management practices.[189]

The State Parties created the *Convention on the Conservation and Management of Highly Migratory Fish Stocks in the Western and Central Pacific Ocean* in order to recognize and address the inherent vulnerabilities of States within the jurisdictional region, especially Small Island Developing States, and including the precautionary principle.[190] In this context, the Convention highlights "the need to avoid adverse impacts on the marine environment, preserve biodiversity, maintain the integrity of marine ecosystems and minimize the risk of long-term or irreversible effects of fishing operations."[191]

4.4.1.2 *Energy*

The objectives of IRENA are "to promote the widespread and increased adoption and the sustainable use of all forms of renewable energy," while taking into account the national interests and priorities of State Parties and reinforcing the environmental, climate change, societal and economic benefits of renewables for national and international society.[192] Indeed, recent activities undertaken by IRENA have highlighted synergies with the SDGs, not only for SDG 7 but more generally for climate change, finance and anti-poverty SDGs as well.[193] In terms of the post-COVID-19 landscape, IRENA's strategy notes the direct national and global correlations between post-COVID-19 recovery plans, shifts to renewable energies across all segments of development, and achievement of the SDGs.[194] Relatedly, the purpose of the *Energy Charter Treaty* is to create "a legal framework in order to promote long-term cooperation in the energy field, based on complementarities and mutual benefits."[195]

188 *Convention for the Conservation of Southern Bluefin Tuna*, *supra* note 167 at art 3.
189 *Convention on the Conservation and Management of Fishery Resources in the South East Atlantic Ocean*, *supra* note 166 at art 3.
190 *Convention on the Conservation and Management of Highly Migratory Fish Stocks in the Western and Central Pacific Ocean*, *supra* note 168 at preamble.
191 Ibid. at preamble.
192 IRENA Statute, *supra* note 169 art II.
193 See IRENA—Report of 10th session, 2020.
194 IRENA Post-COVID Recovery Plan at p 11.
195 *Energy Charter Treaty*, *supra* note 170 at art 2.

The 2001 *Convention of the African Energy Commission* incorporates sustainable development and associated social, economic and environmental concerns into the context of energy policy promotion and attempts at regional governance.[196] This includes the promotion of partnerships and technical assistance from the private sector as well as State Parties and the encouragement of peaceful settlement of disputes arising in the energy sector.[197] The *Protocol on Energy in the SADC Region* functions according to several guiding principles. These include using energy as a tool for economic growth and poverty eradication, ensuring the inclusion of social concerns in energy policy, providing for technological transfer for energy and related sectors, ensuring the inclusion of environmental concerns on energy law and policy, and the peaceful settlement of disputes.[198]

4.4.1.3 *Wastes*

The *Waigani Convention* was created by the State Parties to reflect consensus as to "their responsibility to protect, preserve and improve the environment of the South Pacific for the good health, benefit and enjoyment of present and future generations of the people of the South Pacific."[199] In creating the *Rotterdam Convention*, the State Parties recognized the threats posed by chemicals and pesticides to human health and incorporated sustainable development as a goal for trade and environmental policies relating to chemicals and pesticides to achieve together.[200] With this in mind, the objectives of the *Rotterdam Convention* are the protection of health and the environment in the context of the chemical and pesticide trade using established and shared responsibilities and cooperation efforts between States.[201]

4.4.1.4 *Tourism*

In crafting the *Convention Establishing the Sustainable Tourism Zone of the Caribbean*, the State Parties expressly note the "importance of the concept of sustainability as the basis for protecting biodiversity, culture and the environment, with the human being at the core of our actions, by virtue of favoring an improved distribution of the benefits derived from tourist development."[202]

196 *Convention of the African Energy Commission*, *supra* note 171 art 3.
197 Ibid. at art 3.
198 *Protocol on Energy in the SADC Region*, *supra* note 172 art 2.
199 *Convention to Ban the Importation into Island Countries of Hazardous and Radioactive Wastes and to Control the Transboundary Movement and Management of Hazardous Wastes within the South Pacific Region*, *supra* note 173 at preamble.
200 *Rotterdam Convention*, *supra* note 175 at preamble.
201 Ibid. at art 1.
202 *Convention Establishing the Sustainable Tourism Zone of the Caribbean* (2004) at preamble.

4.4.2 *Governance mechanisms*

4.4.2.1 *Fishing*

Under the terms of the *Convention on the Determination of the Minimum Conditions for Access and Exploitation of Marine Resources within the Maritime Zones,* the Sub-Regional Fisheries Commission is established as a governance feature and vested with oversight and coordination powers.[203] Included in these powers is the ability for the Council of Ministers to the SRFC to act as the preliminary source of potential dispute settlement in instances of disagreements between the States.[204] Should the dispute not be settled through resort to the Council of Ministers to the SRFC or other peaceful settlement efforts, it may then be referred to the International Tribunal on the Law of the Sea (ITLOS) for a final and binding decision.[205]

Under the terms of the original *IATTC Convention*, the Inter-American Tropical Tuna Commission was vested with the authority to engage in investigations regarding the ecological system of the region as well as of the tuna stocks, analysis of information regarding past and current trends in the population of tuna stocks, conducting scientific and other relevant studies, and generating reports and other information.[206] The Commission was further operationalized through the creation of a Director of Investigations, which functions as the investigatory arm of the entity and is assisted by a dedicated Secretariat.[207]

The *Antigua Convention* extends the existence of the Commission, albeit with a more nuanced scope.[208] Among the advances in jurisdiction for the Commission is the determination as to whether covered fish stocks are freely fished or over-fished and how to address over-fishing, the use of analysis for the ecosystems involved in fishing and needed to sustain the fish stocks, the adoption of measures to address and reduce fishing-related waste throughout the area covered, the promotion of "selective, environmentally safe and cost-effective fishing gear and techniques," and the establishment of criteria for the total allowable catch and total allowable fishing capacity.[209] Under the terms of the *Antigua Convention*, a specialized committee structure is established to allow for targeted generation and application of expertise,

203 *Convention on the Determination of the Minimum Conditions for Access and Exploitation of Marine Resources within the Maritime Zones under Jurisdiction of the Member States of the Sub-Regional Fisheries Commission*, *supra* note 159.

204 Ibid. at art 34.

205 Ibid.

206 *Convention for the Establishment of an Inter-American Tropical Tuna Commission*, *supra* note 160 at art 2.

207 Ibid. at art 1.

208 *Convention for the Strengthening of the Inter-American Tropical Tuna Commission* (Antigua Convention), *supra* note 181 at art VI.

209 Ibid. at art VII.

notably the Committee for the Review of Implementation of Measures Adopted by the Commission[210] and the Scientific Advisory Committee.[211] The Secretariat function is carried out by the Administration, which is headed by a Director and is tasked with the primary functions of a standard Secretariat.[212] In addition, an allowance is made for the creation of a specific Scientific Staff to serve the needs of the Scientific Advisory Committee and the Secretariat.[213] Overall, the transparency element of good governance is to be threaded throughout the entirety of the application of the *Antigua Convention* and the work of the Commission. This is especially important in the context of "public dissemination of pertinent non-confidential information; [and] facilitating consultations with, and the effective participation of NGOs, representatives of the fishing industry, particularly the fishing fleet, and other interested bodies and individuals."[214]

The central governance system in the *Convention for the Conservation of Salmon in the North Atlantic Ocean*'s structure is the North Atlantic Salmon Conservation Organization, which was created to "contribute through consultation and co-operation to the conservation, restoration, enhancement and rational management of salmon stocks subject to the Convention, taking into account the best scientific evidence available."[215] Within this system, the principal organs are the Council, a series of three regional Commissions (the North American Commission, the West Greenland Commission and the North-East Atlantic Commission), and the Secretariat.[216] The Council, as the primary decision-making body in the Organization, is charged with extensive information-gathering, analysis, study and reporting requirements for information relating to salmon, coordination of the three Commissions, consultation with States, international organizations and key stakeholders, supervision of the administration, financing and internal affairs of the Organization, and issuing policy recommendations.[217] The Commissions are tasked with undertaking sub-regional consultations on matters relating to salmon, providing suggestions to the Council either as requested or their own, and suggesting regulatory measures for the conduct of salmon fisheries and harvesting.[218] The Secretariat function is carried out under the auspices of the Secretary and includes administrative and technical support.[219]

210 Ibid. at art X.
211 Ibid. at art XI.
212 Ibid. at art XII.
213 Ibid. at art XIII.
214 Ibid. at art XVI.
215 *Convention for the Conservation of Salmon in the North Atlantic Ocean*, *supra* note 161 at art 3(2).
216 Ibid. at art 3(3).
217 Ibid. at art 4.
218 Ibid. at arts 7–8.
219 Ibid. at art 12.

The main governance apparatus for the *Convention* is the North-East Atlantic Commission, which is intended to function as a coordination and information-sharing mechanism for the implementation of the *Convention* and the generation of policies and management practices across the covered territory.[220] The Commission is empowered to make recommendations to State Parties regarding practices and laws and can establish additional committees and sub-organs as deemed appropriate.[221] Over time, the Commission has acted on the latter option in a number of instances, creating specialized committees and the Secretariat to assist in the implementation of the *Convention* and the accomplishment of the *Convention*'s goals.[222]

Under the *Convention for the Conservation of Anadromous Stocks in the North Pacific Ocean*'s terms, the governing entity for implementation of obligations and ensuring cooperation between the State Parties is the Commission. The Commission is geared toward conservation of species in the covered geographical area under the *Convention*'s jurisdiction and the establishment of subsidiary bodies.[223] The Commission is vested with the authority to recommend conservation-related rules to States and the entity as a whole, promote the exchange of information and cooperation with international organizations, propose penalties and remedies for environmental violations, and provide guidance on the application of national laws in the context of commitments under the *Convention*.[224] The *Convention* is overseen on an institutional basis by the Secretariat, under the aegis of the Executive Director, and has administrative and data generation and dissemination requirements.[225]

The governance structure initially used by the *Northwest Atlantic Fisheries Convention* centered on the formalized Commission.[226] Within this structure, the Commission has the ability to create panels dedicated to geographical sub-areas and their support, as well as advisory committees based on specific areas of expertise or subject areas.[227] In terms of administration, the *Convention* establishes a Secretariat under the direction of an Executive Director.[228] In 1978, this structure was superseded by the Northwest Atlantic Fisheries Organization, which is comprised of the Commission as

220 *Convention on Future Multilateral Cooperation in North-East Atlantic Fisheries*, *supra* note 162 at art 4(3).

221 Ibid. at arts 3, 5, 6.

222 InforMEA, *Convention on Future Multilateral Cooperation in North-East Atlantic Fisheries*, available at https://www.informea.org/en/treaties/convention-future-multilateral-cooperation-north-east-atlantic-fisheries.

223 *Convention for the Conservation of Anadromous Stocks in the North Pacific Ocean*, *supra* note 163 at art 8.

224 Ibid. at art 9.

225 Ibid. at art 10.

226 *Northwest Atlantic Fisheries Convention*, *supra* note 164 at art 2.

227 Ibid. at arts 4–5.

228 Ibid. at art 3.

well as the Scientific Council and Standing Committees and subsequently created working groups.[229] Within the Commission apparatus are standing committees on Finance and Administration and International Control.[230] Further, the standing committees under the Scientific Council's aegis are those on Fisheries Science, Fisheries Environment, Research Coordination and Publications.[231]

Under the terms of the *Convention on the Conservation and Management of Pollock Resources in the Central Bering Sea*, the Conference of the Parties is established as the annual decision-making entity and is intended to work together with a designated Scientific and Technical Committee.[232] The CoP establishes the annual allowable harvest levels and catch quotas for pollock, generates conservation and management measures to protect the pollock species and its habitat, creates the Scientific and Technical Committee's work plan, reviews reports and other information generated, and generates guidance for scientific trials and related activities.[233]

The *Convention on the Conservation and Management of Fishery Resources in the South East Atlantic Ocean* is governed under the auspices of the Organization, an entity comprised of the Commission, the Compliance Committee and Scientific Committee, and other committees as created, as well as the Secretariat.[234] The Commission, which meets on an annual basis, is the designated representative body in the Organization.[235] In this capacity, it has the ability to identify and create measures addressing areas of conservation and fish stock management using the precautionary approach, determine the total allowable catches within the *Convention*'s coverage area for the following year, provide a review of data on fish stocks, create "cooperative mechanisms for effective monitoring, control, surveillance and enforcement," provide oversight of committees and ensure that information gathered under the Organization's aegis is widely shared.[236] The Compliance Committee is comprised of representatives from each State Party and is tasked with providing information and advice on compliance-related issues for the Commission, as well as ensuring that State Parties and the Commission follow the rules and procedures set out for the Organization.[237] The Scientific Committee is also comprised of representatives from each

229 *Northwest Atlantic Fisheries Organization, Northwest Atlantic Fisheries Convention* (1949), available at https://www.nafo.int/About-us/ICNAF/icnaf-convention,

230 Ibid.

231 Ibid.

232 *Convention on the Conservation and Management of Pollock Resources in the Central Bering Sea, supra* note 165 at arts 3, 9.

233 Ibid. at art 4.

234 *Convention on the Conservation and Management of Fishery Resources in the South East Atlantic Ocean, supra* note 166 at art 5.

235 Ibid. at art 6.

236 Ibid.

237 Ibid. at art 9.

State Party.[238] It is tasked with providing scientific and technical advice and recommendations to the Commission and to State Parties, promote scientific cooperation between States and the Commission at the technical level, generate criteria and methodology to be used in conservation and management policies, and generate data and reports.[239] To ensure the functioning of the Organization, the Secretariat has been created to serve as the administrative apparatus.[240]

For governance purposes, the highest organ in the system established by the *Convention for the Conservation of Southern Bluefin Tuna* is the Commission for the Conservation of Southern Bluefin Tuna.[241] The Commission is tasked with collecting information on bluefin-related science and data generation, information on legal and regulatory systems used in State Parties for southern bluefin tuna and related ecosystems, *Convention* interpretation and amendment as appropriate, matters referred to it by specialized committees, generating allowable catches for the jurisdictional area covered over time, and the creation of monitoring and compliance systems.[242] To assist in the work of the Commission, the *Convention* created the Scientific Committee as an advisory entity specifically tasked with assessing trends relating to southern bluefin tuna, coordinating research on southern bluefin tuna, reporting on status and ecological issues relating to the *Convention*, and making conservation and associated recommendations to the Commission on southern bluefin tuna.[243] A Secretariat has been established to serve administrative functions, share official documents and information and provide access to the data gathered by the Commission, committees and State Parties.[244]

The *Convention on the Conservation and Management of Highly Migratory Fish Stocks in the Western and Central Pacific Ocean*'s Commission is vested with the authority to develop and implement a set of principles and associated practices for the conservation and management of the fish stocks and the biodiversity supporting them.[245] This includes determining the sustainability status of fish stocks and using it to set the maximum sustained yield of fishery activities allowed per year, minimizing wastes that result from fishing activities, preventing over-fishing and damage to regional biodiversity, assisting artisanal fisheries and fishers, and collecting and sharing data relating to highly migratory fish stocks.[246] Additionally, the Commission

238 Ibid. at art 10.
239 Ibid.
240 Ibid. at art 11.
241 *Convention for the Conservation of Southern Bluefin Tuna*, *supra* note 167 at art 6.
242 Ibid. at art 8.
243 Ibid. at art 9.
244 Ibid. at art 10.
245 *Convention on the Conservation and Management of Highly Migratory Fish Stocks in the Western and Central Pacific Ocean*, *supra* note 168 at art 5.
246 Ibid. at arts 5, 9, 10.

may create subsidiary bodies as deemed appropriate.[247] To assist in the activities of the Commission and the implementation of the *Convention*, a dedicated Secretariat is created.[248]

Two standing committees are established under the terms of the *Convention*. The first of these is the Scientific Committee, which recommends research plans for the Commission and State Parties, reviews information and advice from science experts, encourages technical cooperation, reviews national and organizational data and reports, liaises with other committees and with international organizations and creates reports on relevant topics.[249] The second is the Technical and Compliance Committee, which provides technical information and recommendations for conservation and management compliance, oversight of the *Convention*'s implementation, monitoring and verification practices, and the creation of technical recommendations for fishing and associated activities.[250] The Commission and Committees are required to operate in an open and transparent manner, including making their activities known to international organizations and civil society.[251]

4.4.2.2 *Energy*

There are three foundational organs of IRENA, which together establish the policy orientation and standard activities of the organization.[252] In this system, the supreme organ is the Assembly and the secondary legislative organ is the Council.[253] The Secretariat is the final element of the trio of organs, acting as the core administrative apparatus for IRENA.[254]

In terms of functions, the IRENA *Statute* charges the Secretariat with preparing and submitting draft work programmes and budgets, implementing these work programmes and other IRENA decisions, preparing annual reports, undertaking administrative and technical support, ensuring communications between organs and Member States and providing policy and other advice as requested.[255] Additionally, IRENA has the ability to engage with multiple stakeholders, including non-governmental organizations and private entities, and the importance of establishing links between the organization and private entities has been emphasized for the continued success of the entity in meeting its functions and objectives.[256]

247 Ibid. at art 11.
248 Ibid. at art 15.
249 Ibid. at art 12.
250 Ibid. at art 14.
251 Ibid. at art 21.
252 *IRENA Statute*, *supra* note 169 at art VIII.
253 See ibid. at arts IX, X.
254 Ibid. at art XI.
255 Ibid. at art XI(E).
256 IRENA—Report of 10th session, 2020.

The governance system established by the *Energy Charter Treaty* focuses on two central entities, the Energy Charter Conference and the Secretariat. The Conference is the central organizational body for the *Treaty* and includes activities such as reviewing and facilitating the application of the *Treaty*, creating and overseeing the Secretariat, promoting energy reforms in State Parties, approving proposed Protocols and amendments, negotiating new declarations, creating subsidiary bodies as required and implementing a periodic review process for implementation activities.[257] The Secretariat is comprised of a Secretary-General and designated staff members to assist in managing the operations of the entity.[258] During the course of its implementation, the *Energy Charter Treaty* regime has resulted in the creation of several further subsidiary bodies to assist in meeting the national and organizational obligations.[259] These subsidiary bodies include the Strategy Group, the Modernisation Group, the Working Group on Governance Issues, the Implementation Group, the Budget Committee and the Legal Advisory Committee.[260]

The designated organizational functions vested in the *Convention of the African Energy Commission* include "map[ping] out energy development policies, strategies and plans based on sub-regional, regional and continental development," supervising and encouraging all aspects of energy policy and capacity development, providing technical assistance between States and through the private sector and encouraging the development of the renewable energy sector.[261]

Governance of the Commission is divided between five forms of organs: the Conference of Ministers/authorities responsible for energy in their States, the Executive Board, the Secretariat, the Technical Advisory Board and other, specially created subsidiary bodies.[262] The Conference is designated as the highest authority in the Commission's structure, having the ability to create and oversee policies and work programmes, generate organizations budgets, determine organizational rules of procedure and elect the Executive Board.[263] The Executive Board is a smaller entity that is comprised of representatives of Member States and designated experts in energy.[264] It is tasked with preparing studies related to energy policy and development, the generation of work programmes and reviews of proposed budgets.[265] The Secretariat exists under the supervision of a selected Executive Director,

257 *Energy Charter Treaty*, *supra* note 170 at art 34.
258 Ibid. at art 35.
259 Energy Charter, Energy Charter Treaty, available at https://www.energycharter.org/process/energy-charter-treaty-1994/energy-charter-treaty/.
260 Ibid.
261 *Convention of the African Energy Commission*, *supra* note 171 at art 4.
262 Ibid. at art 6.
263 Ibid. at art 7.
264 Ibid. at art 8.
265 Ibid. at art 8.

who appoints the appropriate staff members to carry out the administrative and technical work of the Commission.[266] The Technical Advisory Board exists to foster cooperation and information sharing between Member States, regional organizations, and UN organs and bodies having expertise in energy and related fields.[267]

Within the institutional mechanisms established for governance under the *SADC Protocol* are the Commission, the Committee of Ministers, the Committee of Senior Officials, the Technical Unit, and designated sub-committees. As part of this structure, the Commission has responsibility for formulating and coordinating a regional energy plan, overseeing and monitoring of the *Protocol*'s implementation and Member State compliance, liaising with other entities from the region and beyond in relation to energy policy and assisting Member States in obtaining financing for energy and related projects.[268] The Committee of Ministers is tasked with establishing energy policy for Member States in the region to implement, appointing the Director of the Technical Unit, providing budget and rules recommendations, recommending amendments to the Protocol text as appropriate and creating additional subsidiary bodies and organs as necessary.[269] One layer beyond this, the Committee of Senior Officials serves a largely advisory function for the Protocol and the organs it establishes.[270] This Committee is also empowered to recommend the conduct of studies and other reports related to energy and associated issues.[271]

The secretariat functions for the *Protocol* are vested in the Technical Unit, which is vested with administrative capacities.[272] Additionally, there are a number of sub-committees established for the purposes of advancing the *Protocol*'s terms. These sub-committees operate under a specific mandate: "(i) address a regional energy need; (ii) unless special circumstances dictate otherwise, they shall be established for the duration of their specific task."[273] They have a dedicated manager to serve as the chair and are accompanied by an administrative apparatus.[274]

4.4.2.3 *Timber*

The *International Tropical Timber Agreement* sets out a governance structure containing the Organization, with members that represent both

266 Ibid. at art 9.
267 Ibid. at art 11.
268 *Protocol on Energy in the SADC Region*, *supra* note 172 at art 4(1).
269 Ibid. at art 4(2).
270 Ibid. at art 4(3).
271 Ibid.
272 Ibid. at art 4(4).
273 Ibid. at art 4(6)(b).
274 Ibid. at art 4(6).

producer and consumer State members, and the International Tropical Timber Council, which functions as the highest authority.[275] The Council meets on an annual basis and is tasked with adopting and overseeing the implementation of rules to ensure the functioning of the Organization, as well as record keeping, appointing the Executive Director and associated staff, and making decisions and recommendations that can become binding on Member States.[276] The Executive Director and staff act as the Secretariat under the terms of the *Agreement*.[277] Another aspect of governance under the *Agreement* is ability to create and utilize subsidiary bodies for specialized issues. Entities convened under the auspices of the *Agreement* include the Committee on Forest Industry, the Committee on Economics, Statistics and Markets, the Committee on Reforestation and Forest Management and the Committee on Finance and Administration.[278] Additionally, the *Agreement* establishes the Bali Partnership Fund "for sustainable management of tropical timber producing forests ... to assist producer members to make the investment necessary to achieve the ... Agreement."[279]

4.4.2.4 *Tourism*

Overall, the administration of the *Convention Establishing the Sustainable Tourism Zone of the Caribbean* is vested in the Secretariat of the Association of Caribbean States. The core governance mechanism created through the Convention is the Special Committee on Sustainable Tourism.[280] Essential functions of this Committee include evaluating the implementation and status of the Zone, examining new proposals for inclusion within the Zone, examining reports and disseminating trends on laws and viability of the Zone as a tool for sustainability and creating recommendations for future legislative or other undertakings.[281]

4.4.2.5 *Wastes*

Governance under the *Waigani Convention* is vested in the Conference of the Parties and the Secretariat.[282] The CoP serves as the primary decision-making apparatus, meeting at least annually to address the prescient issues related to the Convention's implementation. Additionally, the CoP facilitates legislative harmonization between States and the terms of the *Convention*, creates

275 *International Tropical Timber Agreement*, *supra* note 176 at arts 3, 6.
276 Ibid. at art 7.
277 Ibid. at art 14.
278 Ibid. at art 26.
279 Ibid. at art 21.
280 *Convention Establishing the Sustainable Tourism Zone of the Caribbean*, *supra* note 202 at art 4.
281 Ibid. at art 4.
282 *Waigani Convention*, *supra* note 173 at arts 13–14.

and adopts amendments and protocols as required, addresses budgetary issues, creates subsidiary bodies and organs as required and suggests rules and regulations for use by the *Convention* apparatus and State Parties.[283] In addition to administrative functions, the *Waigani Convention* Secretariat serves a role in assisting with efforts to prevent trafficking in prohibited wastes and to implement the national and international prohibitions related to trafficking in wastes.[284]

The Conference of the Parties is the decision-making entity for the *Basel Convention*, providing oversight, compliance review and recommendations and policies for furthering the *Convention*'s terms.[285] A Secretariat is also established to serve administrative and bureaucratic functions.[286] The *Rotterdam Convention* establishes the Conference of the Parties as the primary decision-making body in its governance system, vesting it with oversight and compliance review capacities as well as the ability to generate recommendations.[287] The Secretariat function for the *Rotterdam Convention* is a shared entity between UNEP and the FAO.[288]

4.4.3 *Dispute settlement mechanisms*

4.4.3.1 *Fishing*

In the event of disputes between Member States or a Member State and the IATTC, the first step is for the parties to come together to seek settlement through negotiation or similarly peaceful means.[289] Should this be unsuccessful, the next step is for the States to seek assistance from the good offices of the IATTC to provide a neutral decision on the matter is dispute.[290] In the event neither step is successful, the ultimate recourse established in the IATTC system is for the convening of an ad hoc expert committee, under the auspices of the Commission, which is empowered to issue a non-binding decision.[291]

Although the *Convention* creating the North-East Atlantic Commission does not itself establish a system for the settlement of disputes, it does empower the Commission to create such a system.[292] In the event of a

283 Ibid. at art 13.
284 Ibid. at art 14.
285 *Basel Convention on the Control of Transboundary Movements of Hazardous Wastes and Their Disposal*, *supra* note 174 at art 15.
286 Ibid. at art 16.
287 *Rotterdam Convention*, *supra* note 175 at art 18.
288 Ibid. at art 19.
289 *Convention for the Strengthening of the Inter-American Tropical Tuna Commission (Antigua Convention)*, *supra* note 181 at art XXV(1).
290 Ibid. at art XXV(2).
291 Ibid. at art XXV(3).
292 *Convention on Future Multilateral Cooperation in North-East Atlantic Fisheries*, *supra* note 162 at art 18bis.

dispute between the State Parties to the *Convention on the Conservation and Management of Pollock Resources in the Central Bering Sea*, the designated means of settlement is through conciliation.[293]

Dispute settlement in the context of the *Convention on the Conservation and Management of Fishery Resources in the South East Atlantic Ocean* has three steps depending on the escalating nature of the issues involved.[294] At the most basic level, States are to attempt to resolve disputes through a peaceful and negotiated settlement.[295] Should this fail, the next step is to bring the dispute before the appropriate committee, unless the subject matter of the dispute does not fall into their ambit.[296] And finally, should this step fail, the States may submit the dispute to binding arbitration under the terms of the *Convention*.[297]

Should a dispute arise between the State Parties to the *Convention for the Conservation of Southern Bluefin Tuna*, the first level of dispute settlement is to use "negotiation, inquiry, mediation, conciliation, arbitration, judicial settlement or other peaceful means" of choice by the States.[298] In the event these methods are unsuccessful, the *Convention* provides that the matter can be referred to the International Court of Justice or solved through binding arbitration under terms generated through the Commission and subsequent agreement.[299]

Dispute settlement as set out under the terms of the *Conservation and Management of Highly Migratory Fish Stocks in the Western and Central Pacific Ocean* and in subsequent practices is comprised of reference to the Commission, which may use any peaceful means of settlement agreed upon.[300]

4.4.3.2 *Energy*

As a largely guiding and policy advice entity, the IRENA *Statute* has established a relatively simple dispute settlement system for interpretation and application issues between State Parties. The first step in this system is to encourage the use of peaceful means of settlement, such as good offices and conciliation.[301] Should these methods prove unsuccessful, the Council is then empowered to hear disputes that are deemed appropriate.[302]

293 *Convention on the Conservation and Management of Pollock Resources in the Central Bering Sea*, *supra* note 165 at art 13.

294 *Convention on the Conservation and Management of Fishery Resources in the South East Atlantic Ocean*, *supra* note 166 at art 24.

295 Ibid.

296 Ibid.

297 Ibid.

298 *Convention for the Conservation of Southern Bluefin Tuna*, *supra* note 167 at art 16.

299 Ibid. at art 16.

300 *Convention on the Conservation and Management of Highly Migratory Fish Stocks in the Western and Central Pacific Ocean*, *supra* note 168 at art 31.

301 *IRENA Statute*, *supra* note 169 at art XVI(A).

302 Ibid. at art XVI(B).

Given the nature of the investment-promotion elements of the *Energy Charter Treaty*, there are separate dispute settlement mechanism systems in place for Investor-State disputes and State Party disputes. Investor-State disputes are first to be handled through attempts at peaceful settlement.[303] Should these attempts fail, there is authorization to either refer to the appropriate national court system or to an international arbitral body.[304] Disputes between Member States are first to be subject to attempts at amicable settlement between the parties.[305] Should this fail, the dispute will then progress to an ad hoc tribunal of three judges that is specifically convened to hear the dispute at issue.[306]

The *SADC Protocol* establishes a simplified version of a dispute settlement mechanism for claims between State Parties. From the outset, the use of amicable settlement is to be encouraged and the ultimate goal of dispute resolution.[307] Should this not yield a settlement, the second step would be the convening of an internally organized tribunal to hear the complaint and render a decision.[308] Further, it is possible for an advisory opinion to be issued through some elements of the organ structure.[309]

4.4.3.3 *Timber*

Disputes arising in relation to the *International Tropical Timber Agreement* are to be brought to the Council, which may hear the dispute and issue a binding decision with the caveat that the decision must be taken by consensus.[310]

4.4.3.4 *Tourism*

Matters of treaty interpretation and dispute settlement under the *Convention Establishing the Sustainable Tourism Zone of the Caribbean* are first to be addressed through attempts at peaceful settlement.[311] Should this attempt fail, the matter is to be referred to Ministerial Council of the Association of Caribbean States.[312]

303 *Energy Charter Treaty*, *supra* note 170 at art 26.
304 Ibid.
305 Ibid. at art 27.
306 Ibid.
307 *Protocol on Energy in the SADC Region*, *supra* note 172 at art 12.
308 Ibid.
309 Ibid.
310 *International Tropical Timber Agreement*, *supra* note 176 at art 31.
311 Convention Establishing the Sustainable Tourism Zone of the Caribbean, *supra* note 202 at art 13.
312 Ibid.

4.4.3.5 *Wastes*

A dispute arising under or connected to the *Waigani Convention* is first to be addressed through attempts at negotiation, mediation and peaceful settlement practices.[313] Should this prove unsuccessful, recourse is then available to arbitration though a panel established pursuant to the terms of the *Waigani Convention* or to the ICJ.[314]

Disputes arising out of the *Basel Convention* are to be addressed first through negotiations or other peaceful means and, should these prove unable to generate a settlement, may be referred to the ICJ or to a specially convened arbitral panel.[315] Similarly, disputes arising out of the *Rotterdam Convention* are to be settled, where possible, through negotiation or other peaceful means.[316] As a next step, the dispute may be referred to the ICJ or to a specially created arbitration tribunal.[317] Should these options not progress within a certain period of time, a conciliation committee is to address the dispute within the context of the *Rotterdam Convention* system.[318]

4.4.4 *Hard law elements in governance systems*

4.4.4.1 *Fishing*

Much of the *Convention on the Determination of the Minimum Conditions for Access and Exploitation of Marine Resources within the Maritime Zones under Jurisdiction of the Member States of the Sub-Regional Fisheries Commission* enshrines hard law requirements for States that are geared toward ensuring implementation and entrenchment in law. A key element of the *Convention* is the requirement that States adopt hard law for access to fisheries resources.[319] Another essential area for the *Convention* that has been formulated as hard law in content relates to the conservation and management of the fishing resources in the covered area.[320] These include requirements for obtaining fishing licenses and submitting applications rather than permitting open and unregulated fishing,[321] the linking of provisions on access to fishing vessels and national management and conservation measures and

313 *Waigani Convention, supra* note 173 at art 20.
314 Ibid.
315 *Basel Convention on the Control of Transboundary Movements of Hazardous Wastes and Their Disposal, supra* note 174 at art 20.
316 *Rotterdam Convention, supra* note 175 at art 20.
317 Ibid.
318 Ibid.
319 *Convention on the Determination of the Minimum Conditions for Access and Exploitation of Marine Resources within the Maritime Zones under Jurisdiction of the Member States of the Sub-Regional Fisheries Commission, supra* note 159 at pt. II.
320 Ibid. at pt. III.
321 Ibid. at arts 5–8.

policies relating to fish conservation, protection and restrictions on fishing practices[322] and the prohibition on using dangerous fishing practices.[323] In relation to this, the *Convention* contains elements relating to the regulation of commercial and industrial fishing vessels by flag States and their licensing reviews.[324] In addition to the regulation of larger commercial fishing and associated activities, the *Convention* provides a special set of legal and governance requirements for artisanal fisheries.[325] Further, the *Convention* provides requirements for States to enact laws on illegal, unreported and unregulated fishing within their jurisdictions.[326] The *Convention* includes a significant list of activities which are to be included under national penal and administrative laws.[327]

According to the terms of the *Antigua Convention*, State Parties will take all necessary measures to implement and comply with the terms of the *Convention*, including making changes to domestic laws, submitting vessels under flag State jurisdiction to the terms and obligations of the *Convention*, and implementing sanctions in the event of violations.[328] Further, States are obligated to cooperate and assist in the regulatory, budgeting and fact-finding activities of the Commission.[329]

As a foundational matter, the *Convention for the Conservation of Salmon in the North Atlantic Ocean* establishes a prohibition on salmon fishing in the area outside of the national maritime jurisdiction of State Parties and, even within national maritime jurisdictions, where there are certain circumstances or threats.[330] The Council's decisions are intended to be binding as a matter of law unless a State makes a specific denunciation within the articulated timeframe.[331] Under the terms of the *Convention*, the North-East Atlantic Commission's decisions have a certain period of time during which States may raise their objections to decisions taken before they are considered binding.[332]

The *Convention for the Conservation of Anadromous Stocks in the North Pacific Ocean* establishes prohibitions on certain types of fishing activities as well as limitations on some forms of fishing activities in the covered territory under its jurisdiction and creates regulations for vessels from non-State

322 Ibid. at art 9.
323 Ibid. at art 12.
324 Ibid. at arts 13, 19.
325 Ibid. at arts 20–23.
326 Ibid. at art 25.
327 Ibid. at art 31.
328 *Convention for the Strengthening of the Inter-American Tropical Tuna Commission* (*Antigua Convention*), *supra* note 181 at arts XVIII, XX.
329 Ibid. at art XXIII.
330 *Convention for the Conservation of Salmon in the North Atlantic Ocean*, *supra* note 161 at art 2.
331 Ibid. at arts 13–14.
332 *Convention on Future Multilateral Cooperation in North-East Atlantic Fisheries*, *supra* note 162 at art 12.

Parties operating in the Area.[333] It also requires State Parties to ensure that the terms of the *Convention* are binding on their nationals and their flag ships,[334] however, the actual implementation of this at the national level is a matter of soft law.[335] Also included in the hard law requirements for State Parties is the creation of obligations for cooperation in information sharing and exchange, cooperation in information on law enforcement and cooperation in generating and implementing requirements for scientific research and data collection.[336]

Under the terms of the *Convention on the Conservation and Management of Fishery Resources in the South East Atlantic Ocean*, the Commission and the State Parties are required to establish an observation, inspection, compliance and enforcement system for ensuring that flag vessels fulfill these obligations.[337] The goal is to ensure that compliance is achieved in a non-discriminatory manner that functions through a verification process.[338] Further, the *Convention* requires that State Parties implement the Commission's conservation and management recommendations and that these then become a matter of binding law.[339]

In terms of conservation and management of highly migratory fish stocks, the *Conservation and Management of Highly Migratory Fish Stocks* requires that "the principles and measures for conservation and management … shall be applied by coastal States within areas under national jurisdiction in the Conservation Area in the exercise of their sovereign rights for the purposes of explaining and exploiting, conserving and managing highly migratory fish stocks."[340] In conjunction with this, the *Convention* establishes duties for State Parties to regulate and monitor their flag vessels, particularly those engaged in fishing activities.[341] Connected to the regulation and monitoring requirements are requirements for States to ensure compliance with and enforcement of the *Convention*'s terms. This includes State obligations to investigate and prosecute fishing vessels alleged to be in violation of the national laws and rules which reflect the *Convention*'s terms.[342]

333 *Convention for the Conservation of Anadromous Stocks in the North Pacific Ocean, supra* note 163 at arts 3–4.

334 Ibid. at art 5.

335 Ibid.

336 Ibid. at arts 6–7.

337 *Convention on the Conservation and Management of Fishery Resources in the South East Atlantic Ocean, supra* note 166 at art 16.

338 Ibid.

339 Ibid. at art 23.

340 *Convention on the Conservation and Management of Highly Migratory Fish Stocks in the Western and Central Pacific Ocean, supra* note 168 at arts 7–8.

341 Ibid. at pt. V.

342 Ibid. at art 25.

4.4.4.2 *Energy*

The *Energy Charter Treaty* and implementing bodies have established hard law tenets for national regimes and, to a lesser extent, international regimes. The subjects of these regimes are fields such as the relationship between TRIMs and the energy sector,[343] competition in energy and related sectors,[344] transit of energy materials and products through one or more national jurisdictions,[345] the promotion, protection and treatment of investments in the energy sector,[346] compensation for losses in energy investment under certain circumstances,[347] the appropriation of private energy and associated operations by national governments[348] and the recognition of overall retained sovereignty of national governments over energy resources.[349]

The overall purpose of IRENA is to provide assistance to State Parties in the generation and implementation of binding laws and policies that encourage renewable energy industries and uses. In this sense, the work of IRENA is based in soft law activities at the international level which, in turn, are intended to generate binding, hard laws and norms at the national level.[350] This is emphasized in IRENA's Post-COVID-19 Plan, which reiterates the need for national legislation and implementation with the assistance of IRENA and the larger international community.[351]

In addition to the hard law elements, the *Energy Charter Treaty* also establishes soft law tenets for national and international law. Unlike the hard law elements, which reflect the terms found in other related legal areas, such as trade and investment law, the focus areas of soft law tend to be more responsive to new and emerging needs and subject matters. Critical examples of this include provisions for the promotion of technology transfer,[352] the ability to access capital and facilitate open access to capital for the promotion of investment in the energy sector[353] and the incorporation of environmental concerns into energy and related investment policies and practices.[354]

343 *Energy Charter Treaty*, *supra* note 170 at art 5.
344 Ibid. at art 6.
345 Ibid. at art 7.
346 Ibid. at art 10.
347 Ibid. at art 12.
348 Ibid. at art 13.
349 Ibid. at art 18.
350 *IRENA Statute*, *supra* note 169 generally.
351 IRENA Post-COVID Recovery Plan at p 11.
352 *Energy Charter Treaty*, *supra* note 169 at art 8.
353 Ibid. at art 9.
354 Ibid. at art 19.

4.4.4.3 *Wastes*

Under the terms of the *Waigani Convention*, States are obligated to share information on their laws relating to hazardous waste with the Secretariat as these laws change.[355] This includes sharing information on how States are fulfilling their obligations to prohibit the importation of hazardous wastes and radioactive wastes at the national level as well as their exportation.[356] Accompanying this is the requirement that States provide limitations on and significant regulation of such wastes generated in their national territory.[357] To oversee and coordinate enforcement of these requirements and general compliance with the *Convention*, States are required to establish national authorities and focal points "for the implementation of notification procedures for transboundary movement of hazardous wastes."[358] Further, States must establish what, as a matter of law, constitutes the illegal traffic in hazardous waste and methods of criminalizing it.[359]

To further the objectives of the *Waigani Convention*, States are under an obligation to establish notification procedures for transboundary movement of hazardous waste between Parties, including consent requirements on the part of importing State destinations, exporting State destinations and transit States.[360] To accomplish this, States are to enact laws and rules relating to their own conduct as well as to that of private actors within their jurisdiction.[361] Should there be an issue throughout the course of shipment, States are required to recognize the duty to re-import and take legal measures to codify it.[362] Overall, during all phases of the transportation process, States have the obligation to notify potentially impacted States of accidents or issues which occur.[363] Additionally, there are requirements for States to work with each other and relevant international organizations to ensure that appropriate, safe and environmentally secure measures are taken for transportation and storage of the regulated wastes.[364] The *2004 Guidance Element for Detection, Prevention and Control of Illegal Traffic in Hazardous Wastes* further amplified the hard law elements incumbent upon State Parties to implement, particularly in terms of criminalization and penalties.[365]

355 *Waigani Convention*, *supra* note 173 at art 3.
356 Ibid. at art 4.
357 Ibid.
358 Ibid. at art 5.
359 Ibid. at art 9.
360 Ibid. at art 6.
361 Ibid.
362 Ibid. at art 8.
363 Ibid. at art 7.
364 Ibid. at art 10.
365 See Guidance Element for Detection, Prevention and Control of Illegal Traffic in Hazardous Wastes (2004).

A critical function of the *Basel Convention* is to establish the legal and scientific basis for classification of wastes as hazardous, including designating them as radioactive.[366] Reflecting this, State Parties have an obligation to inform the *Convention* mechanisms of how they have updated their laws and rules to reflect these definitions and plans.[367] In connection, States must share the prohibitions and allowances they have adopted for the importation and exportation of hazardous waste.[368] Included in these requirements are State regulation of the creation and disposal of hazardous wastes at the domestic level, and prohibitions on illegal trafficking in hazardous wastes.[369] Under the *Basel Convention*, States have obligations at all stages of the transboundary shipment of waste, most importantly in terms of providing other States notice of these shipments and notifying as to whether the shipment is to be allowed or prohibited prior to commencement of the shipping process.[370] There is a concomitant duty of re-importation for States involved in the export of wastes.[371] States are required to designate competent national authorities and national focal points for liaison and contact purposes.[372] This complements the requirement that States cooperate with each other in the implementation of the *Basel Convention*, and particularly that they transmit and timely share information on accidents and other issues associated with accidents occurring during the shipment or disposal process.[373]

State Parties to the *Rotterdam Convention* are required to create laws, rules and procedures for severely restricted or banned chemicals and pesticides as well as for severely hazardous pesticide formulations and notification of them, for import restrictions on certain chemicals and for export restrictions on certain chemicals.[374] To assist in the sharing of information and liaising with other States and the *Convention*'s governance systems, State Parties are required to designate competent national focal points and authorities.[375] States are also required to exchange and share information on notification and other restrictions, laws, rules and procedures adopted at the national level in response to the *Convention*, and to provide technical and other available assistance to developing States where possible.[376]

366 *Basel Convention on the Control of Transboundary Movements of Hazardous Wastes and Their Disposal*, *supra* note 174 at art 1.
367 Ibid. at art 3.
368 Ibid. at art 4.
369 Ibid.
370 Ibid. at art 6.
371 Ibid. at art 8.
372 Ibid. at art 5.
373 Ibid. at arts 10, 13.
374 *Rotterdam Convention*, *supra* note 175 at arts 5–6, 10–12, 15.
375 Ibid. at art 4.
376 Ibid. at arts 14–16.

4.4.4.4 *Tourism*

Under the *Convention Establishing the Sustainable Tourism Zone of the Caribbean*, States are obligated to adopt laws and rules necessary to create and implement the Sustainable Tourism Zone in the region and to adopt and coordinate a number of measures relating to it.[377] These measures include topics such as culture and identity, community participation, environmental concerns, technology for sustainability, economic policies and instruments, tourist markets, education, law and legal regulations, implementation of sustainability indicators, air and marine transport, involvement of the private sector in implementing and preserving the Zone and creating protocols and other measures as appropriate.[378] As a corollary, the State Parties have the duty to designate areas within their territorial jurisdiction that should be included in the Sustainable Tourism Zone.[379]

4.4.5 *Soft law elements in governance systems*

4.4.5.1 *Energy*

Generally, IRENA is empowered to undertake activities that result in the promulgation of soft law and associated norms. Under the IRENA *Statute*, these activities are "providing experience for practical applications and policies, offering support on all matters relating to renewable energy and helping countries to benefit from the efficient development and transfer of knowledge and technology,"[380] as well as providing non-binding national law analysis, practices and standards, coordinating governmental and non-governmental interaction, providing policy advice and assistance to states on renewables, providing capacity building assistance, providing assistance on financing for renewables and generating research on renewables and impacts.[381]

The work of the *Convention of the African Energy Commission* is largely focused on providing legal and policy advice to State Parties throughout Africa and in assisting States in creating national laws and rules relating to energy policy.[382] In this sense, the Commission is established to foster regional cooperation and integration while generating mechanisms that focus on soft law rather than on hard law at the organizational level.

Implementation of the *SADC Protocol* is focused on providing legal and policy advice to State Parties throughout the region and in assisting Member

377 *Convention Establishing the Sustainable Tourism Zone of the Caribbean*, *supra* note 202 at art 3.

378 Ibid.

379 Ibid. at art 5.

380 *IRENA Statute*, *supra* note 169 at art IV(A).

381 Ibid. at art IV.

382 See generally *Convention of the African Energy Commission*, *supra* note 171.

States in creating national laws and rules relating to energy policy.[383] In this sense, the *Protocol* was enacted and rendered operational to foster cooperation and integration while generating mechanisms that focus on soft law rather than on hard law at the organizational level.

4.5 Pandemic responses

At the institutional level, many governance systems reviewed in this Chapter have followed the trends of the entities discussed in other chapters by postponing or cancelling their in-person meetings, sometimes moving to an online format and sometimes waiting to reschedule in the future.

The WTO faces an evolving issue in that, from the beginning of the pandemic onward, States have been acting to restrict imports and exports of medical supplies and food stuffs deemed critical and have also banned products from certain States associated with the virus from the outset.[384] This represents a delicate balance between legitimate invocation of the general and safety exceptions in many of the WTO treaty regimes on the one hand and a combination of protectionism and fear on the other.[385] The WTO's response has been to discourage these measures to the extent possible, however it remains to be seen whether the DSB aspect of the governance system will receive a number of complaints regarding actions taken during the pandemic.[386]

In response to the pandemic, the World Bank Group and its affiliated entities have provided additional, targeted financial assistance to States as they seek to ensure that they can meet the needs of their citizens at the public health level and across all sectors.[387] This includes ensuring funding for scientific and other undertakings needed to specifically address the medical and public health needs caused by COVID-19.[388]

The IMF has allocated billions of dollars in support for States as they attempt to address the immediate costs associated with the COVID-19 pandemic, responses to the pandemic and long-term financial issues caused exacerbated by it.[389] Included in the IMF's response planning are efforts to encourage debt reduction, restructuring and forgiveness for States which are facing extreme choices regarding the ability to repay their debt obligations

383 See generally ibid.

384 WTO, Frequently asked questions: The WTO and COVID-19, available at https://www.wto.org/english/tratop_e/covid19_e/faqcovid19_e.htm.

385 Ibid.

386 Ibid.

387 World Bank, The World Bank Group's Response to the COVID-19 (coronavirus) pandemic, available at https://www.worldbank.org/en/who-we-are/news/coronavirus-covid19.

388 Ibid.

389 IMF Factsheet, Surveillance (20 October 2020), available at https://www.imf.org/en/About/Factsheets/IMF-Surveillance.

and the need to provide for their citizens.[390] Further, the IMF has provided State governments and international entities with economic and financial analysis and advisory services throughout the pandemic.[391]

4.6 Trends and summaries

This Chapter has surveyed treaty regimes and concomitant governance mechanisms across a range of topics relating to trade, economic policy, banking and finance and industry regimes. It found that there are significant trends within and across regime classifications that relate to global governance issues and correlate to the SDGs as a whole as well as to particular elements of the SDGs, especially SDGs 7, 8, 9, 11, 12, 13 and 16. Within each section there are varying correlations, however of the strongest overall relate to SDG 16 regarding transparency and good governance as well as SDG 13 and the economic growth aspects of SDG 8.

Throughout the treaty regimes and governance structures discussed in this Chapter there are clear connections between the role that economic development and progress can play as a means of assisting or harming the advancement of environmental concerns, efforts to combat climate change, and sustainable development principles. This is striking as it cuts across individual industries – often those on opposite sides of the production system, geography and interplanetary scope, and includes banking as well as trade. In this way, the treaty regimes and associated governance systems focusing on economic concerns can still be understood as cross-cutting with environmental concerns. At the same time, the emphasis on responsible practices in these industries and sectors – be it setting human rights standards for international banks to use in lending decisions or setting allowable fish catches – indicates the importance of these economic treaty regimes and governance systems as a means of furthering the core concerns of human rights regimes as well.

Sovereignty, and the need to balance it with international goals and ambitions in establishing treaty regimes and governance structures, is another key trend from this Chapter. Economic planning and the regulation of industry practices is a significant element of State practice and sovereign power, especially in the context of trade and finance. And yet, the treaty regimes and governance systems reviewed in this Chapter demonstrate that it is possible to strike a balance that recognizes the durability of sovereignty while giving primacy to the goals of the international community through activities such as internalized dispute settlement systems rather than the resort to court functions and the ability of developing States to receive assistance and technology transfer which makes participation in the global regimes more

390 Ibid.
391 Ibid.

attractive. This balance has been strained during the COVID-19 pandemic, as States are acting to protect their citizens and ensure adequate and continuing access to supplies even where it threatened to undermine trade and financial commitments. However, these issues will be handled within the realm of dedicated governance systems which are widely respected, which itself reaffirms the role of global governance and its importance for current and future international challenges.

The incorporation of transparency and rule of law promotion in the practices of economic regimes is an evident theme within this Chapter and highlights the ways in which these fundamental tenets of SDG 16 can be used across the environmental, social and human rights regimes to generate meaningful law and policy shifts. This is reflected in the use of committee systems that consult with experts and those impacted by proposed economic activities as well as in the generation of guidelines and recommendations for business and financial activities that entrench transparency and respect for laws in their principles. Such trends further the commitment to marginalized and vulnerable communities that can be observed across the chapters and regimes analyzed in this book.

5 Emerging trends and future potentials

The preceding chapters presented a broad spectrum of treaty regimes and governance systems spanning a variety of topics and concerns grouped under the three pillars of sustainable development. The lessons of these chapters provide an understanding of the commonalties and differences in implementing the terms of these treaty regimes and using global governance systems to entrench them in international and national law and policy. At the same time, these chapters noted the challenges faced by each classification of governance system in the face of the COVID-19 pandemic, which will continue to shape the way that global governance systems and the State actors comprising them achieve international responsibilities.

In this Chapter, the lessons of the preceding chapters are brought together to analyze their potential impacts on and ties to the Sustainable Development Goals (SDGs). As noted in the introductory chapter, there are varying schools of thought regarding whether the SDGs are soft law or have hard law components. This Chapter, however, offers an alternative understanding of this relationship. At the domestic level, it is the contention of the Chapter – and this book – that the SDGs reflect many aspects of national law and policy which either exist as suggestions rather than laws or as laws which suffer from enforcement and capacity gaps. At the international level, this book's central assertion is that the argument over whether the SDGs are soft or hard law is extraneous because they can be tied to existing treaty regimes and governance systems. In this way, the SDGs and their targets together are perhaps best viewed as a high-level statement and policy tool that mirrors the international and national commitments already existing for States and the international community.

This conceptualization of the SDGs then allows States and non-State actors to use the SDGs as a consolidated statement of the most pressing and imperative international law treaty regimes and governance systems for the future. They thus incentivize compliance with their terms as well as the terms of the treaty regimes they reflect and can be entrenched and operationalized through the enforcement mechanisms which exist in these instruments. Through this lens, which views the SDGs not as an added layer of obligations but as a supplement to existing treaty regime and governance system-based obligations, it is then possible to conceive of a way for the SDGs to be accomplished even in the midst of a world that will forever be marked by the impacts of the COVID-19 pandemic. By understanding this as well as the ways in which the SDGs weave together various sectors to create a cross-cutting tapestry of governance systems and entrenchment vehicles, it is indeed possible to conceive of a successful system in which, as a matter of law and policy, no one is left behind.

5.1 Application of lessons from environmental treaty regimes to the Sustainable Development Goals

1) A number of the treaty regimes discussed designate environmental threats as common concerns of humankind, extending the reach of their governance systems from purely environmental to issues such as sustainable development and human rights. This can be seen in the incorporation of sustainable development, sustainable use and management of resources, and principles of sustainable development such as the precautionary principle and the polluter pays principle, as fundamental purposes of treaty regime-based governance regimes and the hard and soft law State commitments which they are meant to oversee.

These trends directly relate to SDGs 12 (responsible consumption and production), 13 (climate change its impacts), 14 (life below water), 15 (life on land) as well as the terms of the *2030 Agenda*.[1] Perhaps the most significant example of this comes from the context of the *United Nations Framework Convention on Climate Change* (UNFCCC) system, which included the concept of common but differentiated responsibilities from the outset and is directly tied to SDG 13, which recognized this system as the primary source of international law and governance related to climate change.[2] Similarly, the *Convention on Biological Diversity* (CBD) emphasizes the need for sustainable use of natural resources as an essential objective of the system it has created, including the *Nagoya* and *Cartagena Protocols*.[3] The polluter pays principle and the precautionary principle form a central element of the *Convention on the Protection and Use of Transboundary Watercourses and*

1 See generally *United Nations Framework Convention on Climate Change* (1992).

2 See *2030 Agenda* (2015) at SDG 13. In an official explanatory note, SDG 13 states "Acknowledging that the United Nations Framework Convention on Climate Change is the primary international, intergovernmental forum for negotiating the global response to climate change." Ibid.

3 *Convention on Biological Diversity* (1992) at art 1; *Nagoya Protocol on Access to Genetic Resources and the Fair and Equitable Sharing of Benefits Arising from their Utilization to the Convention on Biological Diversity* (2010) at art 1; *Cartagena Protocol on Biosafety to the Convention on Biological Diversity* (2003) at art 1.

International Lakes[4] and the *Agreement on the Conservation of Albatrosses and Petrels.*[5] Further, the general concern for future generations is another common theme, as evidenced in the *Convention on Migratory Species of Wild Animals,*[6] *Convention on International Trade in Endangered Species* (CITES),[7] and the *Agreement on the Conservation of Cetaceans of the Black Sea, Mediterranean Sea and Contiguous Atlantic Area.*[8]

Additionally, the *Cartagena Protocol*'s focus on human health concerns connection to the terms and targets of SDG 3 as well as SDG 2 in addressing food and associated genetic material access.[9] Concerns regarding human health form essential aspects of the *Vienna Convention*, under which State Parties have an obligation "to protect human health and the environment against adverse effects resulting or likely to result from human activities which modify or are likely to modify the ozone layer."[10] Similar concerns for health and access to adequate food, as well as food safety, underlie the *International Plant Protection Convention*[11] as well as the recently adopted efforts to re-shape the treaty regime's governance focus in the wake of the pandemic and the food security issues that have already arisen.

2) There is a recurrent emphasis on environmental preservation as being tied to peace and the advancement of scientific and cultural knowledge, accompanied by prohibitions on harmful conduct, including militarization of sensitive areas and the protection of sensitive areas in the event of national or regional conflict. This connects to SDG 16 and its many targets as well as to the partnership and civil society involvement aspects of SDG 17.

The central goal of preserving peace through environmental treaties can be seen in the *Antarctic Treaty*, under which States agree to keep the territory free from military use, including weaponization. While this extends to a limited area it does include a number of State Parties, extending the concept of non-militarization of natural resources into multiple national legal systems. Relatedly, State Parties to the *Agreement on the Nile River Basin Cooperation Framework* are required to protect the River and associated areas from harm during armed conflict.[12]

4 *UNECE Convention on the Protection and Use of Transboundary Watercourses and International Lakes* (1992) at arts 2, 3.
5 *Agreement on the Conservation of Albatrosses and Petrels* (2001) at preamble.
6 *Convention on the Conservation of Migratory Species of Wild Animals* (1979) at preamble.
7 *Convention on International Trade in Endangered Species* (1975) at preamble.
8 *Agreement on the Conservation of Cetaceans of the Black Sea, Mediterranean Sea and Contiguous Atlantic Area* (1996) at preamble.
9 *Cartagena Protocol, supra* note 3 at art 1.
10 *Convention for the Protection of the Ozone Layer* (*Vienna Convention*) (1985) at art 2.
11 *International Plant Protection Convention* (1997) at preamble.
12 *Agreement on the Nile River Basin Cooperation Framework* (2010) at arts 12–13.

A critical example of the intersection with SDG 17 can be seen in the *Paris Agreement*, which heavily relied on scientific projections regarding the impacts of different levels of global warming in the articulation of requirements for State Parties and which create space for scientific and technical involvement.[13] This intersection with scientific knowledge and partnership has been seen throughout subsequent CoP decisions, including the Katowice Outcomes in 2018 and the Madrid Outcomes in 2019.[14]

3) Transparency is a vital trend in environmental treaty regimes and governance systems and also reflects SDG 16 and its targets. At the public level, inclusion of requirements for State Parties to engage in public awareness, public education and public participation where there are decisions which will cause impact represents a significant effort to use global governance systems to ensure the protection of individual and community rights. This is works in tandem with requirements for national and, in certain instances, transboundary environmental impact assessments requirements in treaty regimes which are overseen by governance mechanisms.

These measures are intended to assess the environmental damage and threat at the national level – often with a focus on traditional and indigenous communities – as well as the transboundary level where there is a likelihood that the proposed activity would have a cross-border impact. In this context, the other State has the ability to receive information, comment on the plans and receive the final decision regarding the proposed activity. The transboundary aspects of these requirements also address concerns throughout SDGs 14 and 15 regarding shared natural resource systems. Examples of this range from the *Espoo Convention* and *Escazu Convention* provisions regarding environmental impact assessment and public involvement to the many transboundary rivers and seas treaties requiring notification of actions that would potentially impact other States or the shared resource.

4) Environmental treaty regimes and governance systems tend to require that risk assessments or risk measures be created for the purposes of sharing transparent information and understandings with all potentially impacted States, tying directly to SDG 16. Further, many of these treaties, especially those involving maritime resources, require State Parties to share information on real and potential emergencies with State Parties which that be affected, for example through an oil spill as provided for in the *Agreement on Cooperation on Marine Oil Pollution*

13 *Paris Agreement on Climate Change* (2015) at art 2.
14 Katowice Outcomes (2018); Madrid Outcomes (2019).

Preparedness and Response in the Arctic.[15] In this way, there are several levels of global oversight included in the governance planning for activities which have the ability to cause lasting environmental damage and undermine the foundational principles enshrined in many environmental treaty regimes. Again, this links to SDGs 14 and 15, especially the marine concerns addressed in SDG 14 and the concerns for ecosystems which can impact each other that exist throughout both SDGs.

Critical examples of this come from the *Espoo Convention* and its *SEA Protocol*, as well as the recently adopted *Escazu Convention*. As noted above, each of these regimes requires the conduct of domestic environmental impact assessments, with the *SEA Protocol* extending the jurisdictional and topical boundaries of these assessments, while at the same time requiring the consultation and information of States which might be impacted by domestic activities.[16]

Perhaps the most obvious examples of attempts at transnational impact assessments and mitigation come from the pollution-based treaties, since they are inherently premised on the understanding that pollutants do not recognize borders. In creating the *Vienna Convention*, the State Parties highlighted the inherent threat posed to humans and the environment by air pollution and the transboundary spread of pollution.[17] State Parties to the *Stockholm Convention* stressed the need for such a regime due to the transboundary nature of Persistent Organic Pollutants (PoPs), specifically in terms of impacts on migratory species, human and animal health and water and soil resources.[18] In crafting the *Montreal Protocol*, the State Parties stressed that ozone depletion issues are global issues and have a particularly damaging dynamic for developing countries.[19] The years since these treaty regimes were established have only served to emphasize the appropriateness of their concerns, as is demonstrated by SDGs 13, 14 and 15.

5) There are significant trends and similarities in the creation of governance systems across environmental treaty regimes which reflect aspects of SDG 16. Generally, there will be a decision-making entity that is either a CoP or MoP, allowing the State Parties to come together to issue decisions and to engage in negotiations on the most pressing issues facing the regime at the time. Additionally, specialized committees or groups of experts are often convened under the auspices of treaty

15 *Agreement on Cooperation on Marine Oil Pollution Preparedness and Response in the Arctic* (2013) at preamble.
16 *Espoo Convention* (1991) at art 1; *SEA Protocol* (2003) at 1, 3; *Escazu Convention* (2018) at 1.
17 *UNECE 1979 Convention on Long-Range Transboundary Air Pollution* (1979) at preamble.
18 *Stockholm Convention on Persistent Organic Pollutions* (2001) at preamble.
19 *Montreal Protocol on Substances that Deplete the Ozone Layer* (1987) at preamble.

regime-based governance systems and advance SDG 17's partnership and capacity-building aspects.

Successive iterations of CoPs at the UNFCCC and CBD level have demonstrated the ability of this system to generate results that are responsive to the needs of the international community in the face of evolving information to environmental threats, albeit somewhat more slowly that some might hope. The ability to create committees and other advisory entities as part of the governance system for treaty regimes is a significant and shared ability which ensures that these structures are able to receive and make decisions informed by expertise that is, in theory, removed from many of the political concerns found in the CoP process. Similarly, the use of reporting requirements and oversight, monitoring and compliance systems – whether a dedicated Committee on Compliance as used by the UNFCCC under the *Paris Agreement* or a CoP-based review – ensures that transparency is maintained in the international system. All of these highlight the intersection between governance structures that are inclusive of multiple perspectives and insights as well as the priorities and needs of the State Parties. In this way, there is a direct link to SDG 16's prioritization of transparency and inclusion in governance system.

Through the Subsidiary Body for Scientific and Technological Advice established under the UNFCCC system's auspices, scientific updates and knowledge is shared with the State Parties and the UNFCCC system generally and can also be called upon to answer questions from the CoP.[20] To assist in accomplishing the CBD, the Subsidiary Body on Scientific, Technical and Technological Advice was established to provide assistance and guidance on technical points.[21] The *Nagoya Protocol* establishes the Access and Benefit Sharing Clearing-House and Information-Sharing entity with the goal of facilitating the exchange of information and transparency between State Parties[22] and the *Cartagena Protocol* designates the Biosafety Clearing-House as the clearing-house mechanism to be used by State Parties for information sharing,[23] further assisting in the connections between inter-disciplinary interests in environmental issues. Within the context of the *Agreement on the Nile River Basin Cooperation Framework* the Technical Advisory Committee creates programs and policies of the Council and the Organization, makes recommendations to the Council, creates appropriate working groups, and provides technical assistance as needed.[24]

20 UNFCCC, *supra* note 1 at art 9.
21 CBD, *supra* note 3 at art 25.
22 *Nagoya Protocol*, *supra* note 3 at art 14.
23 *Cartagena Protocol*, *supra* note 3 at art 20.
24 *Agreement on the Nile River Basin Cooperation Framework*, *supra* note 12 at art 26.

6) The tiered and escalating approach used by environmental treaty regimes and governance mechanisms in the face of disputes demonstrates the need to balance governance concerns at the international level with the national sovereignty rights that form the bedrock of international law. This sovereignty balance is at the heart of the SDGs as well, particularly SDG 16.

Each level in this process allows States to engage in their own forms of diplomatic settlement while at the same time ensuring that there is an organizational structure for these disputes to use rather than threatening to undermine the entirety of the treaty regime.[25] Further, by often seeking to settle these disputes within the governance system established under the treaty regime, there is a discernible attempt to ensure that they are solved by States or arbitrators with knowledge in the issues involved rather than through a more generalized system.[26]

7) The terms of the treaty regimes tend to emphasize the interlinkages between environmental and economic concerns as a potential source of strength and solidity in terms of generating a consolidated and holistic means to addressing these concerns, linking to SDG 12 as well as the central environmentally focused SDGs.

This is reflected in the financing mechanisms created through many treaty regimes and included in governance systems as well as efforts to increase capacity and to ensure that certain areas of particular ecological value are designated as such and exempted from commercialization. For example, the UNFCCC Financial Mechanism assists in technology transfer and climate change related activities.[27] The Financial Mechanism is currently operationalized through the Green Climate Fund and the Global Environment Facility,[28] further connecting environmental and economic interests. Further, the CBD provides for financial mechanisms to protect and assist developing States in implementing the terms of the *Convention*.[29]

25 See, e.g., UNFCCC, *supra* note 1 at art 14; *Espoo Convention*, *supra* note 16 at art 15; *Escazu Convention*, *supra* note 16 at art 19; *Stockholm Convention on Persistent Organic Pollutions*, *supra* note 18 at art 18; CITES, *supra* note 7 at art XVIII; CMS, *supra* note 6 at art XIII; *Agreement on the Conservation of Gorillas and their Habitats* (2007) at art XII; *Agreement on the Conservation of African-Eurasian Migratory Waterbirds* (1995) at art XII.

26 *United Nations Convention on the Law of the Sea* (1982) at arts 186–187, 191, 279, 284, 287. For other examples, see *Convention for the Protection of the Ozone Layer* (*Vienna Convention*) (1985) at art 11; *Agreement on the Conservation of Cetaceans of the Black Sea, Mediterranean Sea and Contiguous Atlantic Area* (1996) at art XII.

27 UNFCCC, *supra* note 1 at art 11.

28 See Katowice Outcomes, *supra* note 14 at 3/CMA.1.

29 CBD, *supra* note 3 at art 21.

In an effort to ensure that there is responsible and compliant natural resources-based commercial activity in internationalized areas of the oceans, the UNCLOS Enterprise carries out and oversees Area-based activities relating to resource exploration and exploitation, as well as "transporting, processing and marketing of minerals received from the Area."[30] This is closely related to many of the targets in SDG 12 since it is an admission that exploration and exploitation will occur but an attempt to ensure that these activities are conducted in a sustainable manner.

In summary, at the core of each of these treaty regimes and governance systems is the recognition of environmental issues as touching on many sectors and practices but having a wide-ranging impact that requires both general and specific legal and governance systems and responses to having lasting impact.

5.2 Application of lessons from social treaty regimes to the Sustainable Development Goals

1) The strongest correlation between the social treaty regimes and governance systems discussed occurs in terms of SDG 16 given the breadth of its remit, embracing everything from violence reduction to transparency and social inclusion to public participation to reductions in threats from weapons.

While the core human rights treaty regimes and governance systems are a clear example of these connections so are treaty regimes on other areas of social concern. For example, the purposes of Targets 16.4[31] and 16.5[32] are incorporated in the *United Nations Convention against Corruption*,[33] the *United Nations Convention against Transnational Organized Crime*[34] and its *Protocol to Prevent, Suppress and Punish Trafficking in Persons, Especially Women and Children*,[35] *Protocol against the Smuggling of Migrants by Land, Sea and Air*,[36] and *Protocol against the Illicit Manufacturing of and Trafficking in Firearms, Their Parts and Components and Ammunitions*,[37] the *United*

30 UNCLOS, *supra* note 26 at art 170.

31 Target 16.4 ("By 2030, significantly reduce illicit financial and arms flows, strengthen the recovery and return of stolen assets and combat all forms of organized crime").

32 Target 16.5 ("Substantially reduce corruption and bribery in all their forms").

33 *United Nations Convention against Corruption* (2003).

34 *United Nations Convention against Transnational Organized Crime* (2000).

35 *Protocol to Prevent, Suppress and Punish Trafficking in Persons, Especially Women and Children Supplementing the United Nations Convention against Transnational Organized Crime* (2000).

36 *Protocol against the Smuggling of Migrants by Land, Sea and Air Supplementing the United Nations Convention against Transnational Organized Crime* (2000).

37 *Protocol against the Illicit Manufacturing of and Trafficking in Firearms, Their Parts and Components and Ammunitions Supplementing the United Nations Convention against Transnational Organized Crime* (2001).

Nations Convention against Illicit Traffic in Narcotic Drugs and Psychotropic Substances,[38] the *Inter-American Convention against Corruption*,[39] and the *African Union Convention on Preventing and Combating Corruption*.[40]

Additionally, the weapons treaty regimes are directly tied to SDG 16 and its targets by seeking to protect individuals and society from the physical harms posed by arms and weapons as well as from harms associated with conflict. For example, the *Treaty on the Prohibition of Nuclear Weapons* was created by State Parties based on the understanding of the threats posed by nuclear weapons to current and future generations in the transboundary context, as well as the national context, and especially for vulnerable and marginalized groups such as women and children.[41] Based on the experiences of generations of unintended victims, the *Convention on Cluster Munitions* stresses that the use of cluster munitions poses not only a short-term threat but also constitutes a generational threat to civilians long after the fighting has concluded and the conflict has been settled.[42] And, in the *Arms Trade Treaty*, there is an attempt to balance the sovereign right to self-defense with the rights of civilians, particularly vulnerable populations, and the interests of the international community in promoting peace and non-violence.[43]

2) A critical trend in the treaty regimes discussed is their focus on various human rights concerns – be they regarding acts of torture, rights of children, societal ability to progress beyond corruption, the right to health, the right to live without generational threats from weapons, or beyond – and the translation of these concerns into governance structures that are tailored to meet the needs of the populations affected. Again, this represents a significant connection to and entrenchment of SDG 16. Beyond this, however, there are strong connections with SDG 1 (end poverty in all forms everywhere), SDG 3 (good health and well-being), SDG 4 (quality and lifelong education), SDG 5 (gender equality), SDG 6 (clean water and sanitation) and SDG 8 (decent work), and SDG 10 (reduced inequalities), as well as their respect targets.

Examples of this breadth of connections with SDGs can be found in the core human rights treaties, notably the *International Covenant on Civil and Political Rights* (ICCPR),[44] the *International Covenant on Economic, Social and*

38 *United Nations Convention against Illicit Traffic in Narcotic Drugs and Psychotropic Substances* (1988).
39 *Inter-American Convention against Corruption* (1996).
40 *African Union Convention on Preventing and Combating Corruption* (2003).
41 *Treaty on the Prohibition of Nuclear Weapons* (2017) at preamble.
42 *Convention on Cluster Munitions* (2008) at preamble.
43 *Arms Trade Treaty* (2013) at preamble.
44 *International Covenant on Civil and Political Rights* (1966).

Cultural Rights (ICESCR),[45] the *Convention on the Rights of the Child* (CRC),[46] the *International Convention on the Protocol of the Rights of All Migrant Workers and Members of Their Families*,[47] the *International Convention on the Elimination of All Forms of Racial Discrimination* (CERD),[48] the *Convention on the Elimination of All Forms of Discrimination against Women* (CEDAW),[49] the *Convention against Torture and Other Cruel, Inhuman and Degrading Treatment or Punishment*,[50] and the *International Convention on the Protection of All Persons from Enforced Disappearance*,[51] as well as the *American Convention on Human Rights*[52] and the *African Charter on Human Rights and Peoples' Rights*.[53]

3) By allowing private individuals and communities to bring claims regarding human rights violations to regional and international bodies, the core human rights treaties pierced the well-worn veil of international law as the realm of States alone. Indeed, this has created a unique governance structure which attempts to balance sovereignty and the supremacy of the State in international law with the realization that the rights created belong to private actors and that there must be a place for claims regarding infringements on these rights to occur. This gets to the heart of the protections enshrined in the SDGs *per se* and in particular SDG 17 in terms of involving civil society and non-State actors.

Perhaps the most obvious examples of this come from the various human rights committees that have been empowered to hear communications of complaints regarding State Party failure to comply with treaty regimes.[54] The ability of other State Parties or individuals and groups to bring these complaints is itself indicative of the shift in priority and focus between State sovereignty and individuals as the holders of human rights. Beyond this, in the creation of this system the human rights treaty regimes collectively have operationalized a system for review, fact-finding and decision-making on whether violations of guarantees that are included in the intent of the SDGs have occurred.

45 *International Convention on Economic, Social and Cultural Rights* (1966).
46 *Convention on the Rights of the Child* (1989).
47 *International Convention on the Protocol of the Rights of All Migrant Workers and Members of Their Families* (1990).
48 *International Convention on the Elimination of All Forms of Racial Discrimination* (1969).
49 *Convention on the Elimination of All Forms of Discrimination against Women* (1979).
50 *Convention against Torture and Other Cruel, Inhuman and Degrading Treatment or Punishment* (1985).
51 *International Convention on the Protection of All Persons from Enforced Disappearance* (2007).
52 *American Convention on Human Rights* (1969).
53 *African Charter on Human Rights and Peoples' Rights* (1982).
54 See *supra* notes 44 – 51.

4) At the same time, even treaty regimes and governance sectors that have adopted a more traditional international law perspective on governance systems, especially the WHO and FAO which act as formalized international organizations, there is a recognition of the importance of non-State voices in creating highlight technical and specialized policy that is often dependent on knowledge outside that possessed by international policy makers. This further extends the connections between the social treaty regimes and governance systems and SDG 17.

In addition to the WHO and FAO contexts, this can be seen in the criminal regimes, which expand the scope of involvement to include private actors and public servants as well as the state apparatus itself.[55]

5) Social treaty regimes require that domestic entities be either designated or created by State Party governments in order to enforce the terms of the international law instrument at issue. This entrenches the State's commitments under the treaty regime as part of the national governance system while also linking the national governance sector to the global governance system established in the regime.

This duality of governance is both mutually reinforcing and allows States to be held to account when there are failures of governance as a national matter since the failure is in regard to an international commitment. These requirements are directly linked to SDG 16 and associated targets as well as the many SDGs that, as highlighted above, are implicated throughout the social treaty regimes. In the criminal regime context, while the obvious connection is between these treaties and governance systems and SDG 16, the wide-ranging and insidious nature of acts such as corruption implicate the ability to achieve the vast majority of the SDGs.[56]

6) The social treaty regimes emphasized the need to incorporate and act to protect vulnerable and marginalized populations in different contexts and with different needs. However, whether the rights to be protected are those of children today or their grandchildren, the governance systems put in place by these regimes require States to actively report on – and thus, at least in theory, act on – their progress toward achieving their hard law obligations. These governance systems also allow for evolution of their terms as science and technology becomes further advanced

55 *UN Convention against Corruption*, *supra* note 33 at art 7; *UN Convention against Transnational Organized Crime*, *supra* note 34 at arts 5–9, 23; *UN Convention against Illicit Traffic in Narcotic Drugs and Psychotropic Substances*, *supra* note 38 at arts 3, 5, 9; *Inter-American Convention against Corruption*, *supra* note 38 at art III.

56 See generally *UN Convention against Corruption*, *supra* note 33.

while seeking to include the voice of marginalized peoples in their decision-making. As noted above, these protections in themselves address the majority of the SDGs. Further, the reporting and transparency requirements on the governance systems created through the social treaty regimes are intertwined with SDG 16.

Examples from the human rights treaty regimes and governance systems context include reporting and review requirements for the Human Rights Committee under the ICCPR,[57] the Committee on Economic, Social and Cultural Rights under the ICESCR,[58] Committee on the Rights of the Child under CRC,[59] the Committee on the Protection of the Rights of All Migrant Workers and Members of Their Families under the *International Convention on the Protocol of the Rights of All Migrant Workers and Members of Their Families*,[60] the Committee on the Elimination of Racial Discrimination under the *International Convention on the Elimination of All Forms of Racial Discrimination*,[61] the Committee on the Elimination of Discrimination against Women under CEDAW,[62] the Committee against Torture under the *Convention against Torture*,[63] and the Committee on Enforced Disappearances under the *International Convention on the Protection of All Persons from Enforced Disappearance*.[64]

7) The governance systems created by social treaty regimes must be framed against the larger intention of human rights and social treaties to entrench the laws and rules they contain as elements in a durable and evolving human rights system. This system functions as a duality of national and international, which from a governance perspective can seem uneven and yet allows the system to be reinforcing of the overarching global needs and commitments while giving space for national variations and needs provided they do not conflict. In this way, the social treaties offer a durable space to entrench the SDGs in a system that will evolve, thus ensuring that they remain a matter of international law and governance well beyond 2030.

57 ICCPR, *supra* note 44 at arts 28, 40.
58 ICESCR, *supra* note 45 at arts 16–17.
59 *Convention on the Rights of the Child*, *supra* note 46 at arts 43–44.
60 *International Convention on the Protocol of the Rights of All Migrant Workers and Members of Their Families*, *supra* note 47 at arts 72, 73.
61 *International Convention on the Elimination of All Forms of Racial Discrimination*, *supra* note 48 at arts 8–9.
62 CEDAW, *supra* note 49 at arts 17–18.
63 CAT, *supra* note 50 at arts 17, 19.
64 *International Convention on the Protection of All Persons from Enforced Disappearance*, *supra* note 51 at arts 26–27, 29.

Examples of this evolutionary process can be seen in the adoption of protocols which build on the underlying treaty regimes to further particularly relevant issues, such as the *Optional Protocol to the Convention on the Rights of the Child on the Sale of Children, Child Prostitution and Child Pornography*[65] and the *Optional Protocol to the Convention on the Rights of the Child on the Involvement of Children in Armed Conflict.*[66] Additionally, the WHO's *International Health Regulations* are regularly updated and will most likely be updated in the wake of the COVID-19 pandemic to reflect the collective lessons learned from the first implementation of a global pandemic under them.

Further, the commission and court systems used in the Inter-American human rights system and the African human and peoples' rights system represent significant advances in law and jurisprudence by entrenching the cross-cutting terms of their constitutional treaty regimes into a system that evolves to meet the needs and challenges of their respective territorial jurisdictions.[67] By linking many of the SDGs to these entities and their decisions, the SDGs can be seen as becoming more deeply incorporated into the laws and policies of these regions, which in turn generates persuasive legal authority and perhaps even evidence of customary law at the international level.

5.3 Application of lessons from economic treaty regimes to the Sustainable Development Goals

1) Within each of the economic treaty regimes and governance systems there are varying correlations, however of the strongest overall relate to SDG 16 regarding transparency and good governance as well as SDG 13 and the economic growth aspects of SDG 8.

A key example of this can be found in the original GATT text, which stressed that trade and economic advancement "should be conducted with a view to raising standards of living, ensuring full employment and a large and steadily growing volume of real income."[68] Additionally, the World Trade Organization (WTO) *Revised Agreement on Government Procurement* focuses on the need to balance between sovereign interests on the one hand and the concern that these grounds not be used as an excuse for unfairly and illegally assisting domestic businesses on the other while promoting transparency in the procurement process.[69]

65 *Optional Protocol to the Convention on the Rights of the Child on the Sale of Children, Child Prostitution and Child Pornography*, *supra* note 46.

66 *Optional Protocol to the Convention on the Rights of the Child on the Involvement of Children in Armed Conflict*, *supra* note 46.

67 See *American Convention on Human Rights*, *supra* note 38 at Ch VII; *African (Banjul) Charter on Human Rights and Peoples' Rights*, *supra* note 39 at arts 46–59.

68 *General Agreement on Tariffs and Trade* (1949) at preamble.

69 *Revised Agreement on Government Procurement* (1995) at preamble.

2) Throughout the economic treaty regimes and governance systems discussed there are clear connections between the role that economic development and progress can play as a means of assisting or harming the advancement of environmental concerns, efforts to combat climate change, and sustainable development principles. This is striking as it cuts across individual industries – often those on opposite sides of the production system, geography and interplanetary scope – and includes banking as well as trade. In these connections and the responses of the treaty regimes and governance systems to them, there are connections to SDG 2 (achieve food security), SDG 12 (responsible consumption and production), SDG 13 (climate change), SDG 14 (life below water) and SDG 15 (life on land).

In this way, the treaty regimes and associated governance systems focusing on economic concerns can still be understood as cross-cutting with environmental concerns. At the same time, the emphasis on responsible practices in these industries and sectors – be it setting human rights standards for international banks to use in lending decisions or setting allowable fish catches – indicates the importance of these economic treaty regimes and governance systems as a means of furthering the core concerns of human rights regimes as well.

Examples of this can be found in the terms of the WTO *Agreement on Agriculture*, emphasizing the significant connections between environmental concerns and agricultural trade and that the *Agreement* is a regime meant to assist in this interrelationship.[70] Moving into individual industries, these connections between economic regulation and environmental governance are particularly strong in the fishing and energy sectors. While most of the fishing treaty regimes are focused on a region or a resource, taken together these regimes cover the majority of the international community and bind it to at the very least a minimum level of protections.

For instance, the African-led *Convention on the Determination of the Minimum Conditions for Access and Exploitation of Marine Resources within the Maritime Zones* is a concerted effort to bring national laws and rules into accord with existing international law obligations "for the benefit of current and future generations,"[71] and the objective of the Inter-American *Antigua Convention* relating to tropical tuna "is to ensure the long-term conservation and sustainable use of the fish stocks covered by this Convention, in accordance with the relevant rules of international law."[72] In the energy context, the objectives of the International Renewable Energy Agency

70 *Agreement on Agriculture* (1995) at preamble.

71 *Convention on the Determination of the Minimum Conditions for Access and Exploitation of Marine Resources within the Maritime Zones under jurisdiction of the Member States of the Sub-Regional Fisheries Commission* (2012) at preamble.

72 *Convention for the Strengthening of the Inter-American Tropical Tuna Commission* (*Antigua Convention*) (2003) at art II.

(IRENA) are "to promote the widespread and increased adoption and the sustainable use of all forms of renewable energy," while taking into account the national interests and priorities of State Parties and reinforcing the environmental, climate change, societal and economic benefits of renewables for national and international society.[73]

3) Sovereignty and the need to balance it with international goals and ambitions in establishing economic treaty regimes and governance structures is another key trend and intersect with SDG 8 (economic growth), SDG 9 (industry, innovation and infrastructure) and SDG 12. Economic planning and the regulation of industry practices is a significant element of State practice and sovereign power, especially in the context of trade and finance. And yet, the treaty regimes and governance systems reviewed in this chapter demonstrate that it is possible to strike a balance that recognizes the durability of sovereignty while giving primacy to the goals of the international community through activities such as internalized dispute settlement systems rather than the resort to court functions and the ability of developing States to receive assistance and technology transfer which makes participation in the global regimes more attractive.

Examples from the trade context include a number of WTO treaties, such as the *General Agreement on Tariffs and Trade* (GATT), *General Agreement on Trade in Services* (GATS), *Agreement on Agriculture*,[74] the *Revised Agreement on Government Procurement*,[75] *Agreement on Safeguards*,[76] the *Agreement on the Application of Sanitary and Phytosanitary Measures*,[77] the *Agreement on Subsidies and Countervailing Measures*,[78] the *Agreement on Technical Barriers to Trade*,[79] *Agreement on Trade-Related Investment Measures* (TRIMs)[80] and *Agreement on Trade-Related Aspects of Intellectual Property Rights* (TRIPs).[81]

Additionally, the sovereignty balance is at the heart of the *OECD Convention on Combatting Bribery of Foreign Public Officials in International Business Transactions*[82] in that it seeks to address the ways in which corporations which are nationals of a State behave toward actors in another State and setting. The balance between sovereign interests and international

73 *IRENA Statute* (2009) at art II.
74 *Agreement on Agriculture*, *supra* note 70 at 4.
75 *Revised Agreement on Government Procurement*, *supra* note 69 at II.
76 *Agreement on Safeguards* (1995).
77 *Agreement on the Application of Sanitary and Phytosanitary Measures* (1995).
78 *Agreement on Subsidies and Countervailing Measures* (1995).
79 *Agreement on Technical Barriers to Trade* (1995).
80 *TRIMs* (1995).
81 *TRIPs* (1995).
82 *OECD Convention on Combatting Bribery of Foreign Public Officials in International Business Transactions* (1997).

concerns in an evolving yet increasingly active area is emphasized in the series of treaty regimes relating to outer space, namely the *Treaty on Principles Governing the Activities of States in the Exploration and Use of Outer Space, Including the Moon and Other Celestial Bodies*,[83] the *Agreement on the Rescue of Astronauts, the Return of Astronauts and Return of Objects Launched into Outer Space*,[84] the *Convention on International Liability for Damage Caused by Space Objects*,[85] *the Agreement Governing the Activities of States on the Moon and Other Celestial Bodies*,[86] and the *Convention on Registration of Objects Launched into Outer Space*.[87]

4) The balance discussed in trend 3 has been strained during the COVID-19 pandemic, as States are acting to protect their citizens and ensure adequate and continuing access to supplies even where it threatened to undermine trade and financial commitments. However, these issues will be handled within the realm of dedicated governance systems which are widely respected, which itself reaffirms the role of global governance and its importance for current and future international challenges. This is an example of the intersection of these dedicated economic dispute settlement systems with SDG 3 (good health and well-being) and the underlying concerns of State sovereignty.

5) The incorporation of transparency and rule of law promotion in the practices of economic regimes highlights the ways in which these fundamental tenets of SDG 16 can be used across the environmental, social and human rights regimes to generate meaningful law and policy shifts. This is reflected in the use of committee systems that consult with experts and those impacted by proposed economic activities as well as in the generation of guidelines and recommendations for business and financial activities that entrench transparency and respect for laws in their principles.

Included in the instrumentalities of accomplishing this is the WTO Dispute Settlement Body, which provides a trade-expertise based system for the settlement of disputes arising out of WTO laws while ensuring that these

83 *Treaty on Principles Governing the Activities of States in the Exploration and Use of Outer Space, Including the Moon and Other Celestial Bodies*, United Nations, Treaty Series, vol. 610, No. 8843 (1967).

84 *Agreement on the Rescue of Astronauts, the Return of Astronauts and Return of Objects Launched into Outer Space*, United Nations, Treaty Series, vol. 672, No. 9574 (1967).

85 *Convention on International Liability for Damage Caused by Space Objects*, United Nations, Treaty Series, vol. 961, No. 13810 (1972).

86 *Agreement Governing the Activities of States on the Moon and Other Celestial Bodies*, United Nations, Treaty Series, vol. 1363, No. 23002 (1984).

87 *Convention on Registration of Objects Launched into Outer Space*, United Nations, Treaty Series, vol. 1023, No. 15020 (1974).

proceedings are open to other States and that their reports and findings are available at the public level.[88]

6) Across the economic treaty regimes and governance systems there is a consistent focus on including marginalized and vulnerable populations. This connects directly with a number of SDGs, from SDG 1 on poverty to SDG 4 on education and aspects of the rights of the child to SDG 5 on gender equality to SDG 10 on reduced inequalities. Further, given the connections between many marginalized and vulnerable groups and the environment, there are significant connections with SDGs 13, 14 and 15. Finally, Target 16.7, "ensure responsive, inclusive, participatory and representative decision-making at all levels," is directly linked to and advanced by these requirements.

Key examples of these interconnections can be found in the lending practices and rules governing project approval and continued monitoring for international banking and financial organizations such as the World Bank Group and the International Monetary Fund as well as the regional development banks. In the energy sector, the *Protocol on Energy in the SADC Region* uses energy as a tool for economic growth and poverty eradication, ensuring the inclusion of social concerns in energy policy, providing for technological transfer for energy and related sectors, ensuring the inclusion of environmental concerns on energy law and policy, and the peaceful settlement of disputes.[89]

5.4 Impacts of lessons on the post-COVID-19 future

From a governance perspective, perhaps the most immediately impactful response of several treaty regimes was to postpone their scheduled 2020 CoPs to 2021, as planned at the time of writing, along with postponing their intersessional meetings or shifting to an online, condensed intersessional meeting format. Beyond scheduling difficulties, these responses, which are necessary from the public health and security perspectives, have slowed the momentum of many State Parties toward meaningful short-term and long-term environmental commitments and changes, as well as the impacts on social regime issues – notably human rights concerns stemming from the pandemic – and on all aspects of economic regime issues. While adaptive to the needs of the international community that comprises their constituencies, the decisions of the treaty bodies highlight an inherent weakness in the current governance system in terms of the ability to make critical decisions in the context of a CoP structure that is intended to function as an in-person, negotiation-centered entity.

88 See GATT, *supra* note 68.
89 *Protocol on Energy in the SADC Region* (1996) art 2.

The inability to address these issues during a CoP or other structured format which allows fair and transparent decisions to be made threatens to undermine the treaty regimes at issue at the same time that it threatens progress toward achieving the SDGs through these governance systems. Indeed, the High Level Political Forum on the SDGs, traditionally convened during the summer months at the UN headquarters in New York City, went to an online format in 2020, albeit with reduced decision-making powers. In this context, the pandemic has highlighted essential questions regarding the CoP system as well as the importance of recognizing the SDGs as inherently connected to various treaty regimes and governance systems since future limitations on the ability to host a slate of CoPs and similar meetings may result in the need to depend on more limited governance structures to advance the SDGs.

At the same time, the pressures to "build back better" across the world highlight the need to balance a quick economic recovery with one that is sustainable and advances climate related concerns as well as financial needs of national citizenries and the international community. This concept could assist in achieving and incentivizing the SDGs or could result in significant damage to the implementation of the SDGs but, while it is too certain to determine the outcome, it is unlikely that the SDGs will remain on track as they stood at the beginning of 2020. In this context, the actions of treaty regimes and governance systems throughout the environmental, social and economic sectors will heavily influence the ability of States to meet their SDG pledges and the ability of the international community to move the SDG agenda forward. Each treaty regime discussed in the preceding chapters has a role to play in the accomplishment of the SDGs through their abilities to entrench the terms of the SDGs – many of which are at least tacitly entrenched in these regimes already – and to ensure robust oversight and monitoring of these obligations. During a pandemic which has crippled so many aspects of daily life and functions for citizens and States alike, it is perhaps only in the global governance sphere that these types of SDG-related progress can be taken.

Additionally, pandemic responses have shown the increased awareness of States and the international community that many treaty regimes and governance structures, especially those relating to international organization, occupy similar legal and policy space. Rather than creating conflicts, this has been seen as an opportunity for often cross-cutting interactions between these entities in an effort to ensure that the needs of mutual constituencies are met. In this context, the ability of treaty regimes and governance systems to work together can be translated into the potential for more robust entrenchment and governance of the SDGs and their targets across entities in the short- and long-term.

6 Conclusion

The relationship between international law, global governance and the Sustainable Development Goals (SDGs) is highly nuanced and interconnected, as this book has shown. Rather than serving as a hinderance to the achievement of the SDGs or the continued importance of global governance, the preceding chapters have demonstrated the inherently empowering aspects of this relationship for the entrenchment of the SDGs as a matter of law and policy that can last to 2030 and beyond. This is true and, it is asserted, even more important in light of, the COVID-19 pandemic and the aftermath.

This book studied the methods through which international law and its associated innovative global governance mechanisms – such as those found in treaty regimes and their associated domestic authorities/stakeholders – can strengthen, foster and scale up the impacts of treaty regimes and international law on the ability to implement global governance mechanisms. By way of a modern, concrete example, the book examined these questions through a general lens and through the lens of the SDGs. The SDGs were selected as an area of focus because they contain soft and hard law elements, relate to a number of international treaty regime topics and associated governance mechanisms, and offer a blank slate upon which to conduct analysis for current and future implementation. Additionally, the SDGs are time-limited in the sense that they are intended to achieve results by 2030, necessitating the rapid entrenchment of their terms as part of global government mechanisms as well as national governance mechanisms and policies.

At the same time, there exist inherent contradictions between international treaty regimes and principles of international law that function in tandem for global governance mechanisms to be properly implemented. For example, environmental treaties and human rights treaties often speak of furthering essential rights and freedoms, however they can be interpreted as giving primacy to different constituencies, resulting in conflicting implementation of the treaty regimes themselves and of global governance mechanisms. Without determining these areas of contest and highlighting their detrimental impacts, the SDGs and other efforts at global governance will not be able to maximize their legal and societal benefits. Thus, this book addresses the area of confluence as well as gaps and involving treaty regimes and global governance mechanisms in order to offer readers a holistic understanding of the topic.

Chapter 1 of this book set out the basic parameters of the 2015 SDGs as the successors to the Millennium Development Goals (MDGs), the groundbreaking statement regarding the issues following the world into the new millennium in 2000 and the ways in which the international community hoped to address them. As such, it is essential to understand the MDGs before examining the SDGs. From the outset, it should be highlighted that the MDGs, like the SDGs, were time-bound and expired in 2015. This was emphasized as a governance advantage by the United Nations in that it was intended to create a sense of urgency among States and other international actors in terms of implementing commitments made.[1] However, the efficacy of the time-bound system without a significant international hard law element has yet to be fully determined.

In September 2015, the international community officially adopted the next step on the path opened through the MDGs by adopting the *2030 Agenda for Sustainable Development* during the UN General Assembly meeting.[2] This reflected the culmination of several years of attempts to bridge from the successes and challenges of the MDGs and address the issues facing the global community 15 years after the new millennium. In designating the theme as sustainable development, the international community overtly signaled the intent to focus on all three of pillars of sustainable development in the implementation of the SDGs.[3] By embracing the pillars and principles of sustainable development, the SDGs also recognized the inherent links between the pillars.

In Chapters 2–4, this book was organized to parallel the three pillars of sustainable development – environmental, social and economic – before turning to analysis of emerging trends, contradictions and future outcomes from treaty regimes and governance systems discussed to the SDGs in Chapter 5. Within each of the pillar-based chapters, treaties were assigned to one of four topic clusters, and each of these clusters was subsequently analyzed in terms of (1) purposes and objectives of treaties, (2) governance mechanisms used, (3) dispute settlement mechanisms used, (4) hard law elements in governance systems and, where applicable, and (5) soft law elements in governance systems. The intent of each of these categories was to ensure that the critical aspects of organizational structures which promote

1 UN System Task Force on the post-2015 UN Development Agenda, Review of the contributions of the MDG Agenda to foster development: lessons for the post-2015 Development Agenda (2012) at 2.

2 UN General Assembly, *Transforming Our World: The 2030 Agenda for Sustainable Development*, A/RES/70/1 (21 October 2015).

3 Ibid. at preamble.

and entrench the terms of treaty regimes in international and national governance systems are reviewed for areas of overlap and divergence.

In Chapter 2, environmental treaty regimes and associated governance systems were discussed since they represent the pillar with which sustainable development is often associated. And, while environmental concerns in the SDGs tend to be clustered in SDGs 13, 14 and 15, in reality environmental issues are truly cross-cutting, playing a vital role in everything from food security concerns under SDG 2 to clean water under SDG 6 to renewable energy under SDG 7 to peace, justice and strong institutions under SDG 16 and beyond. Indeed, as Chapter 2 demonstrated, environmental treaty regimes are exceptionally diverse in context and content, scope and scale, although united by the ways in which international law has shaped them and how these treaty regimes have established governance systems that allow them legitimacy and the ability to meet the current and future needs of their constituencies.

Chapter 2 reviewed treaty regimes that were categorized into generally focused environmental treaty regimes, pollution-based regimes, species and wildlife regimes and geographically focused regimes. It then provided an overview of the ways in which governance mechanisms contained in the treaties reviewed have responded to and been impacted by the COVID-19 pandemic as an indicator of the strengths and weaknesses of governance systems in the face of a global emergency. Finally, the Chapter reviewed discernible trends across environmental treaty regimes and governance systems which can be used to understand how some SDGs and associated targets are already entrenched in these systems and how these systems may be used as a model for the achievement of the SDGs as long-term legal and policy instruments.

In Chapter 3, social treaty regimes and associated governance systems were reviewed. Social treaty regimes represent a spectrum of legal and governance concerns, as has been highlighted by the COVID-19 pandemic's impacts on health practice and governance as well as on nearly all aspects of the core international human rights system. The connections between social treaty regimes, governance systems and the SDGs are similarly wide-ranging, although the justice and rule of law issues governed by many of the treaty regimes discussed below suggest that SDG 16 is the more all-encompassing SDG in terms of reflecting and furthering the social treaty regimes.

Chapter 3 reviewed treaty regimes that were categorized into core human rights treaty regimes, criminal regimes, health and food regimes, and weapons and hazardous substances regimes. It then provided an overview of the ways in which governance mechanisms contained in the treaties reviewed have responded to and been impacted by the COVID-19 pandemic as an indicator of the strengths and weaknesses of governance systems in the face of a global emergency. Finally, the Chapter reviewed discernible trends across social treaty regimes and governance systems which can be used to understand how some SDGs and associated targets are already entrenched in these systems and how these systems may be used as a model for the achievement of the SDGs as long-term legal and policy instruments.

In Chapter 4, economic regimes and associated governance systems were reviewed. Economic treaty regimes include a wide range of activities, interests and opportunities to craft governance systems. In this setting, it could be expected that various regimes and sectors share little in common in terms of governance systems and goals, however, the opposite is true. Regardless the differences in industry, function and form of governance system, there are core interconnections between the economic aspects of these entities and environmental and social aspects which make the regimes relatable to each other and to regimes set out in Chapters 2 and 3. Additionally, these interconnections demonstrate the ways in which these regimes can be directly connected to and entrench the SDGs.

Chapter 4 reviewed treaty regimes that were categorized into trade regimes, economic policy regimes, banking and finance regimes and industry focused regimes. It then provided an overview of the ways in which governance mechanisms contained in the treaties reviewed have responded to and been impacted by the COVID-19 pandemic as an indicator of the strengths and weaknesses of governance systems in the face of a global emergency. Finally, the Chapter reviewed discernible trends across economic treaty regimes and governance systems which can be used to understand how some SDGs and associated targets are already entrenched in these systems and how these systems may be used as a model for the achievement of the SDGs as long-term legal and policy instruments.

Chapter 5 brought together the lessons of Chapters 2, 3 and 4 to analyze their potential impacts on and ties to the SDGs. As noted in the introductory chapter, there are a number of different arguments in the academic and policy-related literature regarding the status of the SDGs as purely hard law, purely soft law or a combination of the two, however this chapter offers an alternative understanding of this relationship. At the domestic level, it is the contention of the chapter – and this book – that the SDGs reflect many aspects of national law and policy which either exist as suggestions rather than laws or are laws which suffer from enforcement and capacity gaps. At the international level, this book's central assertion is that the argument over whether the SDGs are soft or hard law is extraneous because they can be tied to existing treaty regimes and governance systems, as can many of the targets established for each SDG. In this way, the SDGs and their targets are perhaps best viewed as a high-level statement and policy tool that mirrors the international and national commitments already existing for States and the international community.

Within this conceptualization, the most frequently implicated SDG in terms of entrenchment, durability and versatility of governance systems furthering it is SDG 16. The preceding chapters have demonstrated that SDG 16 is truly cross-cutting in that issues of transparency, accountability, societal incorporation and good governance are not sector or pillar specific but rather are required for any form of treaty regime and governance system to function. At the same time, these are the same considerations that underlie the growth and legitimacy of States and their governance systems at the domestic and even sub-national levels regardless their placement on the development spectrum. From these two perspectives, it is clear that the tenets of SDG 16 exist in – and are reinforced by – international and national laws and can be seen as already entrenching them. Further, the propensity of these legal regimes to include such tenets in systems that are intended to be permanent, or at the very least evolve from a basic point in which they play a critical role, demonstrates the ways in which the internalization of the SDGs within governance systems can outlive the SDGs.

This conceptualization of the SDGs then allows States and non-State actors to use the SDGs as a consolidated statement of the most pressing and imperative international law treaty regimes and governance systems for the future. They thus incentivize compliance with their terms as well as the terms of the treaty regimes they reflect and can be entrenched and operationalized through the enforcement mechanisms which exist in these instruments. Through this lens, which views the SDGs not as an added layer of obligations but as a supplement to existing treaty regime and governance system-based obligations, it is then possible to conceive of a way for the SDGs to be accomplished even in the midst of a world that will forever be marked by the impacts of the COVID-19 pandemic. By understanding this as well as the ways in which the SDGs weave together various sectors to create a cross-cutting tapestry of governance systems and entrenchment vehicles, it is indeed possible to conceive of a successful system in which, as a matter of law and policy, no one is left behind.

Index

For Product Safety Concerns and Information please contact our EU representative GPSR@taylorandfrancis.com
Taylor & Francis Verlag GmbH, Kaufingerstraße 24, 80331 München, Germany

www.ingramcontent.com/pod-product-compliance
Lightning Source LLC
LaVergne TN
LVHW021128300926
849160LV00010B/909

* 9 7 8 0 3 6 7 7 5 3 9 1 7 *